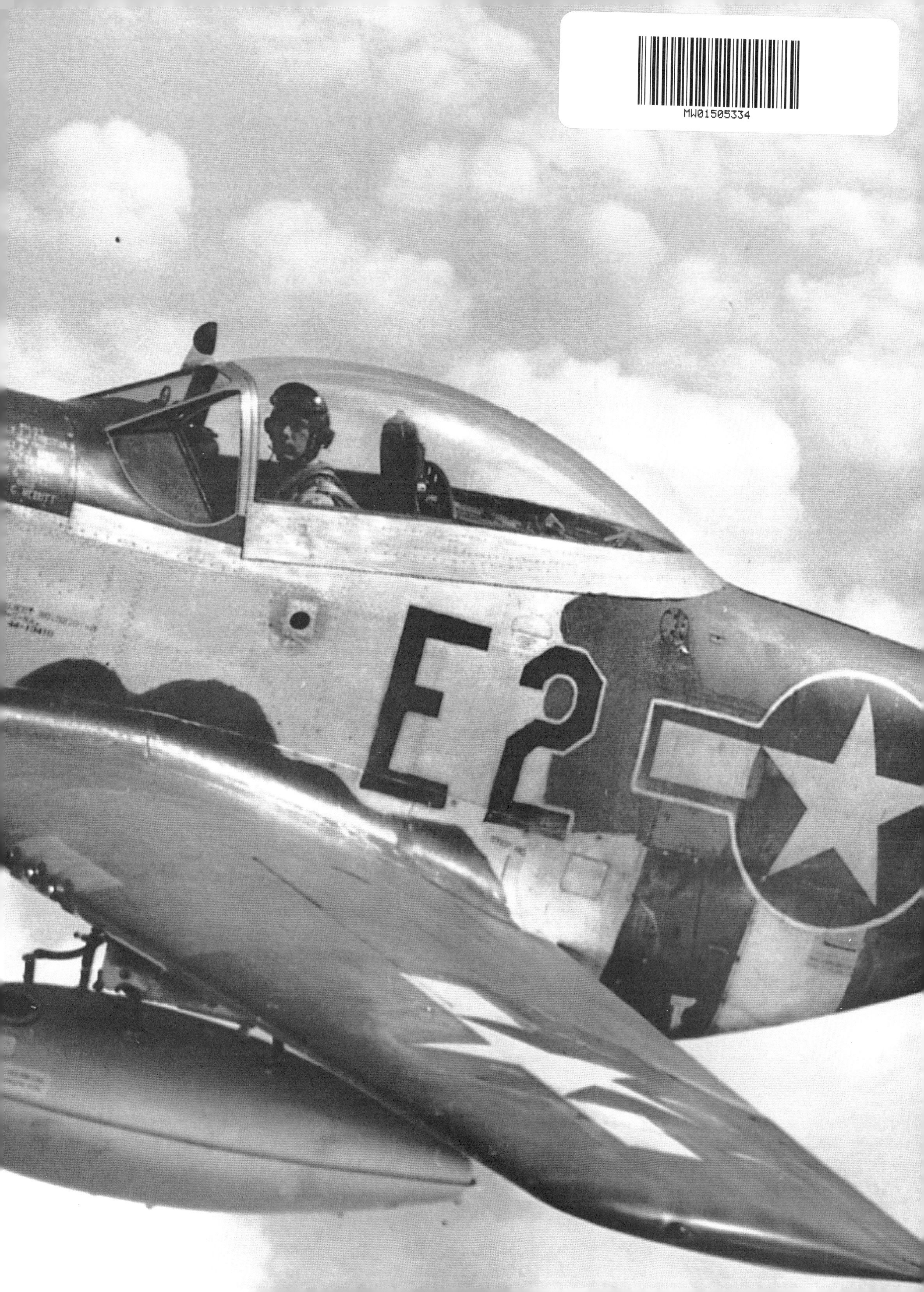
E2

Yellowjackets!

The 361st Fighter Group
in World War II

Yellowjackets!
The 361st Fighter Group
in World War II

Paul B. Cora

Schiffer Military History
Atglen, PA

Dust jacket and aircraft profile artwork by S.W. Ferguson, Colorado Springs, CO.

DALE'S DISTINGUISHED DAY

On May 29, 1944, the 361st Fighter Group flew their first maximum effort with the new P-51 Mustang, and quickly proved the worth of this lethal "Yellowjacket" combination. Future ace Lt. Dale Spencer of the 376th FS, in particular, took an entire formation of Luftwaffe Me 410s to task in full view of the 401st Bomb Group Flying Fortresses that momentarily came under his solitary care. In the span of just thirty seconds, Spencer shot down four of the enemy heavy intereceptors which the bomber crews readily confirmed while the Yellowjackets accounted for ten more *jagdfliegern*. The cover depicts Spencer pulling up over his forth victim as the B-17s stream homeward safely in the distance. Spencer's feat was underscored by his being awarded of the Distinguished Flying Cross.

Dedication
To my parents, who believed

Book design by Robert Biondi.

We are always looking for people to write books on new and related subjects. If you have an idea for a book, please contact us at the address below.

Published by Schiffer Publishing Ltd.
4880 Lower Valley Road
Atglen, PA 19310
Phone: (610) 593-1777
FAX: (610) 593-2002
E-mail: Schifferbk@aol.com.
Visit our web site at: www.schifferbooks.com
Please write for a free catalog.
This book may be purchased from the publisher.
Please include $3.95 postage.
Try your bookstore first.

In Europe, Schiffer books are distributed by:
Bushwood Books
6 Marksbury Ave.
Kew Gardens
Surrey TW9 4JF
England
Phone: 44 (0)208 392-8585
FAX: 44 (0)208 392-9876
E-mail: Bushwd@aol.com.
Free postage in the UK. Europe: air mail at cost.
Try your bookstore first.

Contents

Foreword

I flew B-17s from English bases beginning in April 1943, with three groups: the 351st, 91st, and 384th which I commanded from September 1944 until V-E Day. While I was in the 91st I led the 8th Air Force on the October Schweinfurt Mission when the designated leader, during the assembly, told me to take the lead. Also during my 91st days, I led the first major daylight mission to Berlin. We lost 129 bombers on those two missions, and it became clear that fighter escort was essential to the daylight bombing campaign. It was groups like the 361st that made it possible to continue. The P-51 was, in my judgment, the most important weapon in the European war.

When the 361st came to Bottisham, late in 1943, I learned with surprised pleasure that two of my close friends, Jack Christian and Bill Guckeyson, were in the group, Jack as its commander, and Bill as a captain and flight leader.

Jack Christian, great grandson of the legendary Stonewall Jackson, was a year ahead of me at West Point and a fellow member of the polo team. He graduated with stars on his collar – West Point's equivalent of magna cum laude – and was a member of the exalted regimental staff. In the eyes of the tactical department, Jack was a non-pareil. His friends knew another man, a fun loving fellow adept at circumventing West Point's often unreasonable rules.

Bill Guckeyson, who somehow landed in Jack's group, had graduated in 1942 but the fascinating part of that story is why he came to West Point at all. Bill had graduated from the University of Maryland where he had been student body president, football star sought by the Philadelphia Eagles, and a track champion. For reasons of his own, never clearly explained, he wanted to graduate from West Point and then fly. He could, of course, have saved four years by going straight to flying school, but he had his reasons. No longer eligible for football and track, he starred as a soccer player and captain of that team.

Bottisham was just a few miles from Bassingbourn, so we were able to see one another occasionally, and it was then that I met Joe Kruzel whom I have ever since regarded as a friend.

Jack called me the day Gyke went down, and he was uncharacteristically emotional. Soon after, he and I took a few days leave together. It would be the last time I saw him, for I left soon after on thirty days R and R in the States, and Jack went down in that time.

This is a fine story that Paul Cora has told, one that puts those long ago days in true perspective. It has the additional virtue of being eminently readable.

T.R. Milton
General, USAF (*Ret.*)
Tucson, AZ, April 2001

Acknowledgments

The Author would like to thank the following individuals for their kind assistance in the preparation of this book: Mr. Edward Knickman of the 374th Fighter Squadron who first took the time to tell me about his experiences flying with the 361st Fighter Group; Mr. Steve Gotts of Cambridge, England, who generously lent research materials and guidance from an early stage; Ms. Susanne Lintlemann of the U.S. Military Academy Library for her gracious research assistance; Mr. David Giordano of the National Archives in College Park who, many times, went digging for important records; Mr. Bernard J. Redden of the 361st Fighter Group Association whose support of the project on so many 'fronts' was unflagging from start to finish; MGEN Joseph J. Kruzel, USAF (Ret.) of the 361st Fighter Group Association who lent support to the project in many ways over the past few years; Mr. Rich Espey who gave so much assistance with proofreading the drafts; Mr. Stan Piet who provided excellent copies of many of the 361st Fighter Group's official color photographs; Mrs. Mary Warrington of Cumming, Georgia, who provided research and biographical data on her brother, Maj. George L. Merritt, Jr.; Mrs. Jean Shackelford who provided a number of photographs of Group personnel; Mr. Joseph Zieske Ormond who provided photographs and documents related to 1st Lt. Clarence Zieske; Mr. Laurent Wiart of Arras, France who provided details and photographs of the final resting place of Col. Thomas J.J. Christian, Jr.; General T.R. Milton, USAF (ret.) who kindly read the manuscript and wrote the thoughtful "Foreword" which appears in this book; Mrs. Jeanne B. Cora who devotedly proofread the final draft.

The Author would especially like to thank the following pilots who granted oral interviews on their service with the 361st making this book possible BGEN Harry M. Chapman, Maj. Urban L. Drew, Mr. James Golden, Mr. Edward Knickman, Mr. David C. Landin, Mr. Henry B. Lederer, Mr. George Lichter, Mr. Robert R. Volkman, Mr. Robert C. Wright, and Mr. Leonard A. Wood. The Author would especially like to thank the following individuals who provided written recollections and documents of their service with the 361st making this book possible: Mr. Norman Baer, Mr. Robert O. Bland, Mr. James T. Collins, Mr. James Golden, Mr. George Lichter, MGEN Joseph J. Kruzel, Mr. Bernard J. Redden, Mr. Russell A. Severson, Mr. Marvin Strickler, Mr. Alvin Walther, and Maj. Billy D. Welch.

Introduction

When the 361st Fighter Group was activated in early 1943, the United States Army Air Force was fully engaged in the massive expansion which characterized its storied development during World War II. Around the world its commanders were being tasked with ever-greater operational demands – tactical support of American military operations in every theater, troop transportation, logistical support, reconnaissance, and above all, strategic bombing. It was the concept of strategic bombing – the systematic destruction of an enemy's industrial base, which provided the means of making war – that offered the best hope of bringing speedy victory in the eyes of American air leaders.

In the summer of 1942, the U.S. 8th Air Force had begun arriving in England with the primary goal of carrying out a strategic bombing campaign against Nazi Germany. Though minuscule at first, the 8th Air Force would mature by 1945 into a massive instrument of war capable of dispatching nearly 3,000 combat aircraft against the enemy in a single day.

Unlike their British Allies, the 8th Air Force was committed to operating in daylight in order to fulfill the "precision" bombing aims pressed for by American air chiefs. While daylight visual bombing in good weather provided the best chance of hitting individual targets, daylight also provided the German *Luftwaffe* the opportunity to maximize its air defense capabilities. Though heavily armed and trained to fly in close formations for mutual defense, losses among the 8th's B-17 and B-24 bombers to German fighter aircraft began to increase as more distant targets were attacked over occupied Europe.

1943 was a critical year for the Allies in general, including the strategic bombing campaign against Germany. Among a series of distant, increasingly difficult objectives assailed that year, the Regensburg-Schweinfurt mission of August 17 alone cost the 8th Air Force sixty heavy bombers, and a repeat attack on the Schweinfurt ball-bearings plant in October cost an additional 60 planes and crews. Clearly, losses of the type incurred in the two Schweinfurt raids could not be sustained indefinitely, and in late 1943, such deep penetrations into German airspace by American "heavies" were temporarily halted.

The answer to the survival of heavy bombers over Germany lay in adequate fighter support. Single-seat fighter aircraft dispatched in large numbers along with the B-17s and B-24s would be able to engage German interceptors thus providing protection to the bomber formations. From the earliest days of the campaign, American fighters were employed in escorting the bombers to and from their targets, though it would not be until 1944 that their efforts would be fully effective. First equipped with British Spitfires, and later P-47 Thunderbolts, American fighter groups in England during 1942 and 1943 lacked sufficient range to escort the bombers more than a third of the distance into German air space on deep penetration raids. Once American fighter aircraft departed, the bomber formations sustained their heaviest losses.

Determined as the American air leaders were to make the strategic bombing campaign against Germany successful, they resolved that more men, more units, and improved aircraft would ultimately make the difference between success and failure. Not only would the 8th acquire additional bomber groups, but as 1943 gave way to 1944, the command's fighter strength would also grow dramatically. As aircraft improved, single-engined fighter planes of the Eighth Fighter Command would accompany the "heavies" all the way to their targets and back – a turning point which arrived in the first months of 1944.

As part of this massive effort in the European Theater of Operations, the 361st Fighter Group was formed in early 1943 and trained Stateside for ten months before deploying to England that November. As the last P-47 equipped fighter group to be assigned to the 8th Air Force, the 361st began combat operations in January 1944 and participated in every major effort undertaken by the 8th Air Force until the end of hostilities in Europe the following spring. While the Group's first months of operations were relatively slow, primarily due to the range limitations of their aircraft, but also to their relatively late arrival in the ETO, the transition to the P-51 Mustang fighter in May 1944 placed them in the forefront of bomber escort missions. Accompanying the heavy bombers over occupied Europe, the Group's pilots would do their utmost to protect the B-17s and B-24s in some of the most determined air battles of the war. Fitted out as fighter-bombers, the pilots of the 361st supported the Normandy invasion and the Allied drive across Europe while sustaining some of the Group's heaviest losses. The Battle of the Bulge saw the 361st Fighter Group rapidly transferred to the Continent where it provided top cover for the 9th Air Force as it drove back the German offensive in the Ardennes. Finally, in the spring of 1945 the 361st would protect the bombers from German jets which savagely defied Allied air superiority in the war's waning days. During 441 combat missions, the 361st Fighter Group amassed a total of 226 German aircraft destroyed in the air and 105 on the ground while suffering 81 pilots killed, captured, or missing. This is the story of the 361st – which became known to the bomber crews they escorted as the "Yellowjackets."

one

Birth of a Group

On a clear, sunlit morning in late July 1944, a formation of four P-51 Mustang fighter planes took off from an American Army Air Base at Bottisham, England, and proceeded to climb high above the East Anglian landscape. Resplendent against the blue, cloud-studded sky, the propeller hub and nose section of each Mustang was adorned with a coat of bright yellow paint, readily identifying it as belonging to the 361st Fighter Group, 8th Air Force. Led by Col. Thomas J.J. Christian, Jr., Group Commander of the 361st, the four P-51s soon joined a lone B-17 bomber cruising over eastern England. Each Mustang was equipped with a pair of bulging auxiliary fuel tanks slung beneath the wings, as though headed for a long-range combat mission. Christian's task that morning, however, was simple: satisfying an Army Air Corps photographer in need of close-up airborne shots of American fighter planes in the European Theater of Operations. Following instructions radioed from the bomber, the four P-51s made repeated passes, assuming a variety of formations for the busy photographer. When the task was finished a short time later, the four Mustangs parted company with the B-17, and returned to their base.

For the four Mustang pilots, the photo mission that morning was a brief and unremarkable incident which served only to punctuate the intensive combat operations in which the 361st was engaged that summer of 1944. The photographs themselves, however, would constitute some of the most enduring images of P-51 Mustangs in flight ever produced, and would achieve the status of "classics" symbolizing 8th Air Force fighter operations in World War II.

For Col. Christian, the photo series might have marked a milestone in his career. Having formed, trained and led the 361st from its creation in the States 18 months earlier through 8 months of combat operations over Europe, the impressive im-

age of his own P-51, made famous in the July 1944 photo series, seemed an appropriate tribute to all he had achieved in his 29 years, but he would never know. Within three weeks of the photo mission, Christian would be killed in combat over France.

The 361st Fighter Group would continue on, through much transformation, to finish the war the following spring. Though the young men who came together to form the Group in early 1943 would never forget their first Group Commander, Christian's ultimate sacrifice was one among many that the men of the 361st would make during operations in World War II. Representing the best which their generation had to offer, their achievements and sacrifices would help win the war.

• • •

On February 10, 1943, an order from the 1st Fighter Command carried out at Richmond Army Air Base, Virginia, detached a handful of personnel from the 327th Fighter Group forming the nucleus of a new unit. Designated as the 361st Fighter Group, its primary mission during the following nine months would be to take newly commissioned fighter pilots fresh from flight schools around the country, join them with a small cadre of seasoned pilots, and bring them together with maintenance and service personnel to form a complete fighter group comprised of three fighter squadrons and a headquarters. Once initially assembled and organized, the main focus of all activities would be intensive training and preparation for deployment in combat somewhere in the world by the end of 1943.

Assigned to command the new group was Maj. Thomas, J.J. Christian, Jr., a 27-year-old West Point graduate who had recently returned from combat in the South Pacific. Tall, soft-spoken and characterized by a precise military bearing, Christian would be the outstanding figure in the history of the 361st from its formation until his death in action the following summer. Under his leadership, the small headquarters staff assigned to the 361st would take on the task of organizing and training the new unit from scratch. The raw materials – personnel, equipment, facilities – would soon be forthcoming, but combining those materials into an effective combat-ready fighter group would be left to them.

In his brief career to February 1943, Maj. Christian had acquired a level of background and experience which prepared him for the genuine test of leadership to come. Born the son of a West Point graduate and career army officer in 1915, Thomas J.J. Christian, Jr., had spent his early years growing up on a number of military posts, and later attended the University of Chicago before he was accepted into West Point in the summer of 1935.[1] His entrance into the Military Academy extended the family connection with the school going back to 1842 when his great-grandfather, none other than Thomas J. "Stonewall" Jackson, entered West Point as a Plebe. Being the great-grandson of a Civil War hero, Christian's appointment was reported in *Time Magazine* which announced that "handsome, serious-minded Cadet-select Thomas Jonathan Jackson Christian, Jr., son of a West Pointer (1911) now attached to the War College, and only living great-grandson of one of the Military Academy's most famed graduates" was to report to Fort Sheridan, Illinois, for entrance examinations prior to the fall term.[2] Rising to the top ten percent of his class to graduate 45th of 456 in 1939,[3] his academic record at West Point surpassed his father's, and even that of his great-grandfather, "Stonewall."

Following a brief stint as a 2nd Lt. in the Field Artillery, Christian transferred to the Air Corps in 1940 and after completing advanced pilot training, served as a flight instructor at Randolph Field, Texas, until receiving orders for transfer overseas. Arriving at Clark Field, The Philippines, in April 1941, he joined the 28th Bomb Squadron, 19th Bomb Group as a B-17 pilot.[4]

The rapid pace of events in the Pacific, and America's unpreparedness for war in 1941 were to have dramatic consequences on the course of Lt. Christian's flying career. With nearly half the Philippine-based B-17 force wiped out in the December 8 Japanese attack on Clark Field, it was not long before the small American bomber force in the Philippines effectively ceased to exist.[5] Pilots being desperately needed for the anticipated defense of Australia, Christian was evacuated from Bataan in February 1942 and began training "down under" as a fighter pilot on the Bell P-39 Airacobra. Later promoted to Captain and assigned to the 67th Fighter Squadron in

Thomas J.J. Christian, Jr. photographed as a Cadet at West Point. *USMA Library*

New Caledonia, he would be among the first Army Air Corps pilots to participate in the battle for Guadalcanal when the 67th arrived at Henderson Field shortly after the 1st Marine Division stormed the island. While the land battle for control of Guadalcanal raged around them, Christian and his fellow pilots, equipped with Bell P-400 fighters (the export version of the P-39 built for Britain's Royal Air Force) carried out ground attack sorties against Japanese positions whose distance from the airfield could sometimes be measured in mere hundreds of yards. Operating under extremely primitive conditions, the 67th Fighter Squadron persevered in the face of dire maintenance problems and greatly outclassed aircraft.

During the first weeks of September 1942, as the Marines struggled to maintain their foothold on Guadalcanal against strong Japanese counteroffensives, Christian participated in a number of desperate missions for which he would receive the Silver Star. On September 8, under monsoon conditions, he led another pilot on a dangerous ground attack mission in support of an isolated Marine detachment which was attempting to withdrawal from a coastal raid while under Japanese counterattack.[6] In the midst of the torrential downpour in which Henderson's runway turned to mud, three of the 67th's bomb-laden P-400s attempted to get airborne. While Christian and his wingman succeeded with much difficulty, a third aircraft crashed and burned at the end of the runway. Flying beneath the low, gray ceiling, the two pilots delivered their bomb loads on the Japanese positions and remained over the evacuation beach strafing the Japanese to the limits of their ammunition and fuel. Six days later, as fighting on the ridges around Henderson Field intensified, Christian again participated in a series of dangerous ground-attack sorties in support of the Marines. Streaking over the jungle canopy in repeated strafing runs, two of the squadron's three P-400s were so badly damaged by ground fire that they were forced to make emergency landings.[7]

After logging some sixty hours of combat time over Guadalcanal, Capt. Christian was rotated home in November 1942.[8] Following a brief leave, during which he married Marjorie Lou Ashcroft of Sulpher Springs, Texas,[9] Christian was promoted to Major and assigned to the 327th Fighter Group at Richmond. A short time later, he learned that he would be given command of a new group.

That Christian's command abilities were evident accounted for his assignment to activate the 361st Fighter Group. For those who served under him in the new unit beginning in February 1943, he would exhibit the qualities of an exceptional leader. Joseph J. Kruzel, who served in the 361st as Air Executive Officer and later commanded the Group in the fall of 1944, singled out "Jack" Christian as an outstanding officer. Recalling his early service with the 361st following his retirement from the Air Force as a Major General, Kruzel remarked that Christian's "overall appearance had about it a presence of strict military bearing which alone sufficed to command respect. But this appearance ... coupled with his well above average intelligence, his outstanding judgment, and a knack for expressing himself well both in speech and in writing, were attributes that set him up as a natural leader. He was far and above one of the finest leaders that I've had the experience in knowing. He was fair and just in the handling of his men and when disciplinary action was necessary, he didn't waste any time dishing it out – he didn't particularly like it, but his philosophy was that everything he did was done with the interest of the Group as the basis for that action. His goal was to develop and command the finest fighter group in the Army Air Corps."[10]

Next to Jack Christian, Joseph J. Kruzel would be the most important figure in the 361st Fighter Group's training and combat history through the fall of 1944. Joining the headquarters staff of the 361st exactly one month after the Group was acti-

(L-R) Lt. Col. Christian, Miss Vi Clarke, and Maj. Joe Kruzel photographed in Richmond, Virginia, 1943. Kruzel would marry Vi Clarke the following summer while home from England on leave. *Courtesy J.J. Kruzel*

vated, he, like Christian, brought to Richmond significant flying experience along with recent combat time in the South Pacific.

Born in Wilkes Barre, Pennsylvania, in 1918, Kruzel entered the Army to undertake pilot training after studying pre medicine at a local college for four years. Like Christian, he had ended up in the Philippines shortly before the outbreak of war. "In December 1940, they asked for volunteers...to go out to the Philippines and that was as far away as I could get to see the world so I was one of the volunteers," recalled Kruzel years later. "I was first assigned to an observation squadron – I talked myself out of that [and]into the 28th Bomb Squadron where I flew B-10s. I eventually talked myself into joining the 17th Pursuit Squadron which was commanded by what I consider to be the finest fighter pilot I've ever known – he was the first ace in the Pacific – Lloyd 'Buzz' Wagner."[11] Although war with Japan was clearly on the horizon, Kruzel first learned that the fighting had actually started from a commercial radio broadcast early on the morning of December 8 (December 7 in Hawaii) which announced that Pearl Harbor had been bombed. "The thought that Hawaii would be bombed never entered my mind. We were the ones waiting to be attacked," he commented many years later. "The Japanese planned to attack us sooner than they did...they didn't only because the Japanese bombers on Formosa, north of the Philippines, were unable to take off because of fog."[12] Flying Curtiss P-40s from Nichols Field, Manila, and later from Clark Field (some 50 miles north of Manila), Kruzel carried out twelve combat missions, mostly patrol and reconnaissance during the first weeks of war. Without radar to give early warning of attacks, few interceptions of high-altitude Japanese bombers were possible. Kruzel's last mission in the Philippines was a bombing and strafing attack on Japanese troops landing at Lingayen Gulf on Christmas Eve 1941. Following this sortie, he was ordered to join a group of pilots who would be sent to Australia in order to ferry newly arrived P-40s back to join in the defense of Bataan.

When the Japanese captured the Dutch airfield at Tarakan, Borneo, in early 1942, plans to send Air Corps reinforcements to the Philippines were shelved – Tarakan being a vital refueling stop along the route from Australia. Instead, Joe Kruzel found himself headed to Java as part of the 17th Provisional Pursuit Squadron consisting of "old hands" recently arrived from the Philippines along with pilots fresh from the States. Operating from Blimbing, some 40 miles northwest of Surabaya, the squadron was able to engage Japanese aircraft as they attacked the Dutch East Indies through the end of February 1942. Recalling the Dutch airfield at Blimbing, Kruzel commented that it was so well camouflaged that in five weeks of operations, the Japanese were unable to locate and attack it. "The T-shaped landing area was firm sod with 2-foot-tall hardy stalks planted in rectangular shaped patterns throughout the area making it appear to be a cluster of rice paddies." In the later part of February, Kruzel had his first opportunities to engage enemy aircraft. "I shot down a Nakajima 97 Japanese fighter over Sumatra, and was credited with a Zero who was on the tail of, and shooting at, Walter Cross, my flight leader … I also got credit for a Zero over Bali when we engaged about five of them."[13]

Following Japanese landings on Java, the 17th Provisional Squadron was withdrawn to Australia, and Joe Kruzel, then promoted to Captain, was assigned to the 9th Fighter Squadron in the South Pacific before being rotated home in November 1942. Once back in the States, Capt. Kruzel, like Maj. Christian, was assigned to the 327th Fighter Group with the primary mission of training new pilots for combat. "I didn't particularly like the job," he recalled, "I felt more like I was in a cadet squadron and it seemed to be the order of the day [to] just accumulate hours and get people out but don't have any accidents. And when Jack Christian came through to activate the 361st, I saw my opportunity to get back into combat."[14]

Before serving together at Richmond, Kruzel and Christian were distant acquaintances, and their career paths had crossed shortly before the start of the war. "I had known Jack Christian previously, not very well, but when I went through basic flying school at Randolph, he was one of the Company Commanders, although we were in different companies. Then later, when I became a pilot and … volunteered for duty in the Philippines…we shared the same B.O.Q.[Bachelor Officer's Quarters], and although we were assigned to different units, I did get to know him there." Kruzel recalled that when he approached Maj. Christian at Richmond about the position of Air Executive Officer of the 361st, "I told him I was anxious to go back, and that I was eager for more combat, and I think that he felt that my prior combat experience would help him instill confidence in the pilots."[15] With a distinguished combat record in the Pacific and experience as a Squadron Commander in the 327th Fighter Group, Joe Kruzel would, indeed, prove invaluable in preparing the new pilots of the 361st for overseas deployment.

Among the other officers who would assume key roles within the air echelon of the new Group were the Group Operations Officer, and the Squadron Commanders, all of whom were highly experienced pilots. Capt. Wallace E. Hopkins of Washington, Georgia, had joined the Army in 1939 as an enlisted man, but a year later was accepted as an Aviation Cadet.[16] Arriving at Richmond in the spring of 1943 with a considerable amount of fighter time logged, he was chosen by Maj. Christian to be the Group Operations Officer – a post which he held while flying combat missions through much of the 361st Fighter Group's operational history.

Captain Roy A. Webb of Pampa, Texas, was selected by Christian to command the 374th Fighter Squadron. He arrived at Richmond with several years experience in the Air Corps, including an extended tour in the Caribbean flying P-39s and P-40s.[17] Leading the 374th from its earliest days through its first eight months of combat over Europe, Webb would establish a high reputation within the Group as an air leader, and an enviable personal combat score.

Command of the 375th Fighter Squadron initially fell to Capt. Barry Melloan, though he would depart early on in the Group's stateside training phase. Melloan was succeeded by Capt. George L. Merritt, Jr. of Cumming, Georgia. A graduate of the University of Georgia with a degree in forestry, Merritt had entered the Air Corps in 1941 after a stint with the US Forest Service. He was home on leave following advanced flight training when Pearl Harbor was attacked.[18] Born in 1914, Merritt would be among the oldest of the Group's pilots, but would nonetheless distinguish himself repeatedly in combat, and earn a reputation as one of the most remarkable and aggressive leaders in the history of the 361st.

Capt. Roy B. Caviness of Oil City, Louisiana, would be Christian's choice to lead the 376th Fighter Squadron. A football player at each of the three colleges he attended prior to joining the Air Corps in 1940, Caviness served as a flying instructor after receiving his pilot's wings.[19] Of all the key leaders in the Group's early formation and training, Caviness would remain with the 361st the longest, completing two combat tours and ultimately serving as the Group's last wartime Commander in the Spring of 1945.

Also present on the Group staff from the earliest days was Capt. John M. Stryker of Grand Rapids, Michigan. Stryker had originally joined the Army as an enlisted man in the months before Pearl Harbor and went on to receive a commission following Officer Candidate School (OCS). A dedicated staff officer and able administrator, Stryker would eventually rise from Adjutant to the post of Ground Executive Officer while serving in the 361st through the end of the war. A devoted diarist, Stryker would leave to posterity a daily unit diary summarizing key events in the Group's operational history.[20]

In the first months of 1943, while the bulk of the new pilots who would be assigned to the 361st Fighter Group were still earning their wings, the primary tasks faced by Maj. Christian and his new staff at Richmond involved the establishment of the basic administrative and logistical framework which would ultimately make possible the efficient training, command and control of the Group's three fighter squadrons and supporting units. Additional staff would have to be selected, buildings on the base obtained and allotted, administrative, service, and maintenance personnel would need to be received and billeted, and training routines established so that when the Group reached its full strength of nearly 1,000 officers and enlisted men (including 81 pilots), operational training could begin.

The ground echelon of the 361st consisted of the non-flying staff whose support roles made air operations possible and were among the first personnel to be assigned to the Group. Comprised predominantly of enlisted men, many had volunteered for the Army shortly after America became involved in the war, and a like number had waited patiently for their turn to be inducted. They reported in from Army Air Corps technical schools and units around the country with specialties ranging from aircraft mechanics and instrument repair, to cooks and clerks. Rightly seeing themselves as part of a team, they would readily bask in the achievements of the air echelon throughout the Group's operational history.

The first pilots assigned to the 361st began to arrive in Richmond in the late spring of 1943. Newly graduated from Army flight schools around the country, these young men had, in many cases, volunteered following Pearl Harbor and, by one route or another, had entered the Army's highly competitive flight training program as Aviation Cadets. After successful completion of basic, intermediate, and advanced flight training conducted in the Piper J-3 "Cub," Vultee BT-13, and fi-

Captain John M. Stryker, Adjutant of the 361st Fighter Group seen at Richmond, 1943. Later promoted to Ground Executive Officer, Stryker would remain with the Group into 1945, and, among many other tasks carried out, would be a dedicated unit diarist. *Courtesy J.J. Kruzel*

nally the North American AT-6, they had been awarded their wings and commissioned as 2nd Lieutenants.

Most pilots arrived at Richmond still untested in the aircraft which they would fly in combat overseas: the Republic P-47 Thunderbolt. In the middle of 1943, the P-47 was among the Army Air Corps' first line fighters and was the primary type in use with American combat units then operating from England. Massive, powerful, and immensely strong, the P-47 was a match for *Luftwaffe* opponents at high altitude, and while its performance declined somewhat below 15,000 feet, its rugged construction gave it legendary survivability. To complement the plane's ruggedness was more than adequate firepower in the form of eight .50 caliber machine guns – four mounted in each wing – virtually assuring that any enemy aircraft which came within its sights would receive crippling punishment.

Equipped with a Pratt & Whitney R-2800 radial engine developing more than 2,500 horsepower, flying the P-47 was a challenge to beginners. Recalling years later his first experience flying the Thunderbolt, Henry Lederer, who joined the 374th Squadron in the spring of 1943 as a 2nd Lieutenant, observed that "as a youth, one of the reasons why the best fighter pilots are the young fighter pilots is that you don't really question authority as to putting you into this big machine that's so huge and has so much torque on take-off that, if anything ever happened to the trim on the rudder, your right foot could never hold … a position to make a straight take-off down the center of the runway. You never thought about those things, you had that macho 'Hey, I can do anything … I've gone through a

A Republic P-47D Thunderbolt. Heavy, powerful, and extremely durable, the P-47 was the primary fighter in service with the 8th Air Force in 1943, and was the aircraft with which the 361st would train for combat. *National Archives*

tough training program, and I'm one of the survivors' [attitude]." Despite the daunting first impressions, Lederer, who would continue flying after the war and into the 21st Century, remarked that the P-47 had many good qualities to recommend it. "It was an easy airplane to fly because as long as you went by the numbers – airspeed numbers – you couldn't get into any trouble. Landing, you couldn't get into any trouble if you're any kind of a pilot at all because that landing gear was so wide apart … that you couldn't get a wing in…if your right wheel touched down first." He added, however, that the Thunderbolt was potentially "an overpowering aircraft to fly if you didn't have the time or you didn't have good flight instruction."[21]

The training of the Group's pilots as a unit would be a responsibility in which Joe Kruzel, promoted to Major shortly after assignment with the 361st, played a key role. Recalling the Group's stateside experience in 1943, Kruzel commented that "we just embarked on a continuous training program. We acquired people, we fired a few people , we fought to get some people, we fought to hold some people, we moved around a bit which was a good experience for the later move we made when we came to England."[22] In all, the 361st would make three major moves during training – from Richmond to Langley Field, Virginia, on May 25; Langley to Camp Springs, Maryland (later Andrews AFB) on July 19, and from Camp Springs back to Richmond on October 2, 1943.[23]

Formal operational training for the Group's air echelon began on May 28, 1943, and in the weeks that followed, the pilots assigned to the Group would not merely begin their familiarization with the P-47, but would also begin practicing the essential skills required for overseas deployment in combat. Combat formations would be an important part of the operational routines on actual missions against the enemy and the newly commissioned pilots were rigorously indoctrinated in fighter formations and tactics. The basic combat formation was the two-plane "element" consisting of the leader and his wingman. The element had to function strictly as a team with the wingman's primary job to cover the leader's tail. Two elements comprised a "flight" under a flight leader, and together, three or more flights made up a squadron formation. Depending upon the mission – bomber escort, fighter sweep, ground attack, etc. – a squadron leader could detach individual flights to carry out various tasks. Flying together under the group leader (a role often filled by the Group Commander, but also rotated from mission to mission among the key staff), the squadrons could be deployed as the situation dictated. In a dogfight, it was expected that squadrons and flights would be disrupted and mixed, but above all, the pilots were taught, wingmen must stick with their element leader as a basic matter of survival – two pairs of eyes were always better than one.

Among the other skills honed for overseas deployment were instrument flight, gunnery, and navigation. Instrument skills were essential for flying at night or in conditions in which visibility was restricted – such as in cloud and fog. Without extensive practice at relying strictly on instruments such as the gyro horizon, altimeter, and rate of climb/descent gauges, pilots could easily become disoriented when unable to see the actual horizon. Such disorientation could have rapid and disastrous results. Though they would not know it at the time, their deployment to England, with its notorious weather, would often demand precise instrument skills. Gunnery training, another essential skill, would be carried out at Milleville in southern New Jersey through which the Group would rotate by squadrons. From there the pilots would practice aerial gunnery by shooting at sleeve targets towed by other aircraft, and would also practice shooting at fixed ground targets.

One of the goals of the Group's stateside training was to give relatively inexperienced pilots the opportunity to accumulate flight time in the P-47, an objective that was readily met. At the beginning of the Group's operational training, most of the pilots who had arrived fresh from flight schools had been able to log a few hours in actual fighters, such as the Curtiss P-40, at the end of their Advanced Training. By the middle of October 1943, 51 of the Group's 87 pilots had between 400 and 500 hours logged in fighters, and another 16 pilots had between 500 and 600 hours. Of the remainder, only three on the Group's establishment had less than 400 hours logged flying fighters.[24]

As an interesting side note, unit training requirements included several long cross-country flights intended to simulate combat operations with three squadrons flying together over long distances. One of these took place during the last week of

Henry Lederer of New York City photographed as an Aviation Cadet in April 1943. Commissioned a short time later, Lederer would be assigned to the 374th Fighter Squadron. *Henry B. Lederer*

Below: A P-47 Thunderbolt assigned to the 361st Fighter Group photographed at Camp Springs, Maryland, 1943. Seated in the cockpit is mechanic Russell A. Severson who would serve as a dedicated crew chief in the 374th Fighter Squadron throughout the war. *Russell A. Severson*

Pilots of the 361st Fighter Group seen after landing at Atlanta, Georgia, September 29, 1943. Seated in the center row, second from the left is Maj. Roy Webb, CO of the 374th Squadron. To his left is Maj. Joe Kruzel, and seated to his left is Lt. Col. Christian. Standing at the extreme left is 375th Squadron CO Maj. George Merritt. *Courtesy George Lichter*

September 1943 and saw 36 aircraft fly from Camp Springs Army Air Base to Harding Field, Baton Rouge, Louisiana, from which they participated in large-scale Army maneuvers. The route prepared by the Group operations staff listed Atlanta, Georgia as the first stop where pilots and support personnel would spend the night. "About two weeks before this particular mission," Joe Kruzel recounted years later, "Bobby Jones, of golfing fame, joined our organization as an Intelligence Officer. He was a Captain at the time and happened to be my roommate at Camp Springs Air Base." Learning of the cross-country flight to Louisiana, Jones obtained permission from Lt. Col. Christian to travel to Georgia several days ahead of the Group. When the 36 P-47s along with transports carrying the ground crews landed at Atlanta on the afternoon of September 29, 1943, "Bob Jones was at the airfield to meet us. [He] had the transportation all set up, and rooms for all the pilots and support personnel that flew along in transport at the Ansley Hotel. And also in the lobby of the Hotel there were about 30 to 40 good-looking Atlanta girls that Bobby Jones had arranged to meet us there." Members of the Group who took part in the training flight to Baton Rouge would long remember the pleasant surprise of a reception by Atlanta debutantes, and the thoughtfulness of Capt. Jones. "He was a tremendous individual," remarked Kruzel. "He wanted to go overseas with us, but … just before we left he was transferred to some other organization."[25]

Perhaps during stateside training, the gravity of the task for which they were preparing hit home to a degree. From May 28 through October 15, the Group's pilots would be involved in 26 flying accidents of varying degrees of seriousness. Seven pilots were killed in flying accidents before the 361st went overseas.[26]

By early October, following the return of the 361st to Richmond from Camp Springs, the final phases of training were nearing completion, and it was evident to all that the Group would soon embark for a combat zone somewhere overseas. On October 9, 1943, Richmond's POM (Post Overseas Movement) Inspectors paid a visit, inspecting the administrative and material condition of the Group in order to pinpoint deficiencies for correction prior to embarkation. Following the inspection, as the various deficiencies were addressed, training continued though the pace of events quickened.[27]

On November 4, 1943, after much practice the 361st Fighter Group held its formal Review in which all personnel paraded by unit before a party of reviewing officers from the Richmond Army Air Base. Following this "rite of passage," preparations for the immediate movement to an overseas staging area were stepped up as equipment, from tools to typewriters, was crated up, and buildings were prepared for turnover. On November 10, Maj. Kruzel along with Capt. Wallace Hopkins departed Richmond to serve as the advanced echelon overseas – though their destination was kept secret from the

Officers and men of the 374th Fighter Squadron ready to embark overseas, photographed at Richmond, Virginia, November 11, 1943. *Courtesy George Lichter*

Group at large. At 1730 hours the following day, the 361st departed Richmond Army Air Base and all personnel were marched to a waiting train which took them north to Camp Shanks, New Jersey. Ten days later, the Group again fell in with all its belongings for transportation to a waiting troop-ship.[28] "Wish you could have seen us when we broke camp for the last time in the United States!" wrote 2nd Lt. George Lichter of the 374th Squadron to his parents in Brooklyn, New York. "It was nothing like the moving pictures depict it. Everyone was in good spirits and there was a great deal of joking and horse play. When we started marching to the train, everyone became serious and more or less quiet. After a while, the tension wore off and we were all singing. They even had a band at the station which was still playing as we pulled out."[29]

Boarding the former luxury liner, QUEEN ELIZABETH, the Group's enlisted men and officers settled in for a seven-day sea voyage to the United Kingdom – having been informed of their destination once the ship got underway. By all accounts, the trip was uneventful, though the accommodations were predictably cramped for both officers and enlisted men, the latter being assigned to troop bays in "D" deck while the former were billeted in staterooms. "There are eighteen of us in one room that would ordinarily accommodate two people comfortably," George Lichter wrote home during the voyage. "You can't even turn around without bumping into someone." The food on the trip turned out to be remarkably good, though the schedule of meals took some getting used to. "We only eat two meals a day. One at eight-thirty and the other at six in the evening," Lt. Lichter continued in his letter home. "It is now four-fifteen PM and I'm just about starving to death! From now on, I'm going to make some sandwiches at breakfast to carry me through the day."[30]

On November 29, QUEEN ELIZABETH arrived at Greenock, in Scotland's Clyde Estuary. Unemotionally and succinctly, the Group Adjutant, Capt. John Stryker, summarized the arrival in the European Theater of Operations (ETO) in his unit diary entry for the day: "November 29, 1943. Pulled into harbor in Scotland early morning. Boat dropped anchor at approximately 1000. Quite cold and rainy out. Ate last meal on board ship at 1200. Disembarked at 1345 onto a small ferry. Went to a transient's camp for three hours and had lunch, and boarded train heading for our destination at 2200."[31]

NOTES

[1] United States Military Academy (USMA), "Graduate Record Card for Thomas J.J. Christian, Jr.."

[2] *Time* Magazine, Vol. 10, No. 25, March 11, 1935,.

[3] USMA , ibid.

[4] John M. Stryker, "Group History, 361ˢᵗ Fighter Group" 18 July 1944.

[5] Wesley Frank Craven and James Lea Cate, ed. *The Army Air Forces in World War II Volume One* (Chicago: University of Chicago Press, 1950) pp. 212-13.

[6] Thomas G. Miller. *The Cactus Air Force* (New York: Harper and Row, 1969), p.79.

[7] US Army Air Force Silver Star Citation for Thomas J.J. Christian, Jr., 10 October 1942. Also Miller pp. 79-80, 92.

[8] Stryker, ibid.

[9] USMA, ibid.

[10] Joseph J. Kruzel. Recollections of the 361ˢᵗ Fighter Group tape recorded December 7, 1975, transcribed by Paul. B. Cora, October 2000.

[11] Ibid.

[12] Joseph J. Kruzel, "Narrative," March 5, 2001.

[13] Joseph J. Kruzel, Correspondence with Hugh and Betty Halbert, February 26, 1999.

[14] Kruzel, Recollections, December 7, 1975.

[15] Ibid.

[16] *The Escorter*, (Newspaper of the 361FG Bottisham, England), Vol. 1 # 7) 29 July 1944.

[17] *The Escorter*, (Newspaper of 361FG Bottisham, England, Vol. 1 #3, 1 July 1944), p. 3.

[18] Mary Warrington (sister of George L. Merritt). Interview by author. February 11, 2001.

[19] *The Escorter*, (Vol. 1, #5) 15 July 1944, p 4.

[20] Margot Stryker in John M. Stryker, *361ˢᵗ Fighter Group, 8ᵗʰ Air Force, World War II, A Personal Diary* (361ˢᵗ Fighter Group Association, 1998). Pages un-numbered.

[21] Henry B. Lederer. Interview with author, November 13, 1995.

[22] Kruzel, December 7, 1975.

[23] Jack B. Pearce, "Statistical Summary, 361ˢᵗ Fighter Group," June 1945, p.4.

[24] John M. Stryker, 361 FG Unit Diary entry for October 15, 1943.

[25] Kruzel, December 7, 1975.

[26] Stryker, 361FG Unit Diary.

[27] Ibid.

[28] Ibid.

[29] George Lichter, correspondence with Parents, November 11-29, 1943.

[30] Ibid.

[31] John M. Stryker, 361FG Unit Diary Entry for November 29, 1943.

two

Nissen Huts and Bicycles

When the journey from Greenock finally ended some seventeen hours after it had begun, the officers and men of the 361st had arrived at Bottisham, a small village some six miles east of the university town of Cambridge. Trucked from the rail depot to the airbase which would be their home for the next ten months, the fledgling group, which just one week prior had departed New York, found themselves tasked with the transformation of a small Royal Air Force (RAF) satellite field into an operational fighter base.

The airfield itself had been established some three years earlier as an auxiliary for a nearby RAF bomber base. Originally a grass field, RAF Bottisham's runway was never paved, though it was eventually upgraded with British steel matting known as Sommerfeld Track. Home to a number of Army-Cooperation squadrons of the Royal Air Force through the middle of 1943, it had been used by a variety of aircraft types ranging from delicate Tiger Moth biplanes to American built P-40s and early P-51As in British service. Though an active hub as far as Army-Cooperation was concerned, Bottisham remained a relatively small affair within the RAF, accommodating less than 1,000 personnel at the height of British operations.[1]

With the perimeter track situated immediately adjacent to Bottisham Village and supporting facilities scattered throughout the civilian areas, the life of the airbase and town were closely linked. So it was under the RAF, and so it would remain after the "friendly invasion" of Yanks who arrived at the end of 1943.

While the villagers were certainly accustomed to the constant activity of a nearby military post in wartime, few could have expected the beehive of activity which descended on Bottisham with the arrival of the 361st. Throughout most of the summer of 1943, the field lay dormant after the RAF departed and it was not until November that the first trickle of new occupants arrived. Suddenly on November 30 the Americans began to appear en masse, and not just the 937 officers and men which comprised the 361st. During the first week of December, nearly 800 additional personnel responsible for specialized aircraft repair, signals, ordnance, military police, supply, and the myriad of tasks necessary for the day-to-day functioning of the station, began to appear. In all, more than 1700 American military personnel were assigned to Station F-374 by the end of 1943, a figure approaching twice the maximum RAF complement.[2]

Overall, relations between the villagers and the Americans stationed at Bottisham would remain friendly throughout the Group's deployment there. As one recorded example of cultural exchange, two American Sergeants of Bottisham's 66th Station Composite Squadron accepted an invitation by local villagers at the end of January 1944 to participate in a friendly discussion of the differences between the British and the Americans. "Although nothing was proved and some issues were deliberately evaded," Lt. Robert B. Wentworth, Bottisham's Station Historical Officer recorded, "much was said in a manner which was realistic and, at times conducive to friendly Anglo-American relationships."[3] *Yank*, the US Army's weekly magazine covered this somewhat unique meeting of 100 or so British and Americans in Bottisham. The correspondent attending the meeting noted that the American Servicemen raised points such as the differences in the education systems in Britain and America, as well as the Americans' difficulty in understanding the British accent, particularly over the phone. On the other side of the discussion, a local farmer voiced puzzlement over "the 'conspicuous' habit of gum chewing" among the

Americans, and was also curious to learn the identity of the "comic costume designer for the American Army." A local physician, Dr. A.F. Gilbert, declared that while he had been somewhat shocked by the suddenness of the American arrival in the village, and though he occasionally observed things which "made his hair curl," he admitted that, overall he liked the Americans "very much for their friendliness, generosity and helpfulness, which extends sometimes to the sentimental."[4]

For the newly arrived Americans, the transition to operations in wartime England involved a wide array of adjustments. Perhaps the Station Engineering Officer, Maj. Wesley Parks, spoke for the majority of the new arrivals when he observed that memories of Richmond's temperate warmth "made the cold, damp, and windy climate of England at this season seem like a miserable fate indeed."[5] Summarizing the first weeks of the American presence at Bottisham, Lt. Robert B. Wentworth, Station Historical Officer, noted that personnel of the 361st and attached units "had to get used to British barracks and Nissen huts, complete blackout, bad weather which caused plenty of mild 'flu,' the bucket system of latrines (except in some favorite spots) powdered eggs and dehydrated foods, little 'doll house' stoves which heat when coaxed, a post and a village which somehow had become mixed up to look like one (effective camouflage), long distances from mess hall to work, a certain amount of general bewilderment and such maddening phrases as 'you cawn't miss it.' (but you do)."[6]

Living accommodations for enlisted personnel – typically the corrugated-steel Nissen hut – and a prevailing shortage of coal tended to magnify the less desirable traits of the climate. "The Nissen huts in the enlisted personnel area were functional, but the rationing of coal to heat them left them cold much of the time early on," recalled Bernard J. Redden, a former crew chief in the 375th Squadron. Place mechanically inclined men in a cold, damp living environment, however, and ingenuity soon prevails. "In our hut," Redden continued, "we rigged up a drip system, gravity fed, which allowed waste engine oil or hydraulic fluid to be ignited on a pan in the small pot-bellied stove. Not an entirely safe practice, but…as far as I know none of us ever suffered from pneumonia."[7]

Officer's accommodations at Bottisham were slightly better for the Squadron Commanders and Headquarters Staff since Bottisham Hall, the stately home of a local family, was transformed into their quarters.[8] For Flight Commanders and the average pilot, however, the realities of life at Bottisham were virtually identical to those of the enlisted men. "I guess the biggest things I recall are Nissen huts and bicycles," remarked James R. Golden who reported to Bottisham in January 1944 as replacement pilot "…everybody had a bicycle to get back

Nissen huts and bicycles. Maj. John Stryker seen on his bicycle at Station F-374, Bottisham, Cambridgeshire, 1944. To his left is a corrugated-steel Nissen hut typical of much of the station's living accommodations. *Courtesy J.J. Kruzel*

and forth from where they were sleeping to the lines and most of us were in Nissen huts."[9] George Lichter, who arrived at Bottisham as a Second Lieutenant with the 374th Squadron recalled that the weather conditions required getting used to. "I've never been colder than I was in England in the winter … and we had this little stove in the middle of the Nissen hut which we had somebody fix up to drip oil in it. God, I slept with a hat on, I slept with socks on and winter underwear, and boy, we were bitter cold!"[10] Billy D. Welch, who arrived at Bottisham as a Second Lieutenant in the 376th Squadron ech-

Bottisham Hall, the stately home of a local family which served as living quarters for the Group's headquarters staff and squadron commanders. *Courtesy George Lichter*

oed Lichter's views, adding that the peculiarly British mattresses inherited from the RAF made a distinct impression. "Our
mattresses were English 'biscuits.' These were sofa-like square,
flat pillows," Welch recalled years later. "Three of them were
placed end-to-end on our cots to form a mattress. They had a
tendency to separate while one slept, letting in the cold night
air." Welch eventually solved this inconvenience by sewing
his biscuits together, but cold and damp conditions in general
were a predominant memory for him. "I thought the weather
was always cold, rainy and miserable," he recalled years later.
"I grew up in Florida and never seemed to get used to the English weather."[11]

While the climate had few redeeming qualities in Welch's
memory, he recalled definite compensating niceties associated
with the quaint village of Bottisham. The base, Welch related,
"was on one side of town [and] our quarters were on the other
side, so we had to pass through the village…. One of my more
pleasant memories was the town bakery. When the baker was
baking bread in his open-space clay oven … the aroma permeated the air. Sometimes when returning to our quarters from
the flight line, we would purchase a loaf of his delicious bread.
It was a treat for me and sure tasted better than chow hall bread.
I had never seen an outdoor clay oven before," he added.[12]

At the time of the 361st's arrival at Bottisham, eleven P-
47 Thunderbolts were already at the Station. In the weeks that
followed their numbers would be successively augmented as
more aircraft were flown in. Though the fighters assigned to
the newly arrived Group were the latest P-47D-10 and D-11
models only recently arrived from the States, they were far
from combat-ready. In addition to the initial acceptance inspec-
tions and normal routine maintenance, the ground crews of the
361st, working side-by-side with the 468th Service Squadron
which was also assigned to Bottisham, would be responsible
for implementing an array of some 50 modifications necessary
to bring the aircraft up to 8th Fighter Command operational
standards. These modifications ranged from painting the inte-
rior of the cockpit dark green, to major changes in the electri-
cal and fuel systems. Most of this maintenance was carried out
in the open since hangar space was extremely limited and the
majority of the maintenance shelters were corrugated steel "blister hangars" which resembled enlarged Nissen huts open at
both ends. "Our biggest headache," wrote Maj. Parks, the Station Engineering Officer, several months after the Group had
settled in, "was the installation of fuel and pressure lines for
the belly [auxiliary fuel] tanks. Many a dreary night was spent
by the mechanics in our lone hangar installing fuel pressuriz-
ing systems for belly tanks … Night work was very difficult.
Black-out restrictions prevented the use of the blister hangars

Lt. Billy D. Welch of the 376th Fighter Squadron seen being decorated
at Bottisham in early 1944. *Courtesy Billy D. Welch*

The men who kept them flying: A meeting of the ground crews at
Bottisham, 1944. *Courtesy Russell A. Severson*

because light leaked through the few that had curtains. The
others were impossible. With no curtains plus equipment
stacked inside they merely acted as giant venturis and a local
gale resulted."[13]

To add to the problems of making the Group's 50-plus P-
47s operational within weeks of arrival, maintenance personnel were hampered by the cold, damp English weather, along
with a shortage of tools and winter clothing. In spite of these
deficiencies, wrote Maj. Parks, "the aircraft still had to be made
ready for combat in the shortest time possible. The tools of the
468th Service Squadron were distributed throughout the Fighter
Squadrons and by dint of a great deal of overtime accompanied by a great deal of good-natured cussing, off hand Air Corps
efficiency, and many a shiver, the group was ready for combat

in a little over 3 weeks after its arrival in England. Tools and clothing for men on the line dribbled in, then gushed, and were finally all in the proper hands seven weeks after the arrival of the first airplane. The 'goods wagons' had been lost."[14]

Just as the Group's aircraft required modification before combat operations could begin, the runways inherited from the RAF would need to be upgraded to accommodate the Group's heavy P-47s which would routinely take off by elements and flights in line-abreast formation. "The flying field, with steel mats laid over the grass, was less than ideal," recalled 375th Squadron Crew Chief Bernard J. Redden. "The main runway had a dip in it, so that viewing a take-off from one end of the field, the planes would almost disappear from sight of the viewer before becoming airborne."[15]

Though little could ultimately be done about the noticeable dip which resulted from a former sunken farm road passing through the field, a major program of improvement would be undertaken within the first two months of occupation. After accumulating sufficient quantities of Sommerfield track, alternatively known as pierced-steel-planking (PSP), an intensive upgrade was initiated by Col. Christian and the commander of a detachment of US Army Engineers. Dividing the work force into two teams of approximately 35 men each, a contest for the shortest time in completing the runway improvements was begun at 0930 hours on January 23 and continued round-the-clock for the next 57 hours and ten minutes. Justifiably proud of the speed with which the work was completed, the Engineer detachment commander, Col. I.O. Brent, declared that the project was "never equaled in the ETO or elsewhere by US Troops."[16] Whether equaled or not, the manner in which the runway upgrade was carried out underscores the overriding objective which was to make the Station operational as quickly as was possible.

Lt. George Lichter of the 374th Fighter Squadron. *Courtesy George Lichter*

If the runway was less then ideal from a mechanical standpoint, it had at least one advantage from a station-defense angle – camouflage. The Sommerfield Track allowed grass to grow through the regularly spaced holes in the individual sections, thus causing the runway to blend with the surrounding grass perimeter. Though perhaps beneficial in thwarting a surprise German raider in daylight, this feature was not lost on the Americans during the 361st's early operations at Bottisham. George Lichter, one of the 374th Squadron's original pilots, recalled an unanticipated difficulty the first time he attempted to land at Bottisham after a familiarization flight in December 1943. Spotting the main road from Cambridge, Lichter was initially at a loss to sight the field. "I knew where Bottisham was," Lichter recalled, "and I flew over that road six times on

P-47s, attended by ground crews, warm up for take off, Bottisham in early 1944. Note the 75-gallon belly tanks on the ground near the aircraft. *Courtesy Billy D. Welch*

my first flight and I couldn't find the field. I finally called the tower and said 'send up a flare'!"[17]

While the ground echelon at Bottisham was working to make the station operational, the pilots of the Group's three squadrons and Headquarters section were working to familiarize themselves with their new theater of operations. On December 12, 1943, the pilots at Bottisham began a ground school course intended to familiarize them with operational practices within the 8th Fighter Command, such as navigation and communication procedures. During the following weeks, as aircraft modifications were completed and planes were allotted to the squadrons, the pilots began local familiarization flights. By the end of December orders arrived assigning the Group Commander and Air Executive Officer along with Squadron Commanders and flight leaders to temporary duty with operational Groups. According to the teletyped signal from the 66th Fighter Wing, to which the 361st had been assigned:

> "The Group Commander, Executive [Officer], Squadron Commanders and Flight Leaders of the 361st Group will be ready to participate in combat operations missions with experienced groups of this Wing.... The Group Commander and Squadron Commanders will make up one team and upon completion of their attachment to an operational Group, the remainder of the officers will make up a second team."[18]

Col. Christian and the three Squadron Commanders were assigned to the 78th Fighter Group at Duxford, While Maj. Kruzel and the remaining pilots reported to Metfield for operations with the 353rd Group. During the first week of January 1944, these officers would carry out vital training with their more experienced counterparts, after which they would return to Bottisham to begin final preparations for the combat debut of the 361st.

While flying from Duxford and Metfield, the 361st's leaders from Flight Commanders up would be introduced to bomber escort operations as practiced by the 8th Air Force. Under ideal conditions, the 8th Fighter Command would be able to protect the heavy bombers as they attacked German targets from the time they crossed the enemy coast until the time they left several hours later. The B-17 and B-24 groups were trained to fly in tight formations, stacked by squadrons in "combat boxes" in order to maximize the defensive firepower of the their own guns. Two or more groups of bombers (approximately 35 aircraft each) would be formed into combat wings and these combat wings would fly a prescribed route at high altitude (20,000 to 30,000 feet usually) to their briefed targets and then back

A group of Boeing B-17 Flying Fortresses in a "combat box" formation which afforded maximum defensive firepower for the entire group. *National Archives*

out along a specified withdrawal route. The fighter outfits of the 8th Air Force would be assigned to fly with these combat wings in order to fend off what proved to be the greatest threat to the "heavies" – German fighter aircraft.

The limited range of the P-47 Thunderbolt, which equipped most of the 8th Air Force's fighter groups at the beginning of 1944, was among the biggest concerns of the proponents of the daylight bombing campaign against Germany. Considering the P-47's endurance of a little over 4 hours, the bombers were often required to proceed to their targets without the protection of fighter aircraft beyond the western fringes of Germany. Without this protection, the "heavies" took a pounding, and their losses to German fighters approached unacceptable levels. To the limit of their endurance, however, the P-47 equipped groups of the 8th Fighter Command would escort the bombers for the maximum possible portion of their routes, supporting the bombers during penetration of enemy airspace, within the target area, or along the withdrawal route.

Following the return of the Group's command staff and flight leaders from Duxford and Metfield during the second week of January 1944, the Group undertook final preparations for its first combat mission. Once the 361st was declared operational, inclusion in an actual Field Order could come at any time. The awaited declaration was made on January 15 and it was not long before the teletype machines in Bottisham's headquarters began printing out the Field Orders for the Group's first combat mission. English weather, however, confounded the process so that anticipation led to anticlimax as rain and fog grounded most operations by the 8th Air Force during the third week of January 1944.

Pilots at a pre-mission briefing at Bottisham, 1944. Standing at the extreme left is Maj. Wallace E. Hopkins, Group Operations Officer. Seated in front (l-r) is Group Commander Col. Christian, 374th Squadron CO Maj. Roy A. Webb, and 375th Squadron CO Maj. Merritt. *Courtesy J.J. Kruzel*

It was not until January 21, when the weather had cleared, that the 361st Group would carry out its first combat mission. As Bottisham's pilots assembled in the station briefing room that morning, they learned that the 8th Bomber Command's resources that day would be turned against the then mysterious V-weapon rocket sites, given the codename "Crossbow," in northern France. Though these German rocket-launching bases would not begin their bombardment of England for practically another six months, Allied intelligence ascertained their destructive potential and placed them high on the list of priority targets in the daylight bombing campaign.

8th Air Force Field Order 388, in which the 361st would make its debut, involved nearly 800 B-17s and B-24s assigned to bomb "Crossbow" targets from the Cherbourg area to the Pas de Calais. As one of thirteen fighter groups to take part in the mission, the 361st was assigned to Target Area Support in the Pas de Calais. Simply put, the Group would patrol its assigned area in search of enemy aircraft which might rise from their French bases to intercept the heavy bombers.[19]

The mission would officially begin for the 361st shortly after 1300 hours that afternoon as 52 of the Group's P-47s lifted off in pairs from Bottisham's steel-matted runway. To lead the Group on its first combat sortie was Maj. Ben Rimerman, the experienced Executive Officer of the nearby 353rd Fighter Group. The practice of having newly arrived outfits introduced to combat by an experienced "old hand" not only helped to instill confidence among the ranks of the novice unit, but also helped ensure that Group's role in the operation would, indeed, be carried out. After forming up in squadrons at 4,000 feet over the field, the Group began a steady southeasterly climb toward France. When landfall was made over the French Coast at 1350 hours, the three squadrons were stacked 1500 feet apart, with the high squadron at 19,000 feet. Organized for maximum protection in the tried-and-true "finger four" formation, each flight following its squadron leader, who, in turn followed the Group leader, the 361st patrolled its assigned area for the next 90 minutes.[20] As they scanned the sky, searching for German aircraft, they sighted formations of B-17s on course for their targets in the Pas de Calais. Over St. Omer, German flak rose to meet the bombers, one of which was hit and fell away toward the English Channel where it eventually ditched.[21] These images would be the Group's first glimpses of the air war over Europe during an otherwise uneventful first mission.

When the Group landed back at Bottisham shortly after 1600 hours, eleven of its aircraft had returned early – eight pilots "aborting" due to mechanical failures, and three more detached to escort them back through hostile airspace. Additionally, several of the Group's aircraft were forced to make emergency landings elsewhere due to lack of fuel.

Five of those pilots who were forced to abort on the Group's first mission did so because of "belly tank" failures – fuel from the jettisonable tank fixed to the underside of the aircraft would not feed properly. In most cases, it was Bottisham's runway which was the source of these failures. The uneven surface of the farmland over which the steel matting was laid caused excessive vibration during takeoff that was sometimes enough to loosen or break the fuel line connecting the tank with the aircraft's fuel system. Deprived of the use of the belly tank, the aircraft would not have sufficient range to carry out the mission and the pilot would likely have to turn back early on his own which was deemed an unnecessary risk.

Once combat operations had begun for the 361st on January 21, 1944, the Group would be assigned a role to play in the vast coordinated efforts of the 8th Air Force as it carried out its daylight bombing campaign over Occupied Europe. Weather permitting, the 8th Bomber Command would continue to attack prioritized targets throughout the Continent ranging from factories producing strategic materials, to transportation hubs, and military installations such as the "Crossbow" sites under construction on the French Coast.

After the 361st's second combat mission on January 24, Lt. Col. Christian, and his Air Exec, Maj. Kruzel, took over the task of operational leadership within the Group. Together, these two officers, both of whom had seen combat in the Pacific Theater, would share the burdens of leadership as the novice 361st began its combat tour with the 8th Air Force.

The Group's first combat loss took place during the first of two escort missions carried out by the 361st on January 29. After accompanying a force of B-17s to the vicinity of the German border, the Group, led by Lt. Col. Christian, was heading back toward England when someone spotted an unidentified aircraft well below and Red Flight of the 374th Squadron was dispatched to investigate. After identifying the aircraft as a B-17, Red Flight proceeded toward England independently. When the flight leader deemed that adequate time and distance had been flown and that they were likely over the English Channel, he ordered a let-down through the thick layer of undercast. When the flight broke through the clouds, they found themselves at 800 feet over the heavily fortified French coast. German light flak batteries immediately opened fire on the four P-47s and although they quickly climbed back into the overcast, 2nd Lt. Charles Screws was not with them when they emerged above the cloud layer.[22] Lt. Screws' aircraft had been hit by flak, and the engine of his P-47 began running rough. Unwilling to risk a trip across the icy waters of the English Channel, Screws later reported that "I did a 180 degree turn and flew as far and as fast as I could away from the coastal defense zone. Twenty minutes later, I broke cover over an airfield. They shot at me again and knocked me about…two minutes later I landed, wheels up, in a plowed field. I blew up the IFF [Identification Friend or Foe transmitter] as an FW-190 started to circle … when he left, I went back to the ship and collected my extra pair of socks, medical kit, gloves, and the k-ration chocolate and compass," before setting off into nearby woods.[23]

While the Group's first combat loss undoubtedly drove home the fact that the 361st was now in "a shooting war," no

A 374th Fighter Squadron P-47 Thunderbolt in flight seen from the waist-gunner's position of a B-24 Liberator, 1944. *USAF Museum*

one felt the loss more keenly than Lt. Screws' crew chief, Sgt. Russell Severson. The bond between ground crew and pilot was typically strong and, according to Severson, "As crew chief you just can't imagine how helpless you feel, and very sad, wondering where he was and whether he was alive. I couldn't sleep for many nights." This was only the beginning, however, and the pace of operations at Bottisham continued in spite of the loss. "Luckily, I was given a new pilot and P-47, so you soon get involved with the war again," Severson remarked many years later.[24] Fortunately, however, Screws eventually contacted the French Resistance, eventually making his way across the Pyrenees, to Gibraltar and back to England.[25]

On January 30, the Group was called on to put up two escort missions as over 700 B-17s and B-24s of the 8th Bomber Command attacked targets in Brunswick and Hannover.[26] It would be on the first mission of the day, in which the Group was assigned "penetration support" as the bombers entered enemy airspace, that the 361st would engage German aircraft for the first time. Lt. Col. Christian was to lead on the mission, but was forced to return to base early due to a radio malfunction. Maj. Kruzel took over the lead of the Group's 43 P-47s as they made landfall over the Netherlands at 1100 hours. Though the 361st reached the rendezvous location on time, the assigned bombers were nowhere in sight, so Kruzel took the 375th Squadron and proceeded to climb above a layer of high cloud cover in order to try to locate the bombers. During this maneuver, several Focke Wulf (FW) 190's and Messerschmitt (ME) 109's were spotted just above the clouds and elements of the 375th Squadron gave chase. Capt. John W. Guckeyson was credited with damaging one of the ME-109s.[27]

While detached from the 375th Squadron, the remaining two squadrons, the 374th and 376th, proceeded on course in search of the bombers – a task complicated by the heavy cloud cover that day over much of their route. At 1130 hours in the vicinity of Rheine in western Germany, the 374th Squadron

Lt. Charles Screws of the 374th Fighter Squadron. Forced to crash-land his plane in France on January 29, 1944, Screws was the first combat loss for the 361st Fighter Group. *Courtesy George Lichter*

was orbiting above a layer of cloud cover, still hoping to sight the assigned combat wings of bombers, when vapor contrails were reported several thousand feet above. The squadron went into a defensive "Lufberry" circle as the contrails continued overhead. Suddenly some 20-30 ME-109s dove down on the orbiting P-47s from all directions.

Maj. Roy A. Webb, of Pampa, Texas, the 26-year-old commander of the 374th, watched as several of the Messerschmitts began attacking the rear flight from a 4-o'clock position, breaking up the defensive formation. Webb spotted one of the enemy aircraft on the tail of a P-47 in Blue Flight, and immediately executed a left wing-over which placed him on the tail of the Messerschmitt, whose pilot immediately broke off the attack, diving away to the right and then to the left. Webb, his own flight in trail, stayed with the German, holding his gun sight on the enemy fighter. At 18,000 feet, he was within 400 yards of his target as he depressed the gun trigger on his control stick, sending streams of tracer, armor-piercing and incen-

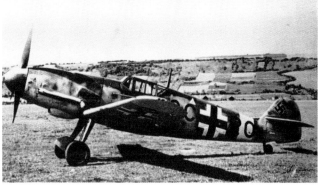

Left: A Focke-Wulf (FW) 190 in flight. The FW-190 would be a frequent German fighter type encountered by the pilots of the 361st. *USAF Museum*
Right: A Messerschmitt (ME) 109. *USAF Museum*

Maj. Roy Webb of the 374th Fighter Squadron poses beneath the cowling of his P-47D "Sweet Thing III" at Bottisham, 1944. *Courtesy Russell A. Severson*

Capt. Robert Sedman of the 374th Fighter Squadron poses beneath the wing of his P-47 at Bottisham, 1944. *Courtesy Russell A. Severson*

diary ammunition from his Thunderbolt's eight .50 caliber machine guns at the diving German. 2nd Lt. Roy P. Lacy of Baltimore, Maryland, was covering his Squadron Commander from above and later reported how "Major Webb closed and began firing at 400 yards and broke off at zero range. Strikes were observed on the canopy, wing roots and tail section. What appeared to be the canopy fell off, and as the enemy aircraft entered a 1,000 foot overcast in a vertical dive, I observed part of the tail section fall off and the plane burst into flames."[28] Based on the evidence of his gun camera film, as well as the observations of Lt. Lacy, Webb would be credited with destroying an enemy aircraft – perhaps the first in the Group's operational history, though it would be impossible to say for sure as several other combats were taking place at the same time.

Capt. Robert Sedman, a 23-year old native of Wheatland, Wyoming, was leading Red Flight of the 374th on the mission and shortly after the Squadron went into its defensive "Lufberry," he saw a German fighter closing on his flight from a 1-o'clock position. Sedman immediately turned into the approaching Messerschmitt and fired a short burst "to check my guns." 2nd Lt. Henry B. Lederer of New York City was flying as Sedman's Wingman and saw a German fighter attacking Yellow Flight of the 374th from dead astern and immediately

called out the Messerschmitt to his leader. Sedman, with Lederer on his wing, turned onto the tail of the ME-109 which quickly broke off its attack and went into a vertical dive in an attempt to get away. "I did a violent push-over and followed the enemy aircraft down," Sedman reported after landing that day. "At about 15,000 feet I opened fire at extreme range and closed to approximately 350 yards, observing hits on the wing roots and fuselage." When down to only 2,000 feet of altitude, Sedman began to pull out of his dive, while watching as the German fighter continued straight down at terminal velocity. Lt. Lederer, who had followed his leader throughout the chase, began his pull out at 8,000 feet as the heavy P-47's airspeed indicator registered 600 MPH. Pulling out of the dive Lederer continued to climb and eventually leveled off at 16,000 feet, temporarily "blacked out" as the "g" force from the maneuver caused blood to flow downward in his body, impairing his vision.[29] Though fairly certain of the critical damage received by the ME-109, and considering the low altitude at which its pilot continued his vertical dive, Sedman later could only claim the German fighter as "Probably Destroyed" since he had neither witnessed a crash, nor captured positive proof of destruction on his gun-camera film.

Lt. Roy P. Lacy of the 374th Fighter Squadron seen in the cockpit of his P-51 at Bottisham, summer 1944. *Courtesy Russell A. Severson*

Lt. Henry B. Lederer of the 374th Fighter Squadron poses on the wing of his P-47 "Duchess of Manhattan" at Bottisham. Note his insulated flying boots designed for high-altitude comfort. *Courtesy Henry B. Lederer*

After climbing up to 11,000 feet on the momentum of his pull-out, Capt. Sedman began calling for the elements of his flight to reform, after they had become scattered in combat. Lt. Lederer had just joined on his wing again when another ME-109 attacked them from abeam at 2 o'clock. The German pilot's speed was so great, however, that he overshot the element of P-47s allowing Sedman to turn onto his tail after applying full throttle. Opening fire at a range of 700 yards and closing to only 150, Sedman's eight .50 caliber machine guns tore into the Messerschmitt, a piece of which flew off and damaged the engine cowling of his Thunderbolt. Sedman and Lederer watched the enemy pilot bail out of his aircraft amid a trail of smoke and flame.[30] Just as the German abandoned his aircraft, Lt. Lederer spotted an ME-109 below and to the left, and after calling for Capt. Sedman to cover him, "went in on the enemy aircraft's tail at about 6,000 [feet] indicating 550 MPH." As he pressed the trigger at a range of 150 yards, Lederer saw strikes and flashes as he repeatedly hit the German fighter. As pieces flew off striking his right wing, cowling, propeller, and windshield, Lederer suddenly noticed another P-47 also firing at the same enemy aircraft.[31] Lt. James Hastin, who had been flying the position of Red Four, had also spotted the ME-109 and attacked the enemy aircraft until forced to break away following an explosion around the Messerschmitt's cockpit. It was then that he spotted Lederer "directly beneath me not more than 10 feet."[32] Though neither of the two attacking pilots witnessed a crash, later assessment of their combat film led to a shared claim for each.

2nd Lt. Joe Latimer of the 374th Squadron would also be able to claim an ME-109 destroyed in the encounter near Rheine. As Blue Flight Leader, Latimer turned his flight in to face attacking German fighters at the start of the fight. After the initial head-on pass he sighted a Messerschmitt dead astern of 2nd Lt. Robert Eckfeldt of Yellow Flight a thousand feet below him. Latimer dove on the ME-109 whose pilot saw the attacking P-47 and broke away in a steep dive. "I had no trouble catching him at 500 MPH," Latimer reported after the combat. After firing approximately 600 rounds of ammunition at the enemy fighter, Latimer saw smoke pouring from the German plane which continued down in a terminal dive. Latimer saw fit to note during the mission debriefing that the German "pilot attempted no evasive action except the high speed dive which to me shows a lack of experience and knowledge of the dive characteristics of the P-47 airplane."[33] Based on the supporting testimony of another pilot in Blue flight, Latimer would be awarded a claim of destroyed.

After approximately 15 minutes, the combat was over and the scattered elements of the 374th Squadron turned west toward England. After landing at Bottisham, the pilots were debriefed and eventually the Squadron would be credited with four enemy aircraft destroyed, one probably destroyed, and two damaged – the first aerial victories in the operational history of the 361st Fighter Group. For this early success, however, the Group traded the loss of one of its pilots. 2nd Lt. Ethelbert Amason, aged 20, of Hargill, Texas, a small town in the Rio Grande Valley, had been flying as the second element leader in Red Flight of the 374th. When the combat started, Amason went out of radio contact and in the excitement of the moment, no one, including his wingman, 2nd Lt. James Hastin, saw what happened to him.

The exact fate of "Bert" Amason would remain a mystery until several years after the war. Unable to obtain any specific information on her brother's disappearance through US Government Channels, Amason's sister, Goldie, began writing letters to the mayors of towns and villages in the eastern Netherlands requesting information on any American aircraft known to have come down on January 30, 1944. Eventually she received a reply from the Mayor of Rijissen, a town some thirteen miles east of Deventer, that an American P-47 had, in fact, crashed nearby on that date. The local villagers had recovered the remains of the pilot and laid them to rest in the local churchyard. After positive identification, Ethelbert Amason's remains were returned to the United States in 1950.[34]

Following the short, sharp engagement on January 30, the month of February would be a time of anti-climax for the 361st. A mere sixteen missions would be flown by the Group during the entire month as operations were frequently hampered by bad weather. In the course of those sixteen missions, contact with enemy aircraft would be made on only three, for a total of six enemy planes claimed destroyed. Still new to the ETO, this relatively slow period would allow the Group to continue its familiarization with routines of bomber escort operations – in effect, the lull before the storm.

Lt. Joe Latimer of the 374th Fighter Squadron poses beside his P-47. Latimer, who was credited with downing an ME-109 on January 30, 1944, would be lost on a disastrous mission some five months later. *Courtesy J.J. Kruzel*

NOTES

[1] John F. Hamlin, *The Histories of RAF Waterbeach and Bottisham*, (Great Britain: Privately published, 1987)pp. 44-47.

[2] Ibid., p. 49.

[3] Headquarters 361st Fighter Group, "Station History – Station F-374" 7 February 1944, p. 3

[4] "The Squawks Get and Airing," *Yank*, May 7, 1944, p.11.

[5] Wesley Parks, "Historical Record, Operational Engineering Sections, (Aircraft) Station F-374," June 1944.

[6] Robert B. Wentworth, "Unit History AAF Station F-374 (361st Fighter Group) For December 1943," March 12, 1944, p.2.

[7] Bernard J. Redden, Correspondence with the Author, February 10, 1996.

[8] Steve Gotts, *Little Friends: A Pictorial History of the 361st Fighter Group* (Dallas, Taylor Publishing Co., 1993), p. 13.

[9] James R. Golden, Interview with the Author, November 27, 1995.

[10] George Lichter, Interview with the Author, September 15, 2000.

[11] Billy D. Welch, Correspondence with the Author, February 13, 2001.

[12] Ibid.

[13] Parks.

[14] Ibid.

[15] Redden.

[16] Robert B. Wentworth, "Engineers from 8th district laying pierced steel runway planking at Station F-374, attachment to "Station History, Station F-374" 7 February 1944.

[17] Lichter.

[18] 8th Air Force, 66th Fighter Wing, Teletype Message 30101A, December 1944.

[19] 8th Fighter Command, "Narrative of Operations," January 21, 1944, p. 2.

[20] Wallace E. Hopkins, "Tactical Commanders Report for 21 January 1944, 361st Fighter Group," January 25, 1944.

[21] 8th Fighter Command, "Narrative of Operations," January 21, 1944, p.2.

[22] 361st Fighter Group, "Mission Summary Report, Field Order 226, " January 29, 1944.

[23] Charles B. Screws, Escape and Evasion Report No. 673, June 5, 1944.

[24] Russell A. Severson, Correspondence with the Author, October 18, 1995.

[25] Screws, Escape and Evasion Report No. 673.

[26] Roger A. Freeman, *The Mighty Eighth War Diary* (New York: Janes, 1981), p. 172.

[27] 361st Fighter Group, "Mission Summary Report, Field Order 221," January 30, 1944.

[28] Roy A. Webb, "Encounter Report," January 30, 1944.

[29] Robert E. Sedman, "Encounter Report," January 30, 1944.

[30] Ibid.

[31] Henry B. Lederer, "Encounter Report," January 30, 1944.

[32] James D. Hastin, "Encounter Report," January 30, 1944.

[33] Joe L. Latimer, "Encounter Report," January 30, 1944.

[34] Bob Burch, "Sound Off," *361st Fighter Group Association Newsletter* (Vol. 13, August 1993), p. 5.

three

"Big Week," Berlin, and Beyond

Four enemy aircraft destroyed and another probable, for the loss of two pilots; at the beginning of February 1944, that was the score which summed up the 361st's initiation into the air war over Europe. While the losses of Lieutenants Screws and Amason brought home the realities of combat to the fledgling Group in its initial combat missions, morale remained high and self-confidence would naturally increase when, by all accounts, they had bested the *Luftwaffe* at the outset.

While the original Group remained largely intact in early 1944, some new faces appeared. 2nd Lt. James R. Golden, a native of Florida, reported to Bottisham during the last week of January 1944 as one of the Group's first replacement pilots. Assigned to the 374th Squadron, which had suffered both of the initial combat losses, Golden was immediately impressed by the tightness of the outfit in contrast to his own lack of experience. "I was just so green, I didn't realize that they hadn't been in combat but a week or two when I got there. But to me, they were all veterans and I was really an absolute neophyte."[1]

Worldwide demands for trained pilots at the beginning of 1944 meant that many of those arriving at active units had minimal experience, and Lt. Golden was no exception. "I had only 60 hours in a P-47 before I went overseas," he later recalled, "and that's not much time! They were shooting us all over there so fast that we really didn't have the amount of training that they wanted us to have – and I was the first replacement pilot in the 361st, and, boy, [I was] at a terrible disadvantage at that time because [I came] out with a minimum 60 hours and these guys have been flying for several months, you know, getting ready to go overseas as a Group."[2] Though Golden had been told at the replacement depot that he would receive further training once he reported to his outfit, little thought had been given to preparation of replacement pilots at Bottisham – after all,

less than five missions had been flown by the 361st at the time of his arrival on January 27, 1944.

With so little time in P-47s, Lt. Golden was surprised to find himself assigned to fly his first combat mission shortly after joining the 374th Squadron. "I was there five days and I looked on the board, and I was [slated] to go – and I hadn't taken a wheel off of the runway! And I remember, on February 2, I went on that trip. It was a very short trip in the Pas De Calais area, which was good because I was not familiar with a lot of the things you do to save fuel and all that sort of thing. I learned quickly that day, that's for sure! I came back from a short mission with almost no fuel and I told the guy I flew with, I said 'Man, my fuel was low!' He said, 'I had over a half a tank left!'" Used to flying stateside with lower octane aviation gas, Golden had failed to use the proper mixture control to maximize fuel economy – a mistake which he would not repeat again.[3]

Inexperienced or not, James Golden would continue to learn on the job during the first months of 1944, though administrative protests over his lack of experience initially barred him from flying. Shortly after his first mission, he recalled that "word came from headquarters that I was not to fly again because I didn't have enough time to be a combat pilot…. I flew mission two, three, mission four, and they came back again and said, 'We told you, he hasn't got enough time to be a combat pilot!' So I was working on my first Air Medal and I was grounded again for not having enough time to fly." In the end, administrative hurdles gave way to operational needs, and Golden resumed logging combat time.[4]

Although the Group experienced a sharp engagement with German fighters on January 30, aerial combat for the 361st would prove elusive during the late winter and early spring of

A P-47D of the 376th Fighter Squadron piloted by Lt. Billy D. Welch, photographed from a B-17 of the 457th Bomb Group, spring 1944. *Courtesy Billy D. Welch*

1944. This was particularly true in the month of February when German aircraft were engaged on just three of sixteen missions – and all of these at the end of the month. Though anticlimactic, the first weeks of February were not sedentary by any means. Whether or not combat was joined, each mission still required vast preparation and attention to detail. Precise timetables had to be set and followed in order to make rendezvous with the assigned bombers at the appointed time. Navigation had to be carefully performed and once its portion of the escort was completed, the Group would have to find its way back to Bottisham in the unpredictable English weather, which was especially so during the winter months.

While the ground crews at Bottisham had been working non-stop since mid-December 1943 to prepare their 70-odd P-47s for combat, the maintenance demands of actual operations were not fully apparent until February 1944. After several weeks of combat flying, ground crews became accustomed to the critical routines necessary for keeping the Group up to strength on a daily basis. For these grease-specked troops who fought the war from England, the unsung but necessary routines which kept the planes in the air, and did much to bring the pilots back home safe, became a way of life for the duration.

Assigned to every aircraft in the Group was a crew chief and an assistant who would serve as the primary maintenance staff for their assigned pilot. From the time the plane returned from a mission until the time it was airborne on its next sortie, these individuals, with the help of various support personnel,

did whatever was necessary to make their plane ready. "When the planes returned from the mission," recalled former 374th Squadron crew chief Russell Severson, "the crews pulled a daily inspection: everything was checked over very carefully. If the guns had been fired, the armorers removed all eight guns and worked all night to have them back in the wings for an early mission – very hard workers. Then we had radio men who kept the radio up to par. We had two expert prop men who worked on the hydromatic prop if something was wrong. If your plane had a 25, 50, 75, or 100-hour inspection, then we'd tow the plane into the hangar and work all night. Sleep was very hard to get."[5]

"Whatever…it took for the aircraft to be flyable by the next mission was done," commented former 374th Squadron Crew Chief Robert Bland. "In rare instances, it might take the balance of the night, even though it was minor work. It was

Lt. James R. Golden photographed in the cockpit of a P-47. Golden was among the first replacement pilots assigned to the 361st Group and arrived at Bottisham in late January 1944. *Courtesy George Lichter*

surprising how small problems could be so out of reach! We wished many times that the guys that designed and built them had to maintain them![6]

Certain regular tasks on the P-47 were far from easy – yet the ground crews were required to persevere regardless. "When they brought in 100 octane gas, we were forced to change spark plugs every other mission" recalled Russell Severson years later. "On a P-47, that's 36 plugs – two in each cylinder. Two of these were located behind the oil coolers; if you had big hands it could take up to an hour for each of those plugs. I saw more than one crew chief throw his wrenches out in the field, but he always picked them up and finished the job … in the back of your mind was [the idea that] your guy was up there all alone with only one engine."[7]

Ground crews were far from finished when their post-mission chores were carried out since the hours prior to a mission also demanded a specific routine for every plane. Arriving on scene well in advance of the scheduled take-off, crew chiefs and assistants would begin a set pre-flight inspection to insure proper functioning of critical systems. After running up the engine for several minutes, a test of both magnetos would be made; a significant drop in magneto RPM's would require in-

374th Fighter Squadron ground crewman at work on a P-51, 1944. Part of a dedicated team, here Crew Chief Russell Severson (right) fuels the aircraft while radio men ensure that the plane's transceiver is in top condition. *Courtesy Russell A. Severson*

vestigation and possibly service. Next, with the arrival of the fuel trucks, the ground crew would oversee the transfer of gasoline to onboard fuel tanks, as well as drop tanks if these were to be used. Squadron armorers would also attend to loading the eight .50 caliber machine guns of each Thunderbolt, as well as the gun camera, and final checks were made to ensure that the plane's gun sight was in working order. After a final cleaning of the canopy to remove dirt specks, which could be mistaken by the pilot for distant aircraft, the ground crews would stand by until the arrival of the pilots just prior to take-off.

"Being England, it was usually raining and the crew chiefs would sit in the nice warm cockpit until the pilots were dropped off. Then we strapped them in and waited for 'start engines.' At this time we told the pilot if there was anything wrong with the plane. If it was minor, I would mark the flight book with a red diagonal, and he would have to sign off on it. They always trusted us and always signed. If there was something seriously wrong, I would red-x the flight book – then no one could fly the plane."[8]

Once the mission had begun, many of the ground crew would attempt to snatch some needed rest – though this often proved difficult. "Sweating out" the mission was a common occupation for crew chiefs and assistants who usually formed a bond with their assigned pilot. The feelings of admiration which the ground crews developed for the fighter pilots whose aircraft they serviced was deep seated and durable. Writing more than fifty years after the end of World War II, former crew chief James T. Collins declared "Of course we all know [that] the real heroes of the 361st Group were the pilots. To this day I stand in awe of their accomplishments…facing death

Pride ran deep throughout the ground echelon. Here "Master Sergeant Thompson checks up on me," wrote former crew chief Russell Severson describing this scene. *Courtesy Russell A. Severson*

or injury day after day, watching their friends go down…. To me they represented the cream of the crop of American youth. It took a very special kind of young man to withstand the pressures of flying daily missions."[9]

The only enemy air opposition witnessed by the 361st during February 1944 occurred in the midst of one of the 8th's most determined efforts up to that time. "Big Week," as it was known, took place over a period of six days beginning February 20, and was intended to deal a major blow to the German aircraft industry through a series of large-scale attacks. A period of clear weather at the end of February allowed the 8th Bomber Command to target the *Luftwaffe* at its root. After a build-up of strength during the winter of 1943-44, hundreds of B-17s and B-24s would be dispatched daily against major aircraft factories and components plants throughout Germany. Bombing in relatively clear weather, results during "Big Week" gave American air strategists cause for optimism. Losses among the bombers, however, were heavy, and over 150 B-17s and B-24s failed to return to their bases during these operations.[10]

Though no claims against enemy aircraft were made during the first three missions put up by the 361st in support of "Big Week" (two on February 20, and a third on February 21), one pilot was lost. On the mission of February 21, as the Group was headed toward Munster to pick up homeward bound "heavies," 2nd Lt. Floyd M. Stegall of the 375th Squadron experienced engine failure near the Dutch-German border. Gliding down over the Zuider Zee, he managed to perform a rough, wheels-up landing near the town of Edam in the Netherlands. Returning to England later in the year, Stegall reported that immediately following his crash-landing, "I saw men running from a village and headed south on a road where I came upon a house. There were two men there and they gave me civilian clothes and took me by bicycle to another house where they hid me. I learned later that the Dutch people had burned my plane." After making contact with the Dutch Resistance, Stegall remained in hiding until the liberation of the Netherlands some seven months later.[11]

The day after Stegall's loss, as the "Big Week" operations continued, enemy fighters were encountered by the 361st in skies over Tilburg in western Germany. 375th Squadron CO Maj. George Merritt scored one of the Group's two victories that day when he spotted a flight of Focke-Wulf 190s below the bomber stream. Picking out one of these, Merritt dove his Thunderbolt, closing the range to within three hundred yards before opening fire. Hit repeatedly, the German fighter slowly rolled over and dove into the ground – the first of some 11 enemy planes eventually credited to the flamboyant Merritt.[12] Four more German fighters fell to the 361st during the remain-

B-17s of the 91st Bomb Group in formation. The 91st was one of the groups that participated in the March 6, 1944 daylight mission to Berlin. *National Archives*

der of "Big Week" – though three of the Group's own pilots failed to return to Bottisham. Lt. Daniel B. Nazzarett of the 376th Squadron was killed over Germany on February 22, and Lt. Dennis B. Weaver, also of the 376th was lost over the North Sea on February 24. Weaver's flight leader, Capt. Wallace B. Frank, later reported that while returning home on the afternoon of the 24th, he spotted a German E-Boat off the Dutch coast and led his flight down on a strafing run. "I was at about 12,000 feet and spiraled down to 6,000 over the boat … the

375th Fighter Squadron CO Maj. George L. Merritt, Jr., at left, is seen participating in a BBC radio broadcast recorded in London on March 9, 1944. During the program, Merritt described his combat with an FW-190 on February 22. At center is Lt. Harry Peacock, and at right is Maj. Bob Pollock, both of Atlanta. The program was later broadcast in Georgia for the benefit of the "folks back home." *Courtesy J.J. Kruzel*

flight went into string formation and I made the first pass," Frank recounted after returning to Bottisham. After leading a second firing pass on the enemy boat, which began to burn fiercely, the attack was broken off and Frank set course for base after one member of the flight reported that he was low on fuel. Though no one reported any damage from German fire, Frank reported that, "About two minutes on course, Lt. Weaver's ship started burning and he bailed out. I circled for an hour giving Maydays and saw Lt. Weaver in his dinghy." Critically low on fuel himself, Frank departed in the hope that Air-Sea Rescue units were on their way to Weaver's assistance. Unfortunately, he was never found and apparently died of exposure.[13]

Despite the losses suffered by the 8th Bomber Command during "Big Week," the first week of March 1944 would be unique for the addition of a monumental prestige target in the daylight bombing offensive against Germany – Berlin. Though American planners had envisioned a daylight raid on the German capital during the preceding autumn, weather complications coupled with a general reluctance to attack the distant, heavily-defended city without fighter escort precluded the enterprise.[14] The arrival of the new long-range P-51 in the ETO (three groups being so equipped by the end of February) gave renewed hope for such a mission, and when meteorologists predicted good weather in early March, the wheels for the first daylight raid on Berlin were set in motion.

Coming after a scrubbed attempt on March 3, and an attack on Berlin area targets by the 3rd Bomb Division on March 4, the first full-scale raid against the city by the 8th Air Force was carried out on March 6, 1944. That morning 730 B-17s and B-24s of the 1st, 2nd and 3rd Bomb Divisions took off for a series of attacks against industrial targets within the German capital. Provoking a savage response from *Luftwaffe* interceptors, the mission of March 6 would go down in history as the single most costly raid of the Second World War. Of the 672 effective bombers which made it into German airspace, 69 were shot down and another 102 received major damage.[15] Nearly 700 American airmen would be listed as missing in action by the end of the day.

The 361st Fighter Group, for its part, was assigned the task of withdrawal support for the 1st Bomb Division during its return from German airspace that afternoon. Departing Bottisham shortly before 1300 hours, the assigned mission took the Group's 39 P-47s across the German border to the vicinity of Dummer Lake where, at 1431 hours, the lead elements of the bomber stream where sighted. The bitter struggle waged by the bombers both to and from their targets was evident to 361st Group Commander, Col. Christian, from the very instant

Group Commander Col. Christian photographed in flight gear at Bottisham, 1944. *Courtesy Robert Volkman*

that the "heavies" appeared. Confusion reigned as ragged, scattered formations of B-17s and B-24s interspersed with one another. Despite the confusion, Christian's understanding of his own mission remained clear as he deployed the individual squadrons under his command. "So many combat wings were scattered over the area, that it was difficult to identify our assigned 1st Division bombers," he later reported. "The 374th Squadron was assigned to escort the first wing of the 1st Division bombers that were encountered.... The remaining two squadrons proceeded to the rear of the bomber columns in search of more combat wings of the 1st Division."[16]

Within five minutes of being detached, elements of the 374th Squadron were in action against German fighters. Capt. Robert E. Sedman, leading White Flight of the 374th, caught sight of an FW-190 flying a perpendicular course just below the bomber stream. Executing a split-s with his flight in trail, Sedman attained a speed advantage on the unsuspecting German pilot and downed the Focke Wulf after riddling its wing roots, fuselage and cockpit with .50 caliber bullets. Sedman's wingman, 2nd Lt. Wayne L. Moore, witnessed his leader's combat, but broke away when he spotted another FW-190 some 1500 feet below. Conscious of the danger in separating himself from his flight, Moore nevertheless dove on the German and closed to within 250 yards of his opponent. After several bursts found their mark, and the right undercarriage of the enemy fighter suddenly deployed, and the stricken plane went into a tight spiral from which it did not recover. After visually following the burning fighter as it spun earthwards, Moore, by then down to a mere 3,000 feet of altitude, turned away to climb and rejoin his squadron [17] The isolated dogfight was almost over before it had begun; the 374th remained with their assigned combat wing until crossing out over the Dutch coast at 1526 hours.[18]

After initially detaching the 374th Squadron when the bombers were first sighted, Col. Christian took what was left of the Group in search of additional 1st Bomb Division combat wings. "At 1445, in the vicinity of Neuenhaus, B-24s were seen under attack by an undetermined number of FW-190s diving in and out of clouds. One of these FW-190s was engaged and destroyed. In the vicinity of Furstenau, at 1455, an undetermined number of FW-190s were seen heavily attacking the rear boxes of bombers. These were engaged and one destroyed. At 1500, in the vicinity of Lingen, another FW-190 was seen making a pass at the bombers. He was also attacked and destroyed. In general, squadrons became split up into flights and sections attempting to identify 1st Division bombers."[19]

Among those who found themselves detached from the rest of their squadron on March 6 was 1st Lt. John M. Bentley of the 376th Squadron. After chasing a pair of FW-190s into a cloud bank, Bentley gave up the search and proceeded to climb back toward the bomber stream – though without his wingman who had become separated during the initial encounter. As he gained altitude, he heard the excited radio traffic from members of the Group engaged in defending the rear box of bombers from German fighters and headed alone toward the scene of the action. "I approached [the rear box] and saw 1 FW-190 that had just come through the bomber formation and was about to make a pass on a B-24 which was going down and heading inland," Bentley reported at debriefing. After spotting Bentley's P-47 closing from behind at high speed, the German broke away in a shallow turn to the left, though not before Bentley brought his Thunderbolt's eight .50 caliber machine guns to bear. "I saw hits on the canopy and wing roots and the enemy aircraft went out of control. He turned sharply to port and headed down. I throttled back and continued to give him short bursts, clearing my tail as I had no cover." Finally, the enemy plane began

A Consolidated B-24 Liberator cut in two by a direct flak it. "One of the most helpless and saddest experiences that one could describe would be the feeling you got when you saw a bomber get hit by flak..." recalled Joe Kruzel. *National Archives*

trailing oily black smoke as it headed earthward, losing its rudder as it picked up speed. After watching the stricken plane disappear into clouds below, Bentley rejoined the escort and headed westward toward home. Though short of fuel as he reached the North Sea, the unmistakable silhouette of a lone B-24, evidently of the 453rd Bomb Group, presented itself several thousand feet below. Leaving the bomber stream, Lt. Bentley approached the Liberator and observed two feathered props as the bomber steadily lost altitude. "I contacted him on channel C and he requested that I obtain a fix on B channel for him as his radio was out. I called on both B and D channels then watched, circling, as the bomber went in the channel. I saw a dinghy afloat with some men in it. I circled as long as my remaining gas permitted then headed for England. I met a launch shortly and contacted it by radio and put it on the correct course."[20]

Lt. Bentley's assistance to the stricken Liberator on March 6 illustrates the sense of dedication and empathy felt by the average fighter pilot toward the bomber crews. Realizing the ease with which a single bomber would be picked off by German fighters, and also appreciating the feelings of despair among the crew of a damaged bomber trying to make its way back home on its own, pilots in the 8th Fighter Command were quick to lend moral and material support to such aircraft. Looking back on his service with the 361st many years later, Joe Kruzel commented that, "...one of the most helpless and saddest experiences that one could describe would be the feeling you got when you saw a bomber get hit by flak ... and there was really nothing you could do about it.... By contrast", he added, "one of the most comforting experiences I expect you could come across other than accomplishing a direct, specific, successful mission, was to spot a lonely B-24 or B-17 coming back from a mission. He may have aborted, he may have been shot up, but he was there alone and he was trying to get back to England and you were perhaps coming back from a target area escort mission and you saw him so you'd tell two, three, four of your aircraft 'go down and escort him' … you'd talk with him and tell him you were going to stick with him as long as your gas could allow you to."[21]

James R. Golden of the 374th Squadron expressed similar sentiments years later writing that "Our primary job was always to protect our 'big friends' … and of course that was satisfying in itself, but too often you had to witness bombers with American boys in them go spinning out of control and smoking towards the ground, hoping to see parachutes come out. You lived in the hope that you were helping to save others from that fate."[22]

Following the March 6 raid on Berlin, the pressure was maintained despite the appalling losses among the B-17s and B-24s. After a day of poor weather in which operations were suspended, another major daylight bombing raid against the German capital was carried out on March 8. In support of this effort, the 361st supplied both penetration and withdrawal cover for the bombers on this long and difficult series of attacks from which another 37 bombers did not return.[23]

While the Group completed an uneventful penetration support mission in the morning of March 8, the afternoon sortie allowed three pilots to make claims against enemy aircraft. One of these was made by Group Air Exec Joe Kruzel, who had recently been promoted to Lieutenant Colonel, and flew on both of the day's missions. Sighting an FW-190 in the vicinity of Dummer Lake in Western Germany, Kruzel and his wingman broke away from the bomber formation and gave chase. The lone German pilot apparently saw the approaching Thunderbolts and attempted to escape at full throttle. Since the end of February, however, the 361st had received a number of P-47D-22 aircraft which, equipped with a new paddle-blade propeller and a water-injection capability, allowed for a temporary boost to the already formidable power plant.[24] "Using full throttle (and water injection)," Kruzel reported after the encounter, "I was closing gradually on him when he suddenly reversed his turn and started into a steep level turn to the right. I closed to within about 300 yards, fired a burst at him, and not being able to hold any more deflection I pulled up over him to his left." Lt. Eugene W. Kinnaird of the 375th Squadron, who was flying as Number 3 in Kruzel's flight, was also able to fire several bursts at the German, who quickly bailed out of the fighter.[25] While Kruzel and Kinnaird would share a claim on the FW 190, Capt. John W. Guckeyson of the 375th, one of three West Pointers from the class of '42 flying in the 361st, was able to down an ME-109.[26]

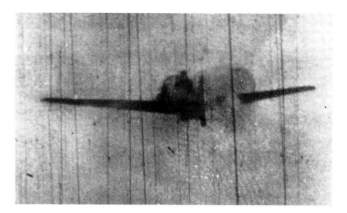

A gun-camera view of an FW-190 at close range. *Courtesy J.J. Kruzel*

While a number of uneventful escort missions were carried out during the middle of month, several pilots of the Group were temporarily detached on March 16 to join an experimental squadron tasked with the study of low-level strafing tactics to be employed against German airfields.[27] Under the leadership of Lt. Col. Glenn Duncan, Commander of the 353rd Fighter Group, the temporary unit was nicknamed "Bill's Buzz Boys" after Maj. Gen. William Kepner who authorized its creation. Since most German airfields heavily defended by light flak, this squadron would practice low level flying in order to develop methods which would result in maximum strafing results with minimal losses when attempting to destroy enemy aircraft on the ground.[28]

The creation of the special strafing unit underscored the emphasis placed on the elimination of German fighter strength by the 8th Fighter Command in the spring of 1944. As an incentive to encourage aggressiveness against the *Luftwaffe* not only in aerial combat, but in deliberate attacks on their bases, the 8th Fighter Command in early 1944 began awarding equal value in personal "scores" to enemy aircraft destroyed on the ground with those shot down in the air. Hence, a pilot intent upon becoming an "ace" could do so strictly by strafing enemy planes on the ground.[29] Doubtless, this new policy was aimed not only at eliminating the primary threat to the bomber offensive – German fighters – but also at achieving air superiority over France and the Low Countries in preparation for the coming invasion of Europe.

It was not long before the 361st found itself demonstrating the new spirit of aggressiveness against the *Luftwaffe* on the ground. On March 17, along with three other P-47 groups of the 8th Fighter Command's 67th Fighter Wing, the 361st was detailed to attack a German airfield in occupied France with the objective of strafing and destroying as many parked aircraft and ground facilities as possible. Led by Col. Christian, newly promoted to full Colonel, 40 of the Group's Thunderbolts took off from Bottisham shortly after 1400 hours and climbed to 18,000 feet while heading for the Normandy coast. The assigned target was Chartres airdrome some 40 miles southwest of Paris. "The original plan had been to proceed from Cabourg [where the Group crossed the French coast] to Alencon, fifty miles west of Chartres, and, from the latter point to launch a coordinated attack on the target on the deck with three eight-ship formations," explained Col. Christian in an after-action report. Fifteen P-47s of the 374th Squadron would remain at altitude acting as top cover while the 375th and 376th squadrons carried out the low-level attack. The element of surprise – a key element in the plan of attack – was quickly lost, however, as the Group was diverted by the 67th Fighter Wing radar control to investigate unidentified aircraft while en route to the planned attack on Chartres. Under the Wing Controller's instructions, Col. Christian's 40 aircraft twice passed over their intended strafing target which fired flak in the Group's direction. Finally, when no enemy aircraft were sighted, the briefed attack was begun.[30]

"The original plan was carried out by two of the eight-ship sections who attacked simultaneously from the west and from the northwest," reported Col. Christian. The two sections led by 376th Squadron CO Maj. Caviness and 375th CO Maj. Merritt respectively were the first to reach the target where they were able to damage several flak towers and set a number of German aircraft on fire as they streaked across the airdrome at low level. After being hit by flak, Maj. Caviness was able to line up on a small high-winged monoplane which he was able to set on fire. Destruction of this aircraft would be shared by several other pilots as well. Maj. Merritt, after shooting up two flak towers in his approach to the field, spotted a taxiing ME-109 which he hit repeatedly bringing it to violent halt. "After

IGHTER STRAFING OF AIRDROMES

AT LUFTWAFFE BASES, WHETHER IN ꟼIED COUNTRIES OR GERMANY IT-, IS NO LONGER PEACEFUL. SOME KILLS ARE SHOWN IN STILL PIC-S TAKEN FROM COMBAT CAMERA FILMS.

A SERIES OF FOUR FRAMES SHOWS BURSTS ON AN ME-110, THE SKID MARK FROM THE TAIL WHEEL OF WHICH IS CLEARLY SEEN.   IN THE SECOND FRAME THE PILOT OR CREW MEMBER IS SEEN ESCAPING BEYOND THE TAIL AND IN THE FINAL FRAME HE IS SPRAWLED FLAT ON THE GROUND.

AIRCRAFT PARKED IN LINE OFFER A PERFECT TARGET FOR GROUND STRAF-ING.

FOLLOWING A P-47 IN, BURSTS ARE SEEN ALL OVER THIS POTEZ-63, FROM THE GUNS OF ANOTHER PLANE.

P-47 ATTACKS A FLAK TOWER.

ANOTHER LOCOMOTIVE STARTS TO EX-PLODE, DURING APRIL, NEARLY 100 LOCOMOTIVES WERE CLAIMED AS DES-TROYED AND EVEN MORE PROBABLY DESTROYED OR DAMAGED.

AN HE-111 WITH IN-LINE ENGINES IS HERE SEEN TAKING BURSTS ON THE NOSE.   NOTE THE ANGLE AT WHICH THE PICTURE IS TAKEN INDI-CATING THE HEIGHT AT WHICH THE STRAFING PLANE WAS FLYING.

ANOTHER ENEMY PLANE IS CLAIMED AS P-47S GO IN ON THE DECK.

A 361st Fighter Group P-47 (frame 4) photographed while shooting up a German flak tower during the March 17, 1944 attack on Chartres Airdrome. This image was captured on the gun camera film of another P-47. *National Archives* passing over, I observed the [enemy aircraft] ground looping to the left, and the landing gear collapsing as the plane was enveloped in a cloud of dust and smoke." Firing at a third flak tower on his exit from the field, Merritt departed the vicinity at low level.[31] Several other pilots succeeded in damaging enemy planes including an FW-190, and a Junkers JU-88 during their individual high-speed passes.[32]

Col. Christian's section was the last to hit the field. "I led the third eight-ship section in a steep dive from Alencon to a point approximately thirty miles south of Chartres and then turned on the deck away from the sun back toward the [airdrome]....I was indicating 350 miles per hour when I hit the field. I fired a short burst at the first hangar, and as I came diagonally across the field, I fired at a smoking object in the middle...which I believe was an airplane already fired upon by other sections of the Group....I was not hit by flak, but my second flight, which passed over directly behind me, received considerable flak damage."[33]

In all, six of the Group's aircraft were hit by German defensive fire while a total of two enemy aircraft were claimed destroyed along with one probable and three damaged along with several buildings and flak towers. Though the tactics employed were intended to minimize the effect of defensive fire from the target, the Germans, by all accounts, were ready and waiting for the 361st – a point which Col. Christian made clear in his report to the 67th Fighter Wing. "...the Group should not be vectored by the Controller in the vicinity of the target prior to the attack," Christian wrote shortly after returning to Bottisham. "The eight bursts of red marker flak, which were fired at us from the target itself twenty minutes prior to our attack, made it perfectly obvious that the ground defenses were well alerted."[34] Luckily, for the Group, the mission provided some relatively cheap lessons which would show dividends down the road.

During the latter part of March 1944, an important group identification feature began to make its appearance on the aircraft of the 361st. When the Group arrived in England at the end of 1943, 8th Fighter Command directives specified a uniform color scheme for its single-engined fighters – an olive drab top coat overall, a grey undersurface on the wings and fuselage, a broad band of white paint on the cowling or nose of the aircraft, and a matching white stripe on the upper surface of each wing and both sides of the rear stabilizer. The only variations from group to group were the squadron identification letter codes assigned by the RAF. At the end of March 1944, however, the 8th's fighter groups were assigned individual noseband colors for purposes of unit identification. While the 56th Fighter Group was assigned a red nose band scheme,

376th Fighter Squadron C.O. Maj. Roy B. Caviness, who led one of the strafing sections at Chartres, receives the Distinguished Flying Cross in a ceremony at Bottisham, spring 1944. *Courtesy J.J. Kruzel*

and the 353rd a black-and-yellow checkered band to name two examples, aircraft of the 361st would be identified by a 24-inch band of bright yellow paint on their cowlings.[35] This distinctive yellow nose feature would remain part of the Group's color scheme throughout the war, giving rise to the nickname "Yellowjackets."

Following the strafing mission to Chartres on March 17, the remainder of the month would be active with eleven escort missions being carried out by the Group. Though uneventful in terms of aerial opposition, the risks were always present. On an otherwise unremarkable trip to escort the "heavies" back from targets in the Berlin area on March 22, 2nd Lt. James Rogers of the 375th Squadron was hit by flak over the Continent and failed tragically in an attempt to nurse his plane back over the English Channel. 2nd Lt. Alton Snyder stayed with Rogers as steadily lost altitude over the sea. "[I] flew his wing giving fixes for him across the Channel at 6,000 feet," Snyder reported when he landed at Bottisham. With his engine alternately cutting out and catching again, Rogers put off an attempted bail-out in the hope of making England, but was forced to ditch his P-47 when less than 1,000 feet of altitude remained. "After he hit," Lt. Snyder continued, "his plane stayed afloat for approximately 1 minute. I noticed what appeared to be a Mae West [inflatable life vest] hanging on the left wing, but when the plane went down there was nothing seen of the Mae West or Lt. Rogers." Breaking off the search when his fuel

A 376th Fighter Squadron P-47 in flight, April 1944. Note the large 150 gallon belly tank. *National Archives*

became critical, Lt. Snyder reported his squadron mate as missing in action.[36]

It would not be until April 8, 1944, that the "Yellowjackets" would next engage German fighters in what would prove to be the Group's most successful day yet. Led by Col. Christian, the mission of April 8 would see the Group's Thunderbolts, for the first time, equipped with the 150 gallon belly tank allowing an added 50 mile combat radius.[37] In support of large-scale bomber raids on industrial targets in northwest Germany, the 361st was assigned to late withdrawal support along the bombers' route home. The Group's three squadrons of P-47s arrived over Dummer Lake at the assigned time of 1430 hours and patrolled the area while awaiting the lead elements of returning bombers.[38] At 1442, rendezvous was made with approximately 200 B-24s of the 2nd Bomb Division returning from attacks on aircraft plants near Brunswick. Within ten minutes, as the formations made their way steadily west, German interceptors commenced attacks on the B-24s.

1st Lt. Alton Snyder, who had stayed with Lt. Rogers until he disappeared on March 22, was leading Yellow Flight of the 375th Squadron "when the bombers called and reported they were being attacked. We immediately went to their assistance. Upon arriving on the bombers' left flank, I bounced a flight of four ME-109s that had just made a pass…." Snyder, along with this wingman, 1st Lt. Scott Naedele, attached to Group Headquarters but flying with the 375th Squadron that day, chased the four Messerschmitts as they dove away, splitting into elements in the process. Singling out one of the enemy fighters, Snyder continued the chase down to 2,000 feet while repeat-

edly scoring hits on the ME-109 from a range of just 150 yards. The German plane spun into the earth below.[39] Lt. Naedele, who had been covering Snyder's tail during the combat, suddenly spotted three more ME-109s flying low on the deck and broke after them so rapidly that his leader failed to pick up on his move. "Then I looked back and saw that I was alone," Naedele recounted after returning to Bottisham, "but it was too late to break off the attack for I was right in the middle of the three enemy aircraft. One of them, evidently their leader, was more aggressive than the other two and turned into me." Naedele and the German pilot soon found themselves in a tight circle in which neither pilot was able to get enough lead to shoot at the other. The other two Germans were apparently inexperienced pilots since, according to Naedele, they "were just stooging around watching us and waiting for an opening." Eventually the German leader broke out of the circle allowing Naedele a clear shot. The German fighter, the cowling of which was "painted black and silver checkerboard," was hit repeatedly and crashed in a ball of fire. The remaining two Messer-

A gun-camera view of an ME-109 being hit at close range. *USAF Museum*

schmitts gave half-hearted chase, but Naedele used his Thunderbolt to full advantage applying maximum power and water injection to climb away at high speed.[40]

During the same engagement, Red Flight of the 375th Squadron watched as a single ME-109, painted black overall with black crosses on a white background adorning the wings, shot down a B-24 before they could get within range. Giving chase as the German dove away, the leader of Red Flight overshot the Messerschmitt during evasive action giving 1st Lt. Eugene Cole, aged 28 from Athens, Ohio, a clear shot. Cole closed from 500 yards to point-blank range and expended nearly 1500 rounds of .50 caliber ammunition, riddling the enemy fighter which began to burn. "The landing gear dropped and black smoke poured from the engine cowling. The [enemy aircraft] went into a vertical dive from 5,000 feet and crashed into the ground."[41]

While the 375th Squadron was engaging bandits, the 374th found itself facing an attack by eight ME-109s on a combat box of B-24s at the rear of the formation. Flying as Yellow Three in the 374th was 1st Lt. Robert Eckfeldt, 22 years old from Belmont, Massachusetts. The son of an Army Major General, "Eggie," as he was known to squadron mates, had attended Harvard for two years before entering the Army, and named his aircraft "The Bald Eagle"- his own nickname within the squadron referencing "the sparseness of hair adorning his head."[42] Picking out three of the attacking Messerschmitts that had gone into a defensive "Lufberry Circle," Lt. Eckfeldt made a careful approach before engaging them. "I followed them down to the deck with my throttle closed, keeping just above their slow spiraling Lufberry and turning with them." When the three Germans had descended to only 100 feet of altitude, Eckfeldt made his attack, singling out a Messerschmitt still in a steep banking turn. Hitting the fighter repeatedly along the top of the fuselage and cockpit, he watched it crash into a field below after which the remaining two German fighters broke away at high speed along the deck.[43] As Eckfeldt took off in pursuit, his wingman, 2nd Lt. Loy C. Vandiver, was forced into violent evasive action when an ME-109 appeared on his tail, as he later described it, "shooting to beat all hell." Fortunately for Vandiver, Capt. Robert Sedman, Red Flight leader, intervened in time to down the Messerschmitt – though Lt. Eckfeldt by then was some distance away and temporarily on his own.[44]

2nd Lt. James Golden, who was flying as Red Two in the 374th Squadron that day (on Capt. Sedman's wing) also found himself alone during the combat. Recalling the mission years later, he related that "I was flying with Sedman and he took off and split-essed down to get into a fight and I took off with him.

As I pulled out, my oxygen mask came off and I started fighting with [it] and lost him … then I sort of pulled up to take a look around and I saw this one plane taking off behind two or three German aircraft … so I bounced down there and got on his wing."[45] The lone P-47 turned out to be that of Lt. Eckfeldt, who was continuing the pursuit of a Messerschmitt at very low level. "I chased him twice across an airdrome at lower than 50 feet and twice around one of the airfield's hangars" Eckfeldt reported after landing that day. "I was within 200 yards of him but I could get no lead so I didn't shoot. He led me through a village and I finally cornered him in a woods by the field in which my first 109 had crashed and it was still burning. He kept dodging behind trees to avoid my fire but I continually turned inside him. Lt. Vandiver and two more 47's joined me and I had run out of ammunition. I left when I saw Lt. Vandiver getting strikes on the ME-109, to come home with another P-47 (Lt. Golden)."[46]

As Eckfeldt and Golden made their way home over Holland, however, another enemy fighter appeared. Recalling the mission years later, Golden recounted that "he and I started back out on the deck, just the two of us, and we had flown twenty minutes or so toward home because we were pretty far in, and about that time a '109 came right across in front of us and "Eggie" took off after him … and we started going around in circles. 'Eggie' was on his tail, and I was on 'Eggie's' tail, and the German was on my tail! And 'Eggie' wasn't shooting, so I got on the radio, which you weren't supposed to do, but I said 'What the hell's the matter, shoot the guy!' And he said 'I haven't got any ammunition left!' So I said 'Get the hell out of the way and at least let me get him off my tail!' And finally, he sort of split out of it and I turned enough to get at least a head-on with the German, and he broke off – fortunately because given a little time I'd have probably broken off, but he blinked first. And at that point … you've got a pretty good chance of getting on their tail but we were low on fuel – man, I tell you we were on vapors!"[47]

Like Lt. Golden, most of the pilots returning to Bottisham on April 8, 1944 did so "on vapors." The use of the 150 gallon drop tank had boosted the Group's combat endurance by a significant margin, but the P-47's capacity for burning fuel, especially in the high rpm settings necessary in a dogfight, was unsurpassed. In all, the 361st was credited with its most successful mission to date with a total of nine enemy aircraft destroyed, two probables, and two damaged. Lost on the mission was 1st Lt. Albert C. Duncan of the 375th Squadron who disappeared during the combat. As a sole clue to his fate, a number of 375th Squadron pilots reported seeing a yellow-nosed P-47 hit over Dummer Lake at 1454 hours.[48]

Though no one ignored the loss of a pilot, or forgot the price that combat flying often exacted, life at Bottisham necessarily went on, and a celebration of the Group's most successful combat operation to date was held on the base that evening. Maj. John Stryker's diary entry for the day summarized the festivities, making note of a "Big party in the Officer's Club tonight – a real rip-roaring one – had nurses over from a station nearby also – went through 59 bottles of Scotch."[49]

With the exception of a brief encounter with enemy aircraft on April 9, during which one pilot in the 375th Squadron was able to claim damage to an FW-190, the middle of the month would be relatively uneventful for the 361st. Most missions, however, usually included some element of drama and for Lieutenants James Golden and Robert Stolzy of the 374th Squadron, April 13 was an example. During one of two missions put up by the "Yellowjackets" that day, Golden and Stolzy

encountered a B-17 on its own over eastern France. Having lost an engine, the bomber was in the unenviable position of having to try to make it back to England on its own, presenting an all-too-easy target for German fighters. Detaching themselves from the Group, Golden and Stolzy chased a German fighter away from the crippled Flying Fortress and then stayed with it as it as it slowly made its way west. When the bomber reached the French coast, it was hit by German flak and lost a second engine giving the pilot no alternative but to ditch in the English Channel. Once down, the crew scrambled into inflatable dinghies while the two P-47 pilots circled at different altitudes giving Mayday calls by radio until British Air-Sea Rescue units reached them. "It was a beautiful sight to see the wake of those two high-speed launches as they sped towards the downed aircraft…" Golden commented years later. "…Bob [Stolzy] and I departed for home landing almost two hours af-

Lieutenants Robert Stolzy and James Golden (second and third from the left, standing) of the 374th Fighter Squadron pose with the crew of the 94th Bomb Group B-17 "Nine Yanks and a Jerk" whom they helped save on April 13, 1944. *Courtesy George Lichter*

ter the rest of our squadron had returned from our assigned mission, again almost out of gas, but what a thrill!" As it turned out, the stricken B-17, named "Nine Yanks and a Jerk", belonged to the 94th Bomb Group based at Bury St. Edmunds. So grateful were the crew to the two Thunderbolt pilots that Stolzy and Golden were invited to the bomber base several weeks later for a reunion with the ten crewman they had helped.[50] A number of publicity photographs were taken on the occasion and, momentarily, the 12 airmen concerned could forget the gravity of their daily tasks. Within a few months, fate would impact the lives of both P-47 pilots; Lt. Golden would become a prisoner of war on June 7, and Lt. Stolzy would be killed less than two weeks after that on the most disastrous mission in the history of the 361st Fighter Group.

An escort mission to northern Germany on April 18, 1944 looked as though it would yield little in the way of action – especially when the 361st arrived at its assigned rendezvous location to pick up returning B-24s of the 2nd Bomb Division and found empty skies. Maj. George Merritt, leading the 375th Squadron that day, reported that the Group spent the majority of its time "milling around Bremen, Hamburg and Bremerhaven … at 23,000 feet trying to [rendezvous] with the assigned bombers. It was later learned that the bombers were some twenty minutes early." Merritt, who would go down in the history of the Group as one of the 361st's most aggressive leaders, rarely lacked a flair for the descriptive, a fact much in evidence in his combat report for the day. "Recall was given at 1620 hours and up until that time things were rather dull and nothing else to look forward to but a long two hour ride back, squirming in your seat every five minutes to keep the old can from becoming numb, or else cook something up to do. After turning to start back we were about half way between Bremen and Bremerhaven at which time the Zwischenahner Lake and airfield stood out like a sore thumb. I saw a small speck creeping off the runway and decided we might as well breeze across the field with one flight to see what was up. I told White Flight to come along with me and Red Flight to give us cover. We pointed our noses at the ground from 23,000 feet and reached the dust about five to eight miles from the field doing close to 500 MPH. During our approach, we lined ourselves up well with objects on the airdrome," Maj. Merritt recounted after returning to base that day. "When we hit the field doing 300 to 350 MPH the first thing I saw was three gun emplacements firing away like mad at us so I pumped a little lead at them and immediately saw two JU-88s parked just to the right of the gun emplacements. Trees and telephone wires around the revetment made it awkward to fire on and disrupted a perfect pass, however some lead found its way into one of the JU-88s and I observed

A close-up of Lieutenants Stolzy and Golden (center)with the pilot and co-pilot of "Nine Yanks and a Jerk." Within two months, both fighter pilots would be lost in combat. *Courtesy James Golden*

some strikes on it. It did not explode before I passed over it but apparently some of the lead found its way into the gas tanks, as the top cover observed it [explode]."[51]

1st Lt. Martin Johnson of Fort Worth, Texas, was flying on Merritt's wing that day and was able to destroy an AR-196 float plane on a lake adjoining the *Luftwaffe* field. After skimming the treetops away from the airdrome, the pair sighted several German locomotives and brought two of them to a halt in strafing attacks.[52] Strafing would evolve into something of a

A 361st Fighter Group ground crewman prepares to load a 500 lb. bomb, complete with a personal message, onto one of the Group's aircraft, spring 1944. *Courtesy George Lichter.*

Lt. Col. Joe Kruzel photographed in flight clothing. Kruzel later described the mission of April 29, 1944 as his most worrisome flying experience of the war. *Courtesy J.J. Kruzel*

Officers and men of Bottisham's meteorology section seen at work in the Group's weather office. *Courtesy George Lichter*

specialty for Lt. Johnson who would ultimately be credited with 8 German planes destroyed on the ground, the most of any pilot in the 361st.

One pilot who attacked Zwischenahner with Merritt and Johnson was Lt. Scott Naedele of Group Headquarters who was flying that day with the 375th Squadron. Despite Maj. Merritt's strafing run on the flak emplacements round the field, Naedele's P-47 was hit and he was forced to bail out becoming a prisoner of war.[53]

The last week of April 1944 was the most combat-intensive period yet for the 361st as the Group attacked German airfields in a planned dive-bombing mission, and then as targets of opportunity. On April 23, the Group's P-47s were equipped with 500 lb bombs in place of belly tanks for dive-bombing attacks on two German airfields in Belgium – Chievres and Denain/Pouvy. Though few of the Group's pilots had had much experience operating the P-47 as a dive bomber, most of the bombs dropped landed within the confines of the two airfields, and while neither field was put out of action, the experience would prove valuable in the months to come.[54] Commenting on the general method of dive-bombing in the P-47, Henry Lederer of the 374th Squadron recalled that the technique was rather rudimentary. "We had a 70 mm recticle with a fixed pip on the cowling, it was a lighted recticle, and that was a machine gun sight, not a bomb sight, and, of course, depending upon the angle at which you approached your target on a dive bombing run, and depending upon your airspeed, and depending upon your pull-up, and depending upon where you released your bombs, they could land anywhere! Of course, we fright-

ened a great many of the enemy, and I think we also frightened ourselves!"[55]

During five successive missions beginning on April 24, German airfields in France were strafed as targets of opportunity during bomber escort missions assigned to the Group. In each case, attacks were limited to one pass by one flight due to the strong presence of light flak defenses surrounding these installations. Increasingly, the Group's pilots reported the use of dummy aircraft by the Germans intended to lure American aircraft against the flak defenses. Ten German aircraft were claimed destroyed and another four damaged during these attacks, for the loss of two pilots.

Final contact with the *Luftwaffe* during the month occurred on April 29, 1944 when Lt. Col. Joe Kruzel led fifty-five of the Group's Thunderbolts on an escort mission fairly deep into central Germany. As a result of unusually strong winds at altitude (commonly called the jet stream) that day, the distance traveled into German airspace was far greater than anyone had planned and nearly led to disaster on the return trip. Considering the mission many years later, Kruzel recalled that the Group flew its planned course over near solid undercast from Bottisham to a point where they believed they would rendezvous with the bombers. While the weather briefing had included warnings about strong easterly winds at altitude, no one had planned for the apparent strength of the jet stream which pushed the Group steadily eastward. "…there wasn't a single German in the sky – no evidence of them. I couldn't even get in touch with the bombers by radio," Kruzel recounted years later. While waiting the for the bombers, however, two unsuspecting Ger-

 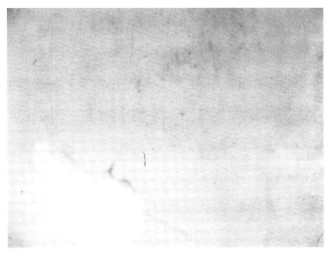

Two gun-camera frames showing the destruction of an ME-109 by Lt. Col. Joe Kruzel. *Courtesy J.J. Kruzel*

man fighters were spotted transiting the area. "When I was circling what was supposed to be the rendezvous area," Kruzel recalled, "I noticed two '109's flying about 3,000 feet below us, so I called them into the Group and I said 'I'm going to go down there and bounce them,' so I'm telling the Group this and of course I'm forgetting at the time that my Number Two man, Stan Rames, was on another channel because I'd had him busy trying to locate the bombers while I was communicating with the Group … Rames had begun to suspect that something unusual was happening because I peeled off from the formation and started making my dive… [and] about the time he saw the aircraft, he turned on to our frequency and he heard me say 'Number 2, you take the guy on the right, I'll take the guy on the left' and he had just enough time to set himself up and fire about the time that I did and we got both of them … I expect we were so far in that they were on a routine training mission and had no idea the Americans would be in so deep that day."

Still in hope that their assigned bombers would appear, the Group loitered in the area for a few more minutes. "And of course that put us further inland, possibly over Poland," Kruzel recalled. "but … failing to even raise the B-17s, I said 'OK Troops, let's go home.' And about the time that we normally got in touch with the British radar and asked for help as to a vector to get home, I called in and identified myself and said we'd appreciate a steer and there was no answer. So I thought maybe I had a poor radio, so I asked for some help from the deputy lead and the other squadron commanders, and … not only could we not get a fix but we couldn't communicate. So I

began to suspect then that something was afoul … we kept on plodding along, plodding along, and we still couldn't raise them. When we did, we were just about … 100 miles further back than I thought we were … My concern was I knew we had a party scheduled at the club that night and I had visions of it being one of the saddest parties of the 8th Fighter Command – commiserating over the loss of 55 aircraft having to land in the North Sea. So I just told everybody to throttle back to get their best fuel consumption and to forget about the enemy and just, each man on his own, milk that airplane back. Well, fortunately, we all made it back – not too much fuel to spare – but I dread to think what would have happened if there'd been a few more Germans about the time we were deep in enemy territory and several of us had tangled with them. I'm sure that some of us would not have made it back because of lack of fuel. But as it turned out, we made the party, we didn't lose anybody and we had two more Germans to add to the 361st's credit."[56]

The end of April 1944 brought with it the close of the first major phase of the 361st's operations in the ETO. While penetrations of German airspace had improved with the use of increasingly greater auxiliary fuel loads, the days of the P-47 at Bottisham were numbered. To reach their full potential in the role of bomber escorts, the "Yellowjackets" would need a new type of aircraft. The beginning of May 1944 would see those aircraft appear at station F-374 in increasingly greater numbers, and would also see the 361st given the means to grow into a truly long-range escort force.

NOTES

[1] James Golden, Interview with the Author, November 27, 1995.

[2] Ibid.

[3] Ibid.

[4] Ibid.

[5] Russell A. Severson, Correspondence with the Author, October 18, 1995.

[6] Robert O. Bland, Correspondence with the Author, October 8, 1995.

[7] Severson.

[8] Ibid.

[9] James T. Collins, correspondence with the author, January 30, 1995.

[10] Roger A. Freeman, *The Mighty 8th War Diary* (New York: Janes, 1981), pp. 183-88.

[11] Floyd M. Stegall, "Escape and Evasion Report No. 1937" October 4, 1944.

[12] George L. Merritt, Jr., "Encounter Report" February 22, 1944.

[13] Wallace B. Frank, "Statement" contained in Missing Aircrew Report No. 1281, February 24, 1944.

[14] Roger A. Freeman, *The Mighty 8th* (London: Janes, 1970) p. 113.

[15] Martin W. Bowman, *Castles in The Air* (Great Britain: Patrick Stephens, 1984) p.123.

[16] Thomas J.J. Christian, Jr., "Tactical Commander's Report," March 10, 1944.

[17] Wayne L. Moore, "Encounter Report," March 6, 1944.

[18] 374th Fighter Squadron, "Mission Summary Report, Field Order 262," March 6, 1944.

[19] Christian, Ibid.

[20] John M. Bentley, "Encounter Report," March 6, 1944.

[21] Joseph J. Kruzel, Recollections of Service With the 361st FG, recorded December 7, 1975, transcribed by Paul B. Cora, October, 2000.

[22] James Golden, Correspondence with the author, December 9, 2000.

[23] Freeman, *War Diary*, p. 196.

[24] Wesley Parks, "Historical Record, Operational Engineering Sections (Aircraft), AAF Station F-374," June 1944.

[25] Joseph J. Kruzel, "Encounter Report," March 8, 1944.

[26] John M. Stryker, 361st FG Unit Diary Entry for March 8, 1944.

[27] Ibid., March 16, 1944.

[28] Freeman, *The Mighty 8th*, p. 126.

[29] Ibid.

[30] Christian, "Combat Report," March 17, 1944.

[31] Merritt, "Combat Report," March 17, 1944.

[32] 361st Fighter Group, "Mission Summary Report, F.O. No. 12 (Wing)," March 17, 1944.

[33] Christian, Ibid.

[34] Ibid.

[35] Freeman, *The Mighty 8th*, p. 292.

[36] Alton B. Snyder, Jr., "Sworn Statement" contained in Missing Aircrew Report # 3403, March 24, 1944.

[37] Gotts, p. 35.

[38] 361st Fighter Group, "Mission Summary Report, Field Order 291," April 8, 1944.

[39] Alton B. Snyder, "Encounter Report," April 8, 1944.

[40] Scott Naedele, "Encounter Report," April 8, 1944.

[41] Eugene Cole, "Encounter Report," April 8, 1944.

[42] *The Escorter* (361 FG Newspaper, Bottisham, England) Vol. 1 #12, September 2, 1944.

[43] Robert Eckfeldt, "Encounter Report," April 8, 1944.

[44] Loy C. Vandiver, "Encounter Report," April 8, 1944.

[45] James Golden, Interview with Author, November 27, 1995.

[46] Eckfeldt, Ibid.

[47] Golden, Ibid.

[48] 361st Fighter Group, "Mission Summary Report, Field Order 291," April 8, 1944.

[49] Stryker, Ibid., April 8, 1944.

[50] Golden, Correspondence with the Author, December 9, 2000.

[51] George L. Merritt, Jr., "Encounter Report," April 18, 1944.

[52] Ibid.

[53] Stryker, April 18, 1944.

[54] 8th Fighter Command, "Narrative of Operations, Field Order 311," April 23, 1944, p.4.

[55] Henry B. Lederer, Interview with the Author, November 13, 1995.

[56] Kruzel, Recollections. December 7, 1975.

four

Long Range Transition

During the first three months of combat operations in the spring of 1944, the pilots of the 361st had carried out their primary mission – bomber escort – to the limits imposed by their equipment. While no one questioned the P-47's exceptional ruggedness, or even its suitability in aerial combat at altitude, the heavy Republic fighter's range proved to be a serious limitation to its use as an escort fighter. Barely able to reach the western fringes of Germany even with auxiliary drop tanks, the 361st's pilots, like those in the majority of 8th Air Force fighter groups, were capable of providing only partial coverage for the bombers on deep penetration raids before having to turn for home. This deficiency was not lost on German fighters who waited until the B-17s and B-24s were beyond the range of their escorts to launch their heaviest attacks.

Symptomatic of the P-47's range limitations, many missions flown by the 361st during the early months of 1944 resulted in little or no contact with the *Luftwaffe*. "The whole time I was flying P-47s I don't think I saw a German airplane," recalled Robert C. Wright, an original 375th Squadron pilot. Wright, who eventually was credited with destroying some 7 German aircraft, described the dilemma which limited range entailed. "[W]ith the P-47…we weren't getting far enough in. The bombers were generally attacked close to the target and with the P-47s we weren't going that far."[1] Wright's impression of the early months was echoed by that of another original pilot, David C. Landin, who completed a combat tour with the 376th Squadron in 1944. "In my time, in the P-47, we saw very little enemy aircraft. We only went to the Zuider Zee which was the end of the run before we had to turn around," he recalled.[2]

Though the spring of 1944 was certainly not without action for the Group, statistics bear out the general view expressed by Wright and Landin. While equipped with the P-47, the 361st conducted some 81 combat missions, the vast majority of which were bomber escort, over occupied Europe. During that period, which lasted from January 21 to May 8, the Group's pilots were credited with 32 German aircraft destroyed in the air, and another 18 in ground strafing. Of the 32 aerial victories, all took place during 11 missions, and the ground-strafing credits were achieved on 10 missions. On just one mission during these months were air victories and ground-strafing claims combined, so for 60 of 81 missions, elements of the *Luftwaffe* were either absent, or unable to be engaged. During the same period, a total of 18 the 361st's pilots failed to return to base – for a rate of 1 loss per 4.5 missions.[3]

By May of 1944, the 361st was slated to undergo a change which would dramatically alter its combat performance. This change would come in the form of a new fighter aircraft, the North American P-51. Sleek, fast, maneuverable, and, above all, capable of an 1100 mile combat radius when equipped with drop tanks, the Mustang was the answer to the long-range escort problem which had plagued the 8th Air Force from its earliest operations.[4]

The P-51 aircraft, known as the Mustang, was a remarkable achievement of inspired aeronautical design and rapid modification. Though destined to make its name with the US Army Air Force, the North American fighter actually owed its origin to a Royal Air Force purchasing scheme in the days of American neutrality. Approaching the North American Aviation company in April 1940, British purchasing agents, at first, wished the American firm to "tool-up" for production of the Curtiss P-40. Convinced that his company could produce a new design, superior to the Curtiss fighter, in the same time which factory modification would require, North American President

A North American P-51B Mustang of the 376th Fighter Squadron in flight, summer 1944. Beginning in May, 1944, the 361st would be re-equipped with the long-range Mustang enabling the Group to participate the deepest penetrations of German airspace. *Courtesy Robert Volkman*

James "Dutch" Kindleberger persuaded the British agents to back the venture. Setting his design staff to the task in the months that followed, Kindleberger was able to keep his promise of producing a prototype in 120 days.[5]

Like the Curtiss P-40, the new design, designated "Mustang" by the British, was a single-seat aircraft powered by a liquid-cooled, in-line engine. Beyond that, the similarities ceased. The outstanding design feature of the Mustang was its low drag "laminar flow" wing, an important innovation characterized by a slim leading wing edge, which, unlike conventional wings, reached its greatest thickness at the center of the wing's cross-section. Visually, the Mustang's signature design feature would be its fuselage air intake beneath the wings which served the engine coolant radiator located beneath the cockpit. Overall, the original prototype exceeded expectations and by 1942, the Mustang Mark I had arrived in Britain. While the first production models delighted British pilots, the Allison engine with which North American had equipped the fighter, was best suited for operations below 12,000 feet. It was not until British engineers mated the American airframe with the Rolls-Royce Merlin engine, which powered the legendary Supermarine Spitfire, that the full potential of the aircraft was realized.[6]

With three internal fuel tanks, and provision for wing-mounted drop tanks, the Merlin-engined Mustang had the range and performance necessary for a truly first-class escort fighter. Although the US Army Air Force purchased small quantities of the Allison-engined P-51A, which were used effectively as fighter-bombers in the Mediterranean, the Merlin-engined

Mustang, designated P-51B, caught the attention of the 8th Air Force.

At the time of the 361st Fighter Group's arrival in England in December 1943, the P-51B was just beginning combat testing with the 354th Fighter Group, an outfit destined to be known as the "Pioneer Mustang" group. During December 1943 and January 1944, the pilots of the 354th would be the first to accompany the bombers deep into German airspace where they would test the Mustang against *Luftwaffe* interceptors. So favorable was the 354th's experience that other 8th Air Force groups were soon clambering to make the transition to the new type. One group commander, the legendary Col. Don Blakeslee of the 4th Fighter Group, even offered to forgo the normal familiarization time mandated for aircraft transition in order to take Mustangs into combat.[7]

Throughout the spring of 1944, fighter groups within the 8th traded their P-47s for P-51s as supplies of the new aircraft and lulls in operational needs made transition possible. By May, the 361st, which had been the last P-47 group to join the 8th (though not the last slated for transition) was ready to exchange their Thunderbolts for long-range Mustangs and on the first day of the month 17 new P-51Bs touched down on Bottisham's steel runway – the first installment of the more than fifty which would be needed to bring the Group fully up to strength.[8]

Bare, almost antiseptic in appearance, the new aircraft arrived in unpainted "Natural Metal Finish" – unadorned save tail numbers, national insignia, and a single matte-black paint strip running atop the cowling from windscreen to propeller hub. Even before Bottisham's pilots could begin familiarization in actual flight, ground crews began applying squadron code letters to the fuselage of each new fighter – B7 for the 374th, E2 for the 375th, and E9 for the 376th. In keeping with the paint scheme adopted for group recognition at the end of March, the Mustangs assigned to the 361st would receive a coat of bright yellow paint on the nose and propeller hub, identifying them as the "Yellowjackets."

Early operations with the P-51 were undertaken with gradually increasing numbers of Mustangs joining the Group's P-47s. The first such mixed force fielded by the 361st participated in escort operations for the "heavies" on May 8, 1944. While nearing the end of their assigned "penetration support" role some 10 miles northeast of Steinhuder Lake in western Germany, the 361st was provided its first opportunity to engage enemy aircraft with one of the new Mustangs. Lt. Leroy H. Sypher of the 375th Squadron would have the honor of first in the Group to be credited with an aerial victory in a P-51, though this was achieved in a slightly unexpected manner. As Sypher later reported, he was flying in Blue Flight of the 375th along with two other P-51s at an altitude of 25,000 feet when he "saw a B-17 losing altitude and being attacked by a number of enemy aircraft." After calling out the bandits, Sypher was

376th Fighter Squadron ground crewmen with one of the Group's shiny, new Mustangs at Bottisham, May 1944. The official caption read "As the wheels of the last flight of a North American P-51 Mustang fighter group left the ground on take-off on a late afternoon, heavy bomber escort mission over Germany, the strains of the 'Star Spangled Banner' sounded through the loud-speakers all over the base. An alert photographer snapped this unusual photograph of ground crew members who were watching the take-off, standing at attention in salute." *National Archives*

told by his flight leader to lead the way. Diving to 12,000 feet, Sypher made a pass at an ME-109 which was firing on the crippled bomber. "I closed from astern and from about 100 to 150 yds and fired a short burst," he reported. "I observed some hits on the right wing root and some smoke." For this, Sypher would be credited with one enemy aircraft damaged. Suddenly, however, the tables were turned as three more Messerschmitts appeared forcing him to break off and head for the deck. "I…hit

Lt. Jefferson K. Wood (l) and Capt. Ezra Smith (r) of the 374th Fighter Squadron pose on the wing of one of the Group's P-51Bs. Wood was one of the 374th's original pilots, while Smith served as Squadron Intelligence Officer. Note the relatively restricted visibility which the P-51B's "birdcage" canopy afforded. *Courtesy George Lichter*

the deck from an altitude of 4,000 feet. The three enemy aircraft who were on my tail followed me down. The first and second enemy aircraft came out still on my tail but the third hit a tree and exploded. I saw a bunch of clouds ahead so I gave it full throttle and RPM's and pulled up into them in a climbing turn. My windshield iced over and I went on instruments, thanks to the clouds I successfully evaded the enemy aircraft."[9] For the crashed German, Sypher was awarded the Group's first kill in a Mustang.

As more P-51s became available, and more pilots completed their check-out in the new fighter, additional Mustangs were assigned to successive missions. On May 11, 20 P-51s were included with 32 Thunderbolts on an uneventful escort mission to the Liege marshalling yard. A third and final mixed-force mission was conducted the next day on another escort to the Liege area, although no enemy aircraft were encountered.[10] Once the last Thunderbolt touched down at Bottisham at a little after 1300 hours, however, the 361st had completed the first phase of its combat operations which had begun some four months earlier. From that point on, the Group would be truly a long-range escort force.

The Group's first all P-51 mission, led by Col. Christian, was carried out on May 13. Assigned withdrawal support for bombers returning from targets in Poland (though poor weather forced them to hit secondary targets in Stettin and Strahlsund in northeastern Germany), the 361st was to rendezvous with their assigned combat wings over Denmark. Though no German fighters were encountered in the four-hour sortie over Northern Europe, the sheer range requirement of the Group's assigned task made it a notable departure from the previous months of operations. As the 361st's Historical Officer recorded, "Pilots were amazed on entering the briefing room prior to this mission to find that their course lay so high up on the wall map that if it were shown in proper relationship to the territory already traversed on previous missions the map would extend above the roof of the building. A pin-up map was used as a temporary expedient and another wall map was later constructed at the other end of the briefing hut."[11]

As the 361st began operations with the P-51, pilots who had recently transitioned from the P-47 soon gained respect for the capabilities of the Mustang, though, in some respects, there was a trade-off. "The two were good for different reasons," recalled David Landin of the 376th Squadron. "The P-47 was just like being in a tank and it was almost invincible....[Thunderbolts] would come home, they would take great damage and still fly; the P-51 wouldn't do that." Though Landin still regarded the Thunderbolt as a fine aircraft, he would concede that in terms of the 361st's primary

In pre-dawn darkness, a 361st ground crewman prepares to install a 108-gallon drop tank beneath the wing of a P-51. These tanks, made of specially treated paper, gave the Mustang an endurance of over seven hours. *Courtesy George Lichter*

mission, the Mustang was a more suitable plane. "With the P-47, with a wing tank or a belly tank, I don't think you could get...over four hours flying time. With the P-51 and wing tanks, I can see some of my missions were seven hours. Without the P-51," Landin concluded, "I'm not sure what the war effort would have resulted in, because the bombers had to be protected and the P-51 was the only aircraft that could do it."[12]

The effect of the transition to the overall character of Group operations was remarkable in only the first two and one-half weeks. In the period lasting from May 13 to 31, 1944, during which the 361st operated P-51s exclusively, the number of enemy aircraft destroyed rose dramatically – approaching 50% of the totals for the entire P-47 operational period. In 15 missions flown during May 13-31, the Group was credited with downing 15 German aircraft and destroying another 8 on the ground. By contrast, in 81 missions conducted from January 21 to May 8, 1944, the 361st received credit for the destruction of 32 German planes in the air, and another 18 in ground strafing.[13]

While the increase in range afforded by the Mustang boosted the likelihood that the Group's pilots would encounter enemy aircraft, thus accounting for an increase in the number of claims, a similar trend in losses was also experienced during the first 15 missions with the P-51. During the period of May 13 to 31, the 361st lost 11 aircraft in combat – one loss per 1.3 missions. By comparison, a total of 18 combat losses were experienced during the 81 Thunderbolt missions flown from 21 January to 8 May – a ratio of 1 loss per 4.5 missions.[14] The rise in losses would continue throughout the summer of 1944; though the trend, in part, reflects the intensity of operations following the D-Day landings, it also underscores Landin's evaluation of the reduced survivability of the P-51 despite its outstanding overall performance.

With the Group fully transitioned, missions calling for deep penetration of German airspace became more commonplace. On May 19, the 361st participated in its first escort mission to Berlin. Led by Maj. Roy B. Caviness, 59 Mustangs left Bottisham shortly after 1130 hours for rendezvous with the B-17s of the 3rd Bomb Division, and with the exception of one P-51 which ditched in the Channel, the Group returned to base nearly six hours later. Though this trip to Berlin was an important "first" in the Group's operational history, a lack of substantial German fighter reaction made for an uneventful, if somewhat long mission.[15]

Two days after the first Berlin escort, the Mustangs of the 361st again returned to the skies over Germany as part of a massive fighter sweep orchestrated by the 8th Fighter Command. Codenamed "Chattanooga," the operation was specifically directed against German railroad locomotives and rolling stock, and involved aircraft from nearly every fighter group in the 8th – more than 600 in all.[16] Dropping down to low level after reaching their assigned patrol areas, the squadrons of each group would fan out to search for German trains. Once spotted, the locomotives would be strafed sending large jets of steam skyward as .50 caliber bullets penetrated their boilers forcing a halt. Once stopped, the fighters could then zero in on tank cars and boxcars which might contain ammunition, fuel or other volatile cargo. These large scale attacks across Germany, it was hoped, would contribute to a breakdown in rail communications and supplies behind German lines – an effort, albeit not

Capt. John W. Guckeyson of the 375th Fighter Squadron. One of the three members of West Point's Class of 1942 assigned to the 361st, Guckeyson was highly regarded for his leadership and aggressiveness in the air. His death in combat would resound throughout the Group. *Courtesy J.J. Kruzel*

permanent, which would aid the Allies in both the east and west.

Though the mission of May 21 would be deemed a success for the "Yellowjackets," with some 22 locomotives claimed destroyed, the operation would be remembered mostly for the loss of Capt. John W. Guckeyson, one of the 375th Squadron's most promising officers. Tall, clean-cut and athletic, Guckeyson had entered West Point in 1938 following a remarkable four years at the University of Maryland where he excelled in football, basketball, baseball, and track which eventually earned him election to the University's Hall of Fame. Though restricted to two years each of baseball and track at West Point due to eligibility rules, Guckeyson nonetheless devoted his energy to soccer at the Military Academy earning the status of All-American.[17] While not noted for academic achievement at West Point, he was elected President of his Class in 1940, 41 and 42.[18]

Joining the Air Corps after graduation in 1942, he eventually accompanied the 361st on its deployment to England in late 1943. Serving as a flight leader in the 375th Squadron, Guckeyson earned a reputation as a bold and skillful pilot eventually credited with destroying 3.8 German aircraft in ground strafing, and another in the air during the spring of 1944.[19]

361st armorers load .50 caliber ammunition into the ammo trays inside the wing of a P-51. The P-51B had only half the firepower of the P-47 – four .50 caliber machine guns. Subsequent models of the Mustang were equipped with six machine guns. *Courtesy Russell A. Severson*

The mission of May 21, however, would prove to Guckeyson's squadron mates the inherent dangers involved in strafing ground targets, as well as the vulnerability of their new aircraft to ground fire. Arriving over their assigned patrol area near Stendal in northeast Germany shortly before 1300 hours, the 375th Squadron's pilots began to search for German trains. As the Group's Mustangs dropped to low level, German defenses came alive and its pilots, "Encountered all types of flak from the vicinity of all cities and towns" and later "…intense, light, accurate flak from many locomotives."[20]

Within a few minutes two moving freight trains were spotted approximately 15 miles south of Stendal. Capt. Guckeyson, leading Blue Flight of the 375th, took his flight down and strafed the railroad cars and locomotives, disabling the engines and bringing the rolling stock to a halt. Continuing south after the first attacks were complete, a third train was spotted along a stretch of double track, this time some twenty miles south of Stendal. Once again, Guckeyson took his flight down to low level for an attack. 1st Lt. Eugene Cole, flying as Blue 3, described what then happened: "While making the third pass at this locomotive I was following Captain Guckeyson in trail, as he broke upward after firing I saw his plane falter and stagger as though out of control at an altitude of approximately 100 feet, then it seemed to fall vertically in a horizontal attitude. I observed the wings and tail disintegrate from the plane as I flew over the crash."[21] Though he couldn't be sure, Cole observed no parachute; indeed saw nothing other than burning wreckage, and consequently reported him as dead. German sources later corroborated, citing the point of impact as being near Tournau, some 5 kilometers west of Stendal. After his body was recovered from the remains of the aircraft on the following day, Capt. Guckeyson was interred in Tournau's community cemetery.[22]

Guckeyson was not the only casualty on May 21. Also lost to flak was Flight Officer Cornelius Hogelin, another member of Guckeyson's flight. Flying only his fifth mission, Hogelin was informed by 1st Lt. Abe Rosenberger that his P-51 appeared to be hit after the strafing run on which Capt. Guckeyson was shot down. "Shortly after leaving the target," Rosenberger later reported, the Mustang "flown by Flight Officer Hogelin was seen to be streaming a thin white vapor. I notified him of the fact by radio and he acknowledged the call saying he was OK. Approximately one hour later on our course home at an altitude of 21,000 feet, the engine…started smoking badly. Losing altitude, he disappeared into the overcast, the top of which was at 16,000 feet." His engine having quit, Hogelin apparently bailed out over the English Channel but was never seen again.[23]

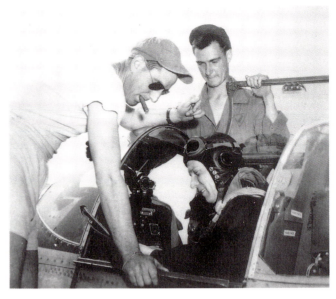

Lt. David C. Landin of the 376th Fighter Squadron, attended by his crew chief and assistant, prepares for take-off in one of the Group's new P-51Bs. *Courtesy David C. Landin*

As would be the case throughout the summer of 1944, the pace of Group operations hardly slackened and on May 24 the 361st returned to Berlin for a second time. Unlike the Group's first mission to the German capital, they were not assigned the usual close escort, but rather were detailed to scout ahead of the bombers to report the weather conditions over the target. So great was the Mustang's range that 361st could loiter over Berlin while awaiting the heavy bombers – which they would then escort out of the target area. Led by Lt. Col. Kruzel, the Group's 44 P-51s arrived over Berlin at 1040 hours and orbited the target area at 24,000 feet while reporting 7/10 low overcast. After the first force of heavy bombers released their loads, the Group then headed for the second force which they reached at 1110 hours. Just as they arrived, a large formation of German fighters – estimated at 75 FW-190s and ME-109s – were spotted above the bomber force. As the Group prepared to engage the enemy force, the German interceptors began a diving attack through the American formation.[24]

As David Landin of the 376th Squadron recalled some fifty years later, "we went to Berlin to tell the bombers what the bombing weather would be, whether they could bomb visually… anyway we were there a half hour before the bombers hit and that was the day that I lost my roommate, Morris Williams. A number of our pilots were shot down because we got hit badly right over Berlin; instead of hitting the bombers either before or after the bomb [run] all of these enemy fighters came and hit them right in Berlin, right in the middle of the flak – which I never could figure out why they did that. They came in higher than we were… they came in right straight through us, right into the bombers. I saw a B-17, for instance, with an enemy fighter stuck like a little mosquito to the side of the bomber going down in flames. It seems real funny but that's what they did; I would have thought that they would have avoided the flak."[25]

The German attack took place shortly after 1100 hours and all three squadrons of the 361st were engaged in the melee which followed. Lt. Morris C. Williams, Landin's roommate, was able to down an ME-109 before his own Mustang was riddled by gunfire. While attempting to nurse the stricken fighter home around 1245 hours, Williams was last heard over the radio by Lt. Sam Wilkerson reporting that his plane was losing fuel, his controls were badly damaged and his compass was useless. Estimating his position as somewhere south of the Zuider Zee in Holland, Williams held out little hope of making it to the coast, let alone across the Channel. "I called and told him to try to make England," reported Wilkerson. "He replied, 'Sam, I got a 109, I'll see you later, goodbye and out.'"[26] Though unknown to his squadron mates until weeks later, Williams ultimately baled out and remained a POW until the end of the war.

While suffering no casualties the 374th Squadron claimed one enemy aircraft probably destroyed in the brief dogfight, while Maj. George Merritt, CO of the 375th, claimed an ME-109 destroyed. The second Berlin mission was most costly for the 375th Squadron as two of its pilots failed to return. 1st Lt. Stanley D. Rames was forced to abandon his P-51 over the town of Altlandsberg just east of Berlin, while 2nd Lt. Warren D. Wherry was killed during the engagement[27] Rames' wingman, 1st Lt. Russell Sobieski, reported that Rames experienced engine trouble following the dogfight, and after attempting to nurse his P-51 westward, radioed that "there was nothing he could do to the plane … His last message was 'Tell my wife I am O.K.' At about 10,000 feet he rolled the ship over and bailed out … the last I saw of him he was running across a field with the chute under his arm."[28]

The culmination of the Mustang transition phase for the 361st came at the end of May on a long escort mission to western Poland. Called upon to provide target area support to the B-17s of the 1st Bomb Division attacking industrial plants, the "Yellowjackets" would find themselves in the right place at the right time to encounter German interceptors. "The day of days in May," as the Group Historical Officer described it, would feature the highest number of Group claims against enemy aircraft to date, and for one pilot in particular, a record for the number of confirmed kills in one mission which would not be broken until September of that year.

The plan outlined by the Eighth Bomber Command for May 29 called for a three-pronged attack on oil and aircraft production facilities throughout Germany and Poland by nearly 900 heavy bombers. Detailed to provide cover to the 3rd Air Task Force which was assigned the destruction of aircraft plants at Posen, Sorau and Cottbus, the "Yellowjackets" would find themselves in airspace further east than ever before. As the Group's historical officer noted at the end of the day, "The pilots were nearer to the Russian Front at that time than they were to England!"[29]

Led by 376th Squadron Commander Maj. Roy Caviness, the 361st put up 41 P-51Bs for the mission, though seven pilots would later abort due to a variety of mechanical problems. With the last flight airborne from Bottisham at 1021 hours, Caviness led the Group in its routine climb out over the North Sea. Heading eastward while climbing, the three squadrons would attempt to rendezvous with their assigned B-17s over Stendal in north-central Germany where they would take over from the fighters assigned to penetration support.[30]

Rendezvousing with the B-17s some fifty miles southeast of Berlin at approximately 1240 hours, Caviness divided his three squadrons among the combat boxes of the heavy bombers as they approached the city of Cottbus which contained one of the targeted aircraft plants. After observing the bombers release their loads from 18,000 feet, the Group accompanied the B-17s along a northerly track, which would take the force over western Poland on the withdrawal route.[31]

Searching the sky above and below for German interceptors, Maj. George Merritt, the ever-zealous 375th Squadron Commander, noticed an enemy aircraft in the vicinity of the Cottbus target. "We were at 25,000 feet over Cottbus airdrome when I observed one aircraft either taking off or buzzing the airdrome immediately after the bombing. I told White and Red Flight about the activity and instructed them to stand by…" Merritt later reported. Dropping down to 15,000 and then 8,000 feet to investigate, Merritt and two flights of his squadron were unable to confirm any German planes on the ground at Cottbus, but when one of his flight leaders spotted a satellite airfield with several parked aircraft less than five miles to the southeast, the targets were too good to pass up. "Red Flight made a pass at the field from the south and missed the field," Merritt related in debriefing. Leading a second flight of P-51s toward the field, Merritt began a strafing run on the stationary German planes. "As we passed over the field at 4,000 feet, I observed a twin engine enemy aircraft parked alone in the south end of the field. It was a beautiful target, and before I knew it, the ship had half rolled and reached the tree tops in a splendid manner about one mile short of the field. Soon the enemy aircraft appeared and I bounced high enough to get a good pass. Approaching it from broadside, I opened fire at 500 yds doing 350 MPH and did not stop until I had passed over it." Seeing what was subsequently identified as a Heinkel HE-111 burst into flames, Merritt was able to claim the first of two ground victories that day. More parked aircraft were spotted and since no flak appeared on the first pass, Maj. Merritt led the flight back for a second strafing run. Lieutenants Robert Wright and Dean Morehouse each were able to claim an aircraft destroyed on the second pass, but as Merritt streaked across the German field firing on another HE-111, he was surprised by a sudden violent jolt. "As I was firing on my second target," he reported, "I must have descended to a little minus altitude as the prop scratched the ground and caused a terrific jar of the airplane. I called Lt.'s Wright and Morehouse to nurse me home, as the vibration almost shook my teeth out."[32]

The mere fact that Maj. Merritt's P-51 was now unusable in combat did not mean that targets of opportunity would be ignored on the trip home. As Wright and Morehouse escorted their leader along the deck on a westerly course for home, several more German airfields were spotted. Shortly after setting course for England, Lt. Wright spotted another German airfield near Luckau. After granting permission for a strafing run, Merritt assumed the role of spectator as Lt. Wright dove in for an attack on the first of several fields. "I observed his pass and saw a smoke column rise after he pulled up, " Merritt later recounted. "He then rejoined me and at once repeated this same procedure on a field believed to be Juterborg. I observed him pass over the field and a smoke column rise. He pulled up slightly and passed over a field just north of there within traffic pattern distance and I observed another smoke column rise."[33]

Credited with four German planes destroyed in strafing, Wright took top honors against ground targets that day, while Maj. Merritt claimed two and Lt. Morehouse another. Recalling the mission some fifty years later, Wright related that "…our Squadron Commander, when he was firing, had gotten so low that it bent the propeller blades on the airplane. Anyway, I was his element leader and Dick Morehouse was his wingman, so we had to stay with him all the way back … Of course there wasn't anything wrong with my airplane … so I was looking around. On the way back we flew practically over three other airfields, and I strafed and got an airplane on each airfield on the way back, and [Maj. Merritt] was flying so slow I didn't have any problem catching up!"[34]

Over in less than twenty minutes, the first phase of the 361st's combat for May 29 had ended by 1315 hours. Detached from the rest of the Group, low on fuel and suffering battle damage, Merritt's flight slowly made its way toward England.

375th Squadron C.O. Maj. George Merritt seen with pilots and ground crew at Bottisham, spring 1944. Note the transparent thigh pocket on Merritt's flying coveralls which would have held hand-written navigational routes and timings necessary for making rendezvous with the bombers and for returning home. *Courtesy George Lichter*

For the 374th and 376th Squadrons, which had remained with the bombers to cover their withdrawal over western Poland, a clash with the *Luftwaffe* had yet to materialize. Still on their drop tanks, the two squadrons continued their routine patterns amid the combat boxes, while eyes continually swept the peripheries in search of enemy aircraft. Led by Major Caviness, the 376th Squadron, radio call sign "Titus," was deployed as top cover to the bombers at 25,000 feet. Some 6,000 feet below the 376th, Maj. Roy Webb's 374th Squadron, call sign "Noggin," was patrolling level with the bombers when at 1330 hours, enemy aircraft were seen making a head-on pass through the B-17s.

"I was leading Noggin Squadron flying at about 18,000 feet to the left hand side of a box of bombers when I noticed 5 plus FW-190's making a pass on the lead box of bombers," Webb reported following the mission. "We immediately dropped wing tanks and dove to attack, squadron intact."[35] Having latched on to the first Focke-Wulf, Webb realized that one of his drop-tanks had hung up refusing to jettison when the release was actuated. A common problem when the gasoline feed tube was secured too tightly, Webb had no choice but to momentarily break off the combat while attempting to shake the tank loose by yawing the aircraft. The first aerial victory, consequently, came to 1st Lt. George Lichter who seized the initiative when his squadron commander was forced to abandon the chase. "Major Webb's right wing tank hung-up and I was able to pass at 12,000 feet and made a 90 degree deflection shot for 350/400 yards … observing no strikes. I turned inside of the enemy aircraft and got on his tail, firing from 300 yds closing to 50 yds observing hits all over the aircraft and noting several pieces flying off … He split-essed and I broke off watching him crash into a wooded area."[36]

Born and raised in Brooklyn, New York, the 22-year-old Lichter had enlisted shortly after Pearl Harbor, and followed a life-long interest in flying by becoming an Army Aviation Cadet. In addition to patriotism, Lichter's desire to close with the enemy was multi-layered. "Being Jewish, I wanted to fight the Germans," he recalled in an interview years later.[37] His enthu-

siasm for combat flying at the time was reflected in letters home, and in describing to his parents the battle on May 29, he declared that "The action took place in Poland and was the best trip I ever took in an airplane." Describing how he shot down the FW-190, Lichter wrote that it "rolled over like a wounded bird and crashed into the ground. After that I saw some parachutes that had come out of one of our bombers and went over to wave at the boys. As I got close I spotted a Jerry plane going straight for them. I headed him off and shot him up pretty good but didn't see him crash. I'm claiming a probably destroyed." Finally, after describing how the intervention of squadron mate 1st Lt. Robert Eckfeldt got another German fighter off his tail, Lichter ended his letter declaring that "I'm sure hoping we get into some more fights like this last one."[38]

After watching Lichter down the FW-190, Maj. Webb was ready to rejoin the bombers. As he began the climb back toward the B-17s, however, he observed another FW-190 shooting at bomber crewman who had abandoned their aircraft. "I

Lt. George Lichter of the 374th Fighter Squadron seated on the wing of his P-51, flanked by his ground crew, May 1944. While serving with the 361st, Lichter named each of his aircraft for his close friend and fellow 374th Squadron pilot Robert Buryl Lind, of Dallas, Texas, who was killed in a training accident in September 1943. *Courtesy George Lichter*

started back toward the bombers when I noticed an FW making passes at approximately 6 parachutes of bomber crews and I immediately tacked on to his tail. He took me from 8,000 feet to the deck…." Webb's violent maneuvering during the chase, however, began to cause the gun stoppages common in the early P-51B. "…slipping and turning made my gun sight go out and three guns jam. I continued following him and fired using my imagination as a gun-sight…we were right on the deck and I was running out of ammunition, he made a tight turn to the right to avoid my tracers which were going just by his canopy on the left and he caught a wing in the trees and cart wheeled on the ground. All of this time there was an FW-190 on my tail who was doing a hell of a lot of firing (but he never hit me)."[39]

It was 1st. Lt. David Callaway of Yellow Flight, after destroying one Focke-Wulf and blacking himself out momentarily in the process, who spotted Webb's predicament between the two German fighters and dove to his assistance. "I could not close on him due to the fact that my engine was cutting out at full throttle. I fired the remainder of my ammunition at approximately 500 yards in an attempt to scare him off Maj. Webb's tail."[40] Although Callaway was unable to see any hits on the German, his effort to ward off the attack apparently succeeded.

1st Lt. Robert Eckfeldt, piloting "Bald Eagle" – his personal P-51B, was also credited with destroying an FW-190 during the sharp engagement which followed the German attack. Having missed the initial order to drop tanks due to radio trouble, Eckfeldt was initially late in the pursuit, but eventually latched on to a highly skillful German pilot. "I switched to "A" Channel and joined 2 ships at about 2,000 feet, one of which turned out to be an FW-190 on Lt. Lichter's tail," Eckfeldt related in debriefing. "When the enemy aircraft saw me coming he dropped flaps. I dropped mine and pulled up along side of him unable to stay on his tail. We jockeyed back and forth at 100 to 130 miles an hour … trying to slide back on to each other's stern. The enemy aircraft then suddenly did a remarkable maneuver, pulling over me and rolling so that he made a head-on pass at me. I started to turn inside of him with flaps and he dived down to the deck. As I was overtaking him, he pulled up to 500 feet and dropped flaps, seeming to stop in mid-air. I put down full flaps to avoid overshooting him." Closing from 200 to 50 yards while holding the trigger down, Eckfeldt was able to see the effects of his four .50 caliber machine guns as debris from the German fighter flew off in his path, marking the impending end of the aircraft.[41]

The Group Operations Officer, Maj. Wallace E. Hopkins, was also able to claim an aerial victory during the engagement of May 29, though his flight began the mission somewhat in-

Lt. Col. Wallace E. Hopkins, 361st Fighter Group Operations Officer, seen on the wing of his personal P-51 "Ferocious Frankie" named for his wife. *Courtesy George Lichter*

auspiciously. "I was leading Noggin Blue Flight, and just prior to rendezvous with the bombers three ships of my flight aborted," Hopkins related following the mission. After joining the group leader's flight, he dove his Mustang in the general pursuit of the bandits, ending up at 2,000 feet looking for enemy aircraft. Catching a lone FW-190 near the deck, he was able to get in a long burst after a series of violent maneuvers just above the treetops. In his own colorful terms, Hopkins described the final moments of the combat. "…I opened up with the old lead and the result was one of the prettiest sights I've ever seen. I observed numerous strikes on his wing-root, which caught fire, then began to disintegrate and fill the otherwise beautiful sky with pieces flying in all directions."[42]

While most of the action had been among the 374th Squadron which had been patrolling at the same level as the bombers at the start of the engagement, elements of the 376th Squadron rapidly dove to investigate after hearing the outbursts of radio chatter from the 374th. When Maj. Webb's call to drop tanks came out, Capt. Wallace Frank, leading Yellow Flight, of the 376th brought his flight down to join the fight. "Our squadron was at 25,000 feet while the bombers were at 18,000 feet. I saw one 'Big Friend' catch fire and called it in at the same time the leader of the low squadron called that there were plenty of bandits in and amongst the bombers. The squadron leader could not see them so I started down. I saw two FW-190s and swung in behind them. My rate of closure was terrific and I opened fire at about 300 yards, zero deflection. I saw strikes all over the tail and fuselage, and I continued firing up to 50 yards seeing strikes on the wing at minimum range. I believe I killed the pilot for as I broke off he went into a shallow dive which terminated in a wooded area with a beautiful explosion." As Frank pulled away, his wingman, 2nd Lt. Will T. Butts, also fired on the Focke-Wulf, scoring hits and earning a share in the claim.[43]

Capt. Frank was not yet finished for the day, however, and the mere fact that an enemy aircraft had been spotted by someone else first was no excuse to sit on the sidelines. After confirming the crash of the previous German, he reported that "I looked for something else and saw another FW-190 with about five of our boys chasing him. The nearest to the FW-190 was about 600 yards so I cut inside him and fired a burst from about 400 yards." As the German pilot split-s'd for the deck and attempted a belly landing, Frank remained in pursuit. "He straightened out and tried to make a crash landing on a dirt road, but did a very sloppy job of it and nosed in from about 30 feet." Seeing no smoke or flames Frank then strafed the aircraft as a means of positively destroying it.[44]

Within the space of a few minutes, the Group's fight in the skies above western Poland was over – finished as quickly as it had started. With drop tanks gone and several minutes at full throttle beginning to show on their fuel gauges, the pilots of the 374th and 376th squadrons joined together in small groups and began to gain some altitude for the flight across Germany to reach home. Overall, the day had been a notable success, particularly for the 374th which was able to claim seven FW-190's destroyed and another five damaged without loss. Although the pilots of the 376th Squadron were only modestly successful in the engagement by comparison, news of the most dramatic achievement of the day would greet them on their return to Bottisham. Detached from the rest of the 376th on a separate task, 21-year-old 2nd Lt. Dale F. Spencer of Clymer, New York, would single-handedly down four German aircraft in a matter of seconds in a remarkable case of being in "the right place at the right time."

Flying the number four position in White Flight of the 376th, Spencer's opportunity came as a result of engine trouble experienced by another pilot. Some thirty minutes prior to the Group's aerial engagement, Lt. Abe Rosenberger of the 375th Squadron, who had joined with Spencer's flight patrolling over the bombers, reported his engine smoking and broke off to head for home. Lt. Spencer, then flying only his eighth combat mis-

Capt. Wallace B. Frank of the 376th Fighter Squadron. One of three members of West Point's Class of 1942 assigned to the 361st, Frank would be captured in France shortly after D-Day, but would be liberated by Allied troops a short time later. *Courtesy J.J. Kruzel*

sion, was ordered by the flight leader to escort Rosenberger back to England. "I broke away from the squadron and circled around west of the bomber track, about 15 minutes, looking for Lt. Rosenberger, but failing to find him, I turned back toward the bombers," Spencer later reported. As he neared the bomber stream, the "A" channel suddenly came alive as a distant Maj. Webb reported bandits and ordered the 374th to break escort. Speeding toward what he hoped would be the location of the dogfight now raging over his headset, Spencer began to approach the combat box of the 401st Bomb Group, whose B-17s were completely unescorted. As he scanned the sky for elements of his Group, he suddenly caught sight of four ME-410s, the rocket-equipped, twin-engined German interceptors, in a shallow climb toward the American formation. Immediately diving to approach the four bandits from behind, Spencer began to close the range in preparation for an attack.[45]

Spectators to the drama now unfolding nearby, the crewmen of the 401st had been warily tracking the approach of the ME-410's before Spencer's arrival on the scene. "At 1329 hours,

A Messerschmitt ME-410 in flight, seen from behind. This type of aircraft was frequently used by the *Luftwaffe* as a rocket-firing day interceptor. This captured example bears British markings. *National Archives*

in the vicinity of Woldenburg, Germany, four ME-410's appeared, flying parallel to our formation and in the same direction, at a speed I estimated to be 200 MPH," reported Maj. Ralph White, Group Leader of the 401st, to his Intelligence Officer after landing. "They were approximately 1500 yards away, flying echeloned to the left and were looking us over. We had been watching them come up and at first I had though they were B-17s because of their perfect formation. At that particular time, there were no friendly escorting fighters around and I expected them to start lobbing rockets into our Group formation. Approximately 20 seconds before the ME-410s were parallel to us, I observed a single P-51 Mustang fighter come up…from slightly below and to their rear. He seemed to be throttled back and was not observed by the ME-410's who were intent upon our formation."[46]

Approaching carefully from the blind spot below and behind the four Messerschmitts, Lt. Spencer closed on the number 4 enemy aircraft flying rearmost in the formation until "I could see the black cross on No. 1's fuselage," before opening fire.[47] The number 4 Messerschmitt erupted in smoke and flame as a result of a two-second burst fired by Spencer. Immediately the remaining three ME-410s broke into a steep dive to the right in a frantic attempt to dodge the attacking P-51. Within seconds, however, Spencer dispatched the number 3 enemy aircraft and was firing on the remaining two, both of which crashed and burned. "I never saw such an exhibition in my life," reported Capt. Scribner Dailey, the Deputy Group Leader of the 401st Bomb Group that day, "…the P-51 had shot down three of the 410's before a full five seconds time had elapsed."[48]

Amid the speed and excitement of the action, Spencer was not sure if he had downed the fourth ME-410, though eyewitnesses from the 401st shortly confirmed that he had, in fact destroyed all four enemy aircraft. So amazed and thankful for the determined defense of their formation by the single P-51 pilot, that the leaders of the 401st Bomb Group threw a party with Spencer as guest of honor at their Deenethorpe base four days later.[49]

The mission of May 29, 1944 was the culminating event of the Group's P-51 transitional period, demonstrating the full potential of the new long-range fighter. As the pilots of the Group recounted the highly successful mission in the days that

Lt. Dale F. Spencer of the 376th Fighter Squadron. Spencer would be the highest scoring "ace" in the 361st Fighter Group. *Courtesy Robert Volkman*

followed, they were treated to an encounter with a figure from the past. 1st Lt. Charles Screws, the first pilot lost in combat by the Group, returned to Bottisham after a harrowing escape from German-occupied France, a story which he recounted to the Group's pilots shortly after his return. "How he made his escape is a secret, but it's quite a thrilling story," squadron mate George Lichter wrote to his parents in Brooklyn after hearing Screws' account. Though his fellow pilots were undoubtedly glad to see Screws back at Bottisham, Lichter's letter hinted at some potentially embarrassing moments in that "We had given him up for lost and some of the men were even wearing his clothes."[50]

NOTES

[1] Robert C. Wright, Interview with the Author, August 27, 1994.

[2] David C. Landin, Interview with the Author, October 15, 1994.

[3] Steve Gotts, *Little Friends: A Pictorial History of the 361st Fighter Group in World War II.* (Dallas: Taylor Publishing Co., 1993) pp. 165-168.

[4] William N. Hess, *P-51: Bomber Escort* (New York: Ballantine Books, 1971), p. 73.

[5] Ibid., pp. 10-11.

[6] Ibid., p. 49.

[7] Grover C. Hall, Jr., *1000 Destroyed: The Life and Times of the 4th Fighter Group* (Dallas: Morgan Aviation Books, 1946), p. 80.

[8] Gotts, p. 39.

[9] Leroy H. Sypher, "Encounter Report," May 8, 1944.

[10] Robert B. Wentworth, "Station History, Station F-374 (361st Fighter Group) For May 1944," June 1, 1944, p. 6.

[11] Ibid., p. 7.

[12] Landin.

[13] Gotts, pp. 165-66.

[14] Ibid.

[15] Wentworth, p. 7.

[16] Roger A. Freeman, *The Mighty 8th War Diary* (New York: Janes, 1981), p. 248.

[17] *Bethesda Record*, July 1, 1944.

[18] United States Military Academy, "Graduating Class Questionnaire" for John W. Guckeyson, 1942.

[19] Gotts, p. 172.

[20] 361st Fighter Group, "Mission Summary Report, Field Order 344," May 21, 1944.

[21] Eugene Cole, "Sworn Statement," contained in Missing Aircrew Report #05002, May 22, 1944.

[22] "Report on Capture of Enemy Air Forces," May 21, 1944, contained in Missing Aircrew Report #05002.

[23] Abe P. Rosenberger, "Sworn Statement" contained in Missing Aircrew Report #4959, May 22, 1944.

[24] 361st Fighter Group, "Mission Summary Report, Field Order 349," May 24, 1944.

[25] Landin.

[26] Sam C. Wilkerson, Jr., "Sworn Statement," contained in Missing Aircrew Report # 5116, May 25, 1944.

[27] 375th Fighter Squadron, "Mission Summary Report, Field Order 349," May 24, 1944.

[28] Russell J. Sobieski, "Sworn Statement" contained in Missing Aircrew Report # 5118, May 24, 1944.

[29] Wentworth, p. 11.

[30] 361st Fighter Group, "Mission Summary Report," May 29, 1944.

[31] Ibid.

[32] George L. Merritt, Jr., "Combat Report," May 29, 1944.

[33] Ibid.,

[34] Wright.

[35] Roy A. Webb, "Encounter Report," May 29, 1944.

[36] George Lichter, "Encounter Report," May 29, 1944.

[37] George Lichter, Interview with the Author, September 14, 2000.

[38] George Lichter, correspondence with Parents, May 30, 1944.

[39] Webb, Ibid.

[40] David Callaway, "Encounter Report," May 29, 1944.

[41] Robert Eckfeldt, "Encounter Report," May 29, 1944.

[42] Wallace E. Hopkins, "Encounter Report," May 29, 1944.

[43] Wallace B. Frank, "Encounter Report," May 29, 1944.

[44] Ibid.

[45] Dale F. Spencer, "Encounter Report," May 29, 1944.

[46] 401st Bomb Group, "Statement of Maj. Ralph J. White, Group Leader," May 31, 1944.

[47] Spencer, Ibid.

[48] 401st Bomb Group, "Statement of Capt. Scribner C. Dailey, Deputy Group Leader," May 31, 1944.

[49] Stryker, June 4, 1944.

[50] Lichter, correspondence with parents, May 30, 1944.

five

Summer of '44

Part 1: Operation Overlord

Operation Overlord, the long-awaited invasion of France, was in many ways the watershed of the European War. Before its execution, the conflict's length was purely a matter for speculation; once Allied troops were firmly established in Normandy, however, the defeat of Germany seemed a much more timely prospect. True, no one was expecting a "walkover" in France, but an unmistakable feeling of progress permeated the Allied camp in the middle part of 1944.

For the Army Air Forces based in England, the coming drive across France would introduce new demands into day-to-day operations. To meet the anticipated ground-support needs for the campaign, the 9th (Tactical) Air Force had been created in late 1943. Equipped with a variety of fighter and bomber aircraft, the 9th's primary task would be tactical support of the ground troops in their advance across western Europe.

Despite the creation of this separate tactical force, the 8th Air Force, whose principal task from inception had been the strategic attack on German industry, would have to adapt to the necessities of the land campaign. The "heavies" – accustomed to operating against distant targets deep within the Reich – would be employed increasingly against targets in France and the Low Countries by the late spring of 1944. Not only would the bombers be "softening" the actual infrastructure of German defenses in Occupied Europe, but their frequent attacks on the Pas de Calais region would actively contribute to the deception of German intelligence about the invasion's true location.

For the 8th Fighter Command, the D-Day period would be defined by an important operational transition. While the job of high-altitude escort would remain its paramount reason for being, the 8th's fighter groups would increasingly adopt the fighter-bomber role in attacks on the German transportation web in France.

Though the mission of long-range escort would continue as a primary task for the "Yellowjackets," they too would be impacted by the need for fighter-bomber operations in support of the invasion. Beginning with D-Day itself, and lasting through early September, the invasion summer would be the most intense period of operations in the Group's history. In 96 days from June 6 through September 9, an average of one mission per day would be carried out by the 361st, and multi-mission days became commonplace. Of these 96 missions, 25 were ground-attack sorties involving bombing and strafing of German transportation targets and installations, as opposed to a mere 6 such missions in the 103 carried out prior to D-Day.[1] Losses, too, rose dramatically in the summer of '44 and 32 pilots would fail to return to Bottisham in the same 96-day period. Among those who would meet their end in the skies over France would be the ever-eager Maj. Merritt, CO of the 375th Fighter Squadron, and also, to the disbelief of all, Col. Christian who had formed and led the Group since its creation.

Above all, the summer of '44 would be a season of change for the "Yellowjackets." Replacement pilots would arrive in increasing numbers at Bottisham, not only to fill the slots of those missing in action, but also to take over from the old hands who would be rapidly finishing their tours as the summer months came to a close. The Group which emerged in the fall of 1944 would not be the same as that which had first assembled at Richmond in 1943.

The anticipation of D-Day was present at Bottisham in the weeks before the invasion, though it did not entirely dominate the consciousness of the Group's personnel. The routines and rhythm of combat operations had been established for five months by the middle of May and although rumors of the great operation abounded, events on the ground in France seemed unlikely to completely alter time-tested methods. Aircraft would still need to be serviced, fueled and armed, pilots would still be briefed and dispatched in the same fashion, and the routines of administration would persist. In short, the Group had been "at war" since January and had honed the process of day-to-day operations to a high rate of efficiency. Most commonly, the invasion was looked to as a positive step toward shortening the war – particularly for the ground echelon who would typically remain overseas for the duration. From a pilot's standpoint, the invasion offered more than simply additional mission credits – it would be a chance to observe first-hand what promised to be one of the war's pivotal events, as well as come to grips with the *Luftwaffe* which, it was believed, might well respond to the landings *en masse*.

Details of the coming invasion, particularly among the rank-and-file of the Air Corps in England, were cloaked in secrecy, yet clues to the imminence of D-Day revealed themselves to the careful observer. At Bottisham throughout May 1944, concerns over potential German spoiling attacks, or retaliation following the invasion, led to a discernible increase in base security. Beginning on May 11, a series of chemical and defense readiness exercises were initiated, and although an apparently humorous episode, in which the Group Commander was caught by the station Chemical Officer without his gas mask during a drill, was gleefully noted in the unit diary, the threat of attack was taken seriously. In one of several staff meetings convened for base-security issues during the month, Col. Christian emphasized the importance of perimeter anti-aircraft defenses citing that an estimated 6,000 German airborne troops gave the enemy the capability to "drop 50 on this field, simultaneously invading every fighter station in Great Britain."[2] While 24-hour liberty passes became increasingly difficult to come by as the month progressed, perhaps the most unmistakable hint of the nearness of D-Day was a standing order issued on May 27 requiring that small arms and gas masks be carried by Group personnel at all times. "Weapons are not worn off the station yet" recorded the Group's Historical Officer though he added that, "they probably will be soon."[3]

Among the pilots of the 361st, anticipation of the invasion was solidified in the month before D-Day by evidence not readily apparent to the ground echelon. "We could see it on missions – the buildup along the south shore of England, and we had an inkling that it was coming," reflected Henry Lederer of the 374th Squadron some fifty years later. "And, of course," he added, "we were warned by intelligence not to say a word – either amongst ourselves or over the air."[4] Echoing Lederer's

Summer of '44: Lt. Jesse Adkins of the 374th Fighter Squadron poses beside what would become an increasingly familiar weapon during the Allied drive across France – a 500 lb general purpose bomb. Note, to his right, in the distance, one of the "blister" hangars used by ground crews for maintenance at Bottisham. *Courtesy J.J. Kruzel*

Lt. Henry B. Lederer of the 374th Squadron with his ground crew at Bottisham, summer 1944. *Courtesy Henry B. Lederer*

recollection, former pilot David Landin of the 376th Squadron remarked that having seen the assembled ships and materiel along the Channel coast, the nearness of the invasion "was pretty obvious.... plus," he continued, "you'd talk to people, and you knew the island was just loaded with supplies and servicemen. So you knew it was coming, you just didn't know when it was coming."[5]

The first week in June saw the 361st putting up an invasion-related escort mission virtually every day. Throughout the week, the "heavies" attacked coastal defenses in the Pas de

D-Day Briefing: Pilots of the 361st photographed in the briefing room late on the evening of June 5, 1944. Seated at the extreme right is Lt. Col. Roy Webb, CO of the 374th Squadron. To his right, Capt. George Rew; to his right, Lt. Col. Wallace E. Hopkins, Group Operations Officer. *Courtesy J.J. Kruzel*

Capt. John M. Ellis, Jr., Group Intelligence Officer, points to the map used for the D-Day briefing showing the role the 361st would play in the massive air operations which would support the invasion. *Courtesy J.J. Kruzel*

Calais region as part of the Allied deception plan, or attempted to knock out various transportation targets in northeastern and north-central France. On the evening of June 4, the Group accompanied five B-24s of the 458th Bomb Group making their second attempt to knock out a series of bridges on the Seine River. The attack was made using a newly introduced and highly secret radio-controlled bombing technique code-named AZON.[6] Though the 361st was able to claim one ME-109 destroyed on the mission, Lt. Walter Kozicki of the 376th Squadron was shot down by a Messerschmitt and bailed out over France. After successfully evading capture and making contact with the French Resistance, Kozicki returned to England in August 1944.[7]

On June 5, an escort mission to the Pas de Calais region was carried out, though no enemy aircraft were sighted. The heavy bombers gave the appearance of carrying out "softening-up" preparations in the Pas de Calais as part of an elaborate deception plan which concealed the real invasion areas in Normandy. As the last of the Group's 48 participating Mustangs touched down at Bottisham around 1130 that morning, there was yet no clue as to the imminence of the landings, and the waiting ground crews began their post-mission maintenance as soon as the planes reached their hardstands. By late afternoon, however, instructions were passed among the Group's crew chiefs for the now-familiar D-Day paint scheme. To prevent aircraft recognition problems on the morning of the invasion, zebra-stripes – officially 18 inches wide, alternating three-white and two-black along the fuselage and wings – were to be painted on every Allied aircraft save the "heavies."[8] No aircraft so marked would fly until Overlord was in motion.

As former 374th Squadron crew chief Robert O. Bland recalled, the time constraints for the paint scheme came as a bit of a surprise for the ground crews. "We were given precise measurements and we all got together and helped each other. Sometime in the early evening we had completed several of the aircraft when Major Webb came by in his jeep and inquired how things were going. Then he dropped the bombshell! They all had to be finished by midnight with drop tanks installed and ready to go by early morning! He didn't state the purpose, but we put two and two together and 'guessed' that it was the big push! Measurements were guessed at from that point in time!"[9]

For those at Bottisham not tasked with post-mission maintenance chores, the coming of evening on June 5 brought with it the pursuit of various recreational activities both on and off base. While these continued more or less as usual, word began to spread that something was afoot. "Yeah, you just had a gut feeling it was going to happen," recalled native Floridian James Golden of the 374th, "and we sure knew the night before though, my Lord have mercy! We were down to some little ole' stage show that somebody was putting on the base and they said, you know, there's a briefing tonight at, as I recall, 11 – 11:30, and you knew that was it."[10]

For those who did manage to get away, the return to Bottisham at the end of the liberty run brought with it the near end of speculation. Key staff were ordered to report to Group Operations immediately and pilots were instructed to assemble in the Mess Hall by 23:30 hours. Lingering doubts were finally put to rest when Group Commander Col. Christian arrived to deliver the briefing. Taking center stage shortly after

Midnight, the 28-year-old Colonel proceeded to outline the Group's role in the great operation. For nearly the next 24 hours, he informed them, a maximum effort would be put up by every group in the 8th Fighter Command, not to mention the "heavies," troop carriers, the 9th Air Force units, and the RAF. In a short time, C-47s and towed gliders would be transporting the first invasion troops – the combined Allied Airborne forces-who would jump into Normandy. Heavy bombers would attack the invasion beaches in the early hours of the morning, and aircraft of the 9th Air Force and RAF would patrol the Channel and Normandy coast throughout the landing operations. Any aircraft, save the heavy bombers, not adorned with zebra stripes would be fair game.

For the 361st, alongside other units of the 8th Fighter Command, the task would be to provide an aerial cordon well inland from the beaches, in positions to intercept any *Luftwaffe* response to the landings. In the absence of enemy aircraft they would also seek out and strafe enemy traffic along the roads and railroads of German-occupied France. To achieve continuous coverage, the groups would be split into "A" and "B" sections, alternating patrols throughout the day. The 361st, for its part, was assigned a patrol area 40 miles south of Caen between Argentan, Mortain and Mayenne.[11] With a total of six missions scheduled for June 6, every pilot in the Group would have a chance to participate in the D-Day patrols. The first of these, slated to begin shortly after 0300 hours, would be led by Col. Christian and would consist of 34 P-51s of the 374th and 375th squadrons. Fitted with drop tanks, they would remain up for some six hours before returning to base where the aircraft would be refueled, rearmed and taken up again by fresh pilots.

By 0300, the preparation for the first mission was complete and those assigned to fly were gathered at the flight line for a few pre-flight words with their crew chiefs. When start-engine time arrived they were strapped into their cockpits by attending ground crew – many exchanging a quick handshake before the historic flight, and pressed their starting buttons bringing thirty-four 12-cylinder Merlins to life. In what would later prove to be a twist of fate, 2nd Lt. James Golden of the 374th was surprised by the appearance of Squadron CO Maj. Webb on his wing moments before take off. "I was getting ready to take off in the early morning hours … on D-Day, and he comes running and he says 'I gotta have your aircraft cause mine's out and I'm not going to miss this show!' So I crawl out of the cockpit and he crawls in and away he goes." Assigned to fly as deputy group leader, Webb would complete the mission, while Golden would wait until 1800 hours that evening to fly his first D-Day sortie – during which he would earn the dubi-

376th Squadron pilots study maps prior to taking off on D-Day. At center is Capt. Wallace B. Frank. *Courtesy George Lichter*

ous distinction of last Allied airman to be shot down on June 6, 1944.[12]

Left standing on the flight line as the Group's Mustangs took off to gingerly form up in darkness for the flight south, Golden was convinced that regardless of the Germans, his squadron mates would have a difficult task ahead. Looking back some fifty years later, he remarked that the uncertain weather conditions coupled with the pre-dawn departure of the first mission introduced unique complications. "The weather was very, very funny. It was bad, and then it cleared up with a nice moon sitting up there around midnight or one o'clock, and then when the time came to take off the weather was awful, just awful. How they flew all those airplanes through that weather in the dark is just beyond me. The thing that just impressed me was ... when that mission was back, we hadn't lost anybody – I just couldn't believe it!"[13]

Despite the difficulties of forming up in darkness, Col. Christian and 28 of his pilots (six had aborted due to mechanical trouble) arrived on time over Argentan to begin their patrol. The mission was charged with expectation yet the 361st's D-Day experience, much like that of every other group in the 8th, was something of an anti-climax. For much of their four-hour patrol, the terrain below was obscured by near-solid undercast. Scanning the air for Germans, they were met with only the occasional glimpse of other American fighters overlapping in their patrols, and scattered concentrations of flak over Argentan and Mortain. Once the fuel from their drop tanks had been expended, elements of both squadrons let down below the cloud-layer to search for targets of opportunity and were able to strafe a mixed-bag of trucks, locomotives, and a few parked aircraft at an airdrome near Flers. By 0830, the two squadrons had completed their patrol and headed north toward Fecamp for the flight home. The specified course out, well east of the invasion beaches, was necessary to avoid recognition problems over Normandy, and would be followed by each successive patrol.

The cycle of take-offs and returns at Bottisham continued throughout the day at a relentless pace. At 0617, while the first patrol was over France, the Group's second mission left Bottisham for its eventual relief. A third patrol departed base at 1057, followed by three more at 1208, 1318, and 1812, all bound for the same patrol area south of Caen. Though ground controllers remained poised to vector patrolling fighters to intercept any suspicious radar contacts, no massive German response took place. The few enemy aircraft spotted by the Group were generally hedge-hopping to avoid detection or nearing an airdrome for landing. At 1945 hours during the final mission

of the day, Capt. George Rew of the 374th Squadron shared a ground claim with Lt. Vernon Richards after spotting four ME-109s on the deck near St. Vendomes. "As we went down," Rew later recounted, "two of them put down their wheels and landed in open fields half a mile apart. Lt. Richards and I hit one just as he stopped rolling and four white nosed P-51s got the other 109s that landed."[14]

On the same mission, the 375th Squadron was vectored to Tours to investigate reported enemy air activity. As the squadron neared the city, a JU-88 was spotted landing at a German airdrome, with a second on final approach. In characteristic style, 375th Squadron CO Maj. Merritt reported that "We were at three o'clock to this aircraft at a distance of about two miles. Immediately, I made plans to destroy this one in the air. Unfortunately, he just kissed the ground the moment I got to him … [I] opened fire at 400 yards doing 350 miles per hour … the

Armorers on the 374th Fighter Squadron flight line load ammunition trays. Note the fresh, prominent "invasion stripes" on the aircraft. *National Archives*

approach was from broadside. The first firing was short, and some bullets passed over the target due to the necessity of maneuvering into firing position. A good number of strikes were observed on the fuselage and cockpit area, and flames immediately appeared which should show in the films." After setting the twin-engine bomber on fire, Merritt was forced to break off by intense light flak as German batteries around the field opened up on his P-51. "One gun installation suddenly put up a continuous cone of tracers during my approach so fierce that I turned the ship on its wingtip to avoid passing through it," he added.[15] Always ready to engage the enemy, Merritt had built up a reputation as a dedicated and aggressive squadron commander. The JU-88 strafed at Tours would be his eleventh and final victory, and the mission his second to last.

Though the predicted air battles in response to the invasion failed to materialize, the price of operations on June 6 was not low for the 361st. In each of the final three missions of the day, one aircraft failed to return to Bottisham – two of them succumbing to German ground fire. Flying at low-level near Chartres around 1415 hours, 1st Lt. Lawrence B. Perry of the 375th Squadron was killed when his P-51 suddenly burst into flame after being hit by flak.[16] The second casualty occurred some 45 minutes later when 2nd Lt. William D. Willett's plane was hit during a strafing attack. "I first noticed Lt. Willett's ship streaming glycol right after he made a pass at an armored vehicle." reported 1st Lt. Ray S. White of the 376th. "It was pouring down rain and the visibility was terrible. I called him and told him he was hit and to get some altitude. He did not answer. He called his leader, Lt. Lane, and said he thought he hit something. I called him again and again to get some altitude so he could bail out. He stuck right on the deck until his engine quit." Attempting a belly landing in a field, Willet's plane overshot, ploughed headlong into a treeline and finally reached a crunching halt on its side.[17]

The last pilot to be lost on D-Day was 2nd Lt. James R. Golden of the 374th Squadron, who had been bumped from the first mission at 0300 that morning. It was shortly after 2100 hours when Golden pulled up from strafing a train and noticed black smoke trailing from his aircraft and rapidly dropping oil pressure. He called to his wingman, 1st Lt. Edward Murdy, to look him over. "When I looked in his direction I could see that the entire left side of his plane was covered with oil," Murdy reported after returning to base. "I advised that he throttle back and I followed along giving him his headings." Unable to cut the distance by crossing out over Normandy, Golden was forced to head toward Dieppe and within fifteen minutes, his engine seized-up, forcing him to bale out well short of the coast. Murdy reported that he saw Golden clear the plane before passing into

A Junkers JU-88 bomber. *National Archives*

the undercast and glimpsed the burning wreckage after diving below the clouds. No parachute, however, was sighted.[18]

Recalling the incident some fifty years later, Golden described the bailout itself as a brush with death. "I tell you, the difference in an official report and what's going on down in there is really amazing … I went out with my [parachute] leg straps unbuckled somehow. I finally put one foot on the side scrambling to get out, and the wind just took me the rest of the way, and I was tumbling and trying to find the rip cord and it was not there! So I was still tumbling and I'd heard somebody say if you started scissoring your feet you could straighten out, so I tried to straighten out and I did… I was falling down and I could see that chute blowing out behind me … and I reached up and caught the pack with my left hand and pushed it down far enough to get the rip cord. When the chute popped, no leg straps! So I went through the chute, the big buckle – the breast buckle – caught my face and clipped me in the chin and eyebrow. Even playing football, I had the bad habit of sticking my tongue out, and when the thing hit me on the chin, I just bit a hunk – and that bleeds like a stuck pig!…I really was not totally conscious of what I had done, because I hit the ground and I was reaching to get my chute off so I could run, and the chute was lying on the ground. The only thing I had hooked on me was the dinghy strap – the rest of it was gone! And, I tell you, I almost fainted right there when I realized that I had gone through the chute and held on to that chute harness with my arms until I hit the ground!"[19]

Quickly hiding himself in a trash pit not far from where he landed, Lt. Golden resolved to remain perfectly still until he was completely sure it was safe to come out. Unfortunately, a German military camp lay nearby and it was only a matter of minutes before *Wehrmacht* troops were searching for him. For the first night he was able to stay hidden, but on the following morning his luck ran out. Assisted by two French civilians, he had been taken inside a nearby house when the Germans returned and captured him. Interrogated and sent to Germany, Golden would remain at *Stalag Luft III* for many of the war's remaining months.[20]

Ground crews of the 361st watch as a P-51 touches down on Bottisham's steel-matted runway following a mission over France, June 6, 1944. *National Archives*

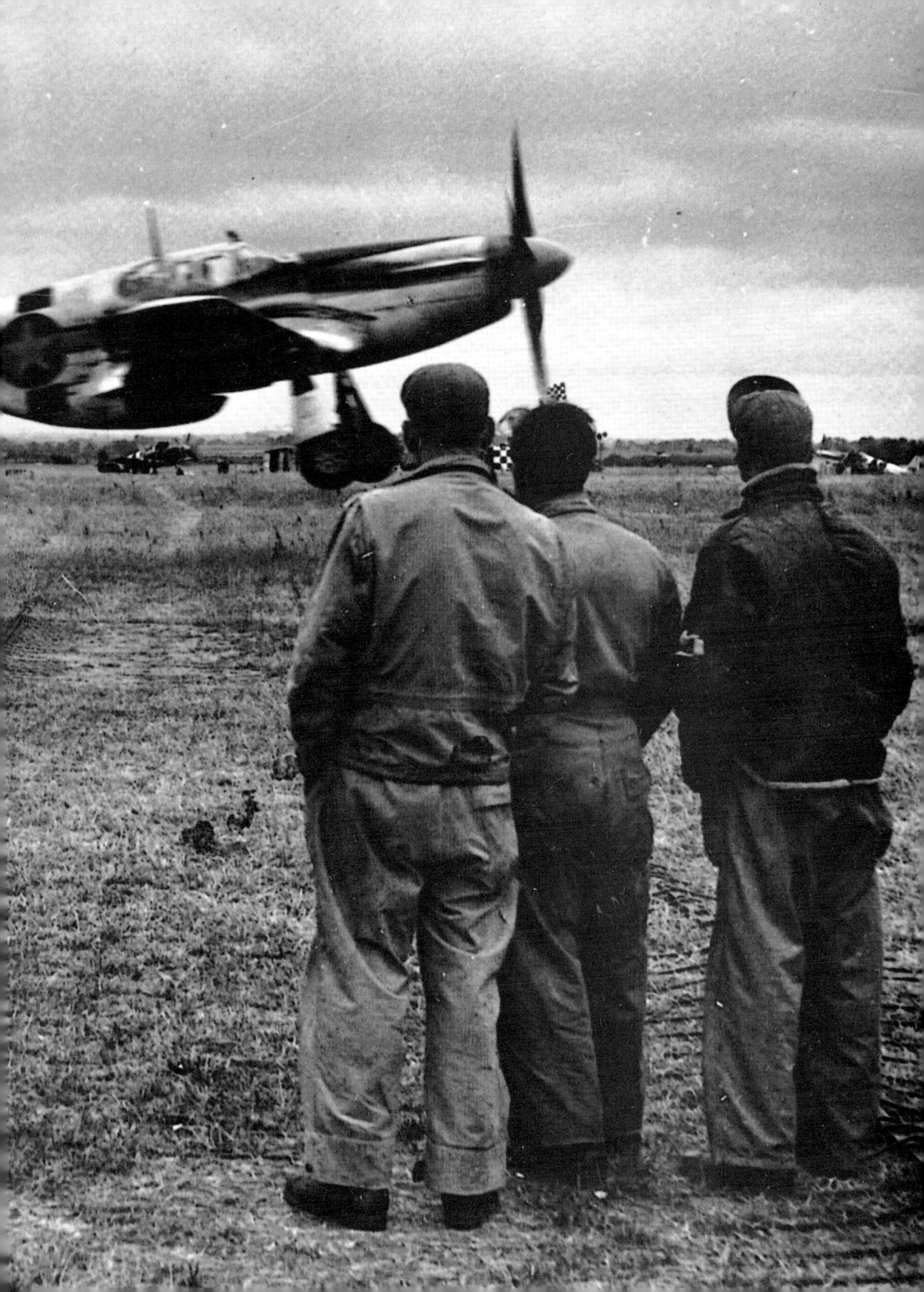

When the final mission of June 6 returned to Bottisham at 2239, nearly 24 hours had passed since the Group first learned of the invasion's impending launch. With little in the way of first-hand information from the beaches, the station was cheered by radio broadcasts which announced that the ground troops had, in fact, been able to establish a beachhead in Normandy by the evening of D-Day.

For the ground crews charged with repairing, servicing and arming the Group's aircraft, little more than a passing acknowledgment of the initial success of Overlord could be offered. For them, the fever pitch of activity brought by the invasion had begun on the afternoon of June 5 – and had continued non-stop through the following day. Indeed, for the better part of a week after the landings, multi-mission days would be the norm, and rest would be difficult to obtain. "The crew chiefs didn't sleep at all for over 48 hours," recalled Russell Severson, a former crew chief in the 374th Squadron. "Finally, the assistant crew chiefs, who had been sent in to sleep, relieved us. I still had a hard time sleeping, but when I did, the CO couldn't wake me – I felt like I was drugged!"[21]

Part 2: Second Front

Though D-Day was the pivotal event of the war in Europe, it was, in itself, a mere beginning. Following the establishment of the beachhead in Normandy on June 6, the liberation of France, spawned by the invasion, would occupy the bulk of Allied efforts throughout the summer of '44.

Though much of the ground-attack work undertaken by the Army Air Forces would be carried out by 9th Air Force units – many transferring to bases and strips on the Continent as Allied holdings in France expanded – the 8th Air Force would continue to support the ground campaign as needed. This was particularly true during the first half of June as American troops pressed toward the initial major objective in the Battle of Normandy – the capture of Cherbourg.

For those pilots and ground crews at Bottisham who might still have been unsure of the meaning of the term "maximum effort," the days that followed the invasion would clarify it. A mere five hours after the last D-Day mission had returned to Station F-374, the first of four ground-attack efforts put up by the 361st on June 7 was enroute to skies over Normandy. As would be the case throughout the coming days, the task of the "Yellowjackets" would be to interdict German road and rail traffic behind the front, in theory barring the daylight movement of enemy reinforcements. Sometimes armed with bombs, sometimes with machine guns alone, the Group's flights and squadrons would crisscross the French countryside south of the beachhead attempting to deny daylight movement – by foot, truck, tank or train – to the Germans.

Though ground-fire alone would take its toll on low-level missions, ground obstacles and debris from explosions would also be persistent hazards. Bombing and strafing a variety of ground targets throughout the day, it was on the final mission of June 7 that the dangers of low-level strafing were made most painfully clear. Leading a fighter-bomber sweep near Nantes, some 125 miles southwest of the Allied beachhead, Maj. George Merritt ordered a strafing attack on a group of German vehicles spotted along a rural road. Leading his flight in the first pass, Merritt had skimmed the treetops of an adjacent wood before lining up on the parked vehicles. Just as he and his trailing wingmen commenced the strafing run, the 375th Squadron CO's aircraft was suddenly seen to cartwheel and crash. "The pass was made over [the] woods where Major Merritt hit a

A flight of Mustangs prepares to take off from Bottisham on a combat mission, June 1944. The aircraft closest to the camera is Col. Christian's P-51B "Lou III" equipped with a British Malcolm Hood canopy which provided greater visibility than the standard "bird cage" canopy. Christian's P-51D, the well-known "Lou IV" succeeded this aircraft as his personal mount. *Courtesy George Lichter*

post, skipped off the road and exploded," Reported his shocked wingman, 2nd Lt. Sherman Armsby. "He landed upside down in a field in a ball of fire," the report abruptly ended, no more description being necessary.[22] Perhaps no more aggressive and colorful squadron CO flew with the 361st in the course of the war. Always ready to engage and shoot down Germans, Merritt's combat career, spanning five aerial and six ground victories, ended in a way that would become increasingly familiar in the summer of '44 – quickly and violently.

For six days following the invasion, save June 9 when weather conditions precluded flying, the Group put up two or more missions per day over France, either escorting bombers against tactical targets, or operating as fighter-bombers behind German lines. Two of the Group's pilots who were forced down and captured during this period underwent dramatically different turns of fate. During the second of three missions on June 8, in which elements of the Group dive-bombed targets in France, 1st Lt. James Hastin of the 374th Squadron was forced to bail out of his P-51 which caught fire in the explosion of a train he was strafing.

After evading capture and making contact with the French Resistance, Hastin was clandestinely taken to Paris several weeks later where, along with several other Allied airmen, he was betrayed and turned over to the *Gestapo*. Despite their status as Prisoners of War, Hastin, along with 167 other Allied airmen, was shipped to the concentration camp at Buchenwald when the *Gestapo* prison at Frenes was evacuated in mid August. "We were told by the inmates at the camp that the only way out of the place was up the chimney," Hastin wrote years later. After two months of the brutal conditions at Buchenwald, he was finally turned over to the *Luftwaffe* and sent to *Stalag Luft III* in East Prussia.[23] Two days after Lt. Hastin went down, Capt. Wallace B. Frank of the 376th Squadron was lost on a strafing mission over northern France. One of three members of West Point's Class of 1942 who were assigned to the 361st, Capt. Frank suffered a broken leg after bailing out of his P-51 and was convalescing in a German hospital in France several weeks later when American troops liberated him.[24]

By June 13, single daily missions resumed as the norm for the 361st, and on that day an escort mission over France yielded four ME-109s shot down for no losses. It was not until June 18 that the Group returned to German airspace as part of the 8th Air Force's first attack on strategic targets since the start of the invasion.[25]

The costliest mission in the 361st Fighter Group's history occurred on June 19 when five pilots of the 374th Squadron failed to return from a mission over France – although their loss was not due to enemy action. Aside from the normal hazards of combat flying, the weather alone over England and western Europe could often prove deadly; this was exactly the case that day. Led by Lt. Col. Joe Kruzel, the 361st was attempting to rendezvous with bombers in the Bordeaux region when the pilots encountered thick cloud formations rising well above 20,000 feet impairing visibility so badly that wingmen had difficulty even seeing their element leaders. Closing up as tightly as possible in order to remain in visual contact, unsuccessful attempts were made to climb above the clouds after which Kruzel ordered his pilots to abort and head for home.[26]

Evidence suggests that before the planes could disperse in the near-zero visibility, a series of collisions involving aircraft of the 374th Squadron took place. "We were over France in close formation headed southward trying to descend below dense storm clouds when a flight leader screamed that he had vertigo," wrote former pilot Glenn Fielding of the 374th to a former crew-chief many years later. "More than one leader must have been involved. When I lost sight of my leader from 25 ft. away I peeled-off and came home alone."[27] Killed on this mission were Capt. Joe Latimer, and Lieutenants David Callaway, Lawrence Downey, Walter Sargent, and Robert Stolzy.[28]

Despite the setback dealt by the weather on June 19, the pace of operations at Bottisham did not slacken, and the majority of the Group's contact with the *Luftwaffe* during June took place in the last ten days of the month. On June 20, the "Yellowjackets" put up two missions – the first escorting B-24s to western Poland, during which Group Commander Col. Christian was able to direct a successful strafing attack on Putnitz Airdrome. After observing several columns of smoke rising from the field following the strafing runs of two other flights, Christian led his wingmen down for a pass at a German seaplane observed in a lake just north of the airdrome. "At 1035," the Group Commander later recounted, "I told my flight to follow me and made a pass, from east to west, across the lake … [and] fired several long bursts at what I believe was an HE-115 anchored about fifty yards offshore. I saw many tracers coming up from the flak position northeast of the field (to which I was by that time exposed) so I broke sharply to the North and withdrew…I saw the seaplane settling in the water and finally sink."[29]

Killed in the strafing attack at Putnitz was 2nd Lt. Miles Elliott of Shelton, Washington, whose P-51 was badly hit over the airdrome. As Lt. William Rogers of the 375th Squadron later reported, Elliott called by radio after pulling up from strafing, saying "he was hit in the gas tank and had gas in the cockpit…. He asked what direction to go and somebody told him to bail out over the woods west of the field." Though his aircraft was seen pulling up to gain altitude by several members of his

A close-up view of Col. Christian piloting his personal P-51D "Lou IV." It was this aircraft that he flew when he attacked and sank a German float plane near Putnitz Airdrome. *National Archives*

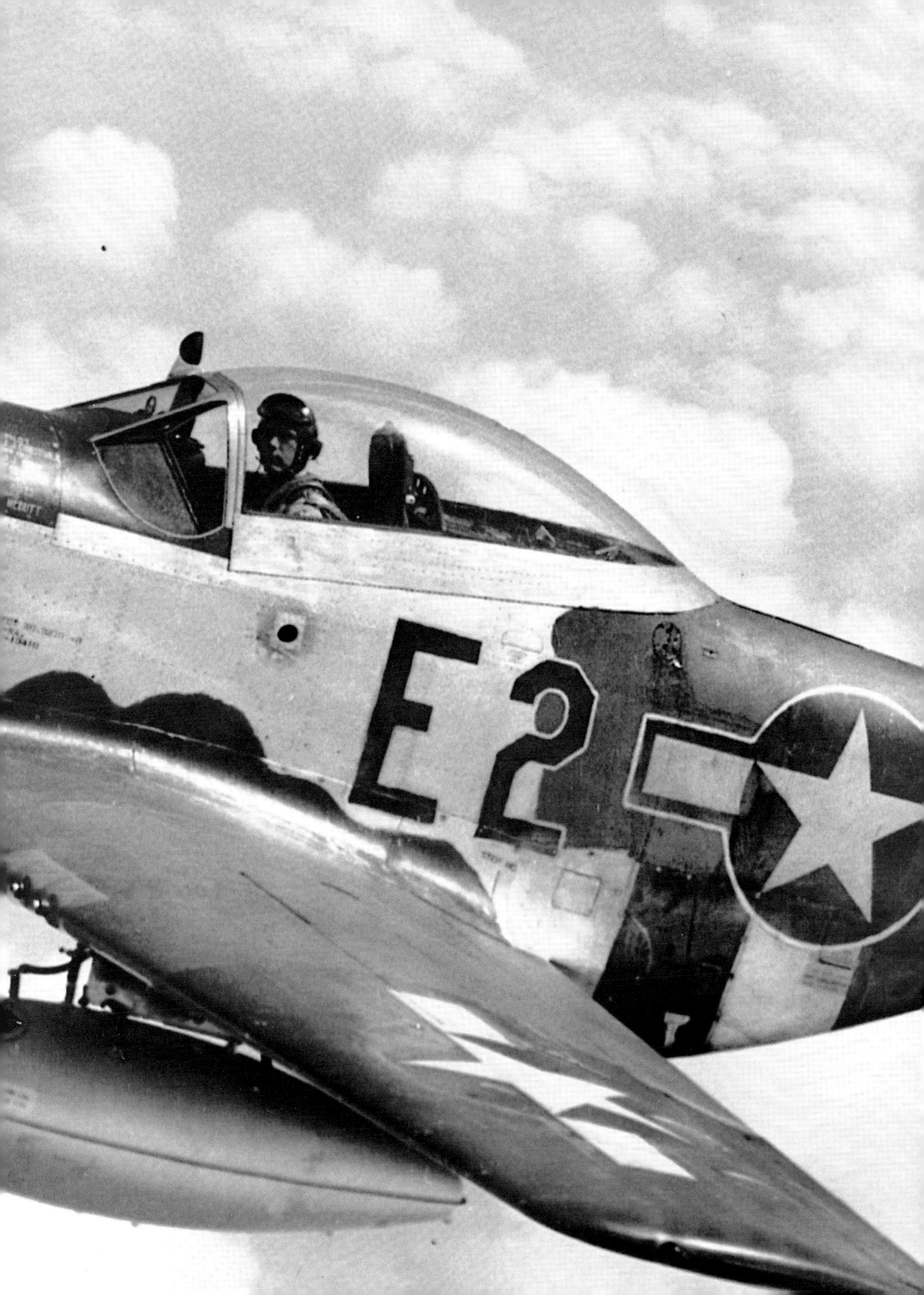
E2

flight, Elliott was apparently unable to bail out before his aircraft crashed.[30]

Though encounters with German fighters over France were a relative rarity for the "Yellowjackets" during the summer of '44, the early morning hours of June 25 held a notable exception. Detailed to escort B-17s against transportation targets in France, Lt. Col. Joe Kruzel was leading the Group toward the rendezvous point near Caen in conditions of unusually good visibility when he spotted what appeared to be a running dogfight several thousand feet below. Without hesitating, Kruzel took the 375th Squadron down from 21,000 feet to investigate and encountered "a scattered jumble of P-38s, 109s, 190s and flak from 5,000 feet down to the deck. We released our external tanks, split the squadron into flights and joined the combat. It was difficult to determine the exact number of P-38s and [enemy aircraft] present as they were very low and scattered over a fairly large area, flying in ones and small groups of two and three."[31]

Spotting a lone P-38 in pursuit of an FW-190, which was gradually outdistancing the twin-engined Lightning, Kruzel placed his recently received P-51D into a shallow dive, pushed the throttle to the firewall and joined the chase. After passing the P-38 he closed to within range of the Focke-Wulf and fired a burst at the German only to have his electric gun sight immediately fail. In an interesting commentary on one of the unexpected shortcomings of the early D-model Mustang, Kruzel described his attempts to bring down the German over the course of several minutes. "[F]rom that point on, it was hit and miss – I tried using my ring and bead but in the P-51D it is set too low, and in lining up the ring and bead your visibility over the nose of the plane is limited making low flying on the treetops dangerous." Undaunted, Kruzel stayed with the Focke-Wulf through a series of evasive maneuvers firing bursts from close range. When the German pilot pulled up into a steep climbing turn, however, several hits were scored after which the pilot and/or canopy – Kruzel could not be sure which – were seen to fly from the stricken plane which then crashed and burned.[32]

After downing the FW-190, Kruzel then attempted to reform the Group – to the extent possible – in order to begin the assigned escort. In this he would have only limited success as elements of all three squadrons were dispersed along the deck in a series of individual combats. 2nd Lt. Urban L. Drew of the 375th – who was destined to achieve the distinction of "ace" with the "Yellowjackets" – would gain his first aerial victory that day when his element leader's luck ran out. Having only begun his combat tour on June 16, Drew was flying as wingman to 1st Lt. Martin Johnson who latched onto an ME-109 in the

2nd Lt. Miles Elliott of the 375th Fighter Squadron who was killed June 20, 1944 after strafing Putnitz Airdrome. This photograph, taken several weeks earlier, shows Elliott displaying soot residue on the underside of his P-51 following a low-level strafing attack on a German railroad locomotive. *National Archives*

opening moments of the battle. Closing to within range of the German, Johnson fired several short bursts when three of his P-51B's four guns jammed preventing effective fire against the violently dodging Messerschmitt. Realizing the futility of his single gun, Johnson pulled up and called for his wingman to engage.[33]

"'Johnnie' was almost through with his tour and he'd never shot down an airplane in the air," Drew related years later. "He had several on the ground that he had credit for – but he was desperate to get one in the air and it looked like this was the first one because this guy was just down behind his armor plate on the treetops … [he] pulled up and I pulled off to the side to watch it – to confirm it – and all his guns jammed and with a few well chosen four letter words he said 'Drew, take him.'"[34] Closing to 100 yards in each of two passes, Drew riddled the Messerschmitt which finally nosed into the ground and exploded – the first of what would be six aerial victories in his tour with the 361st.

Elsewhere in the 375th, 2nd Lt. Jack S. Crandell was able to claim two ME-109s destroyed after becoming separated from his flight. Following a momentary delay in dropping his tanks,

Lt. Col. Joe Kruzel's P-51D "Vi" seen at Bottisham, June 1944. It was while flying this aircraft on the mission of June 25, 1944, that his electric gun sight went out exposing the difficulty of using the ring and bead sight on the D model Mustang. Note the three Japanese "kill" flags along with two German flags just below the windscreen. *Courtesy J.J. Kruzel*

Lt. Col. Roy Webb of the 374th Fighter Squadron poses on the wing of his personal P-51D "Sweet Thing IV." *Courtesy Russell A. Severson*

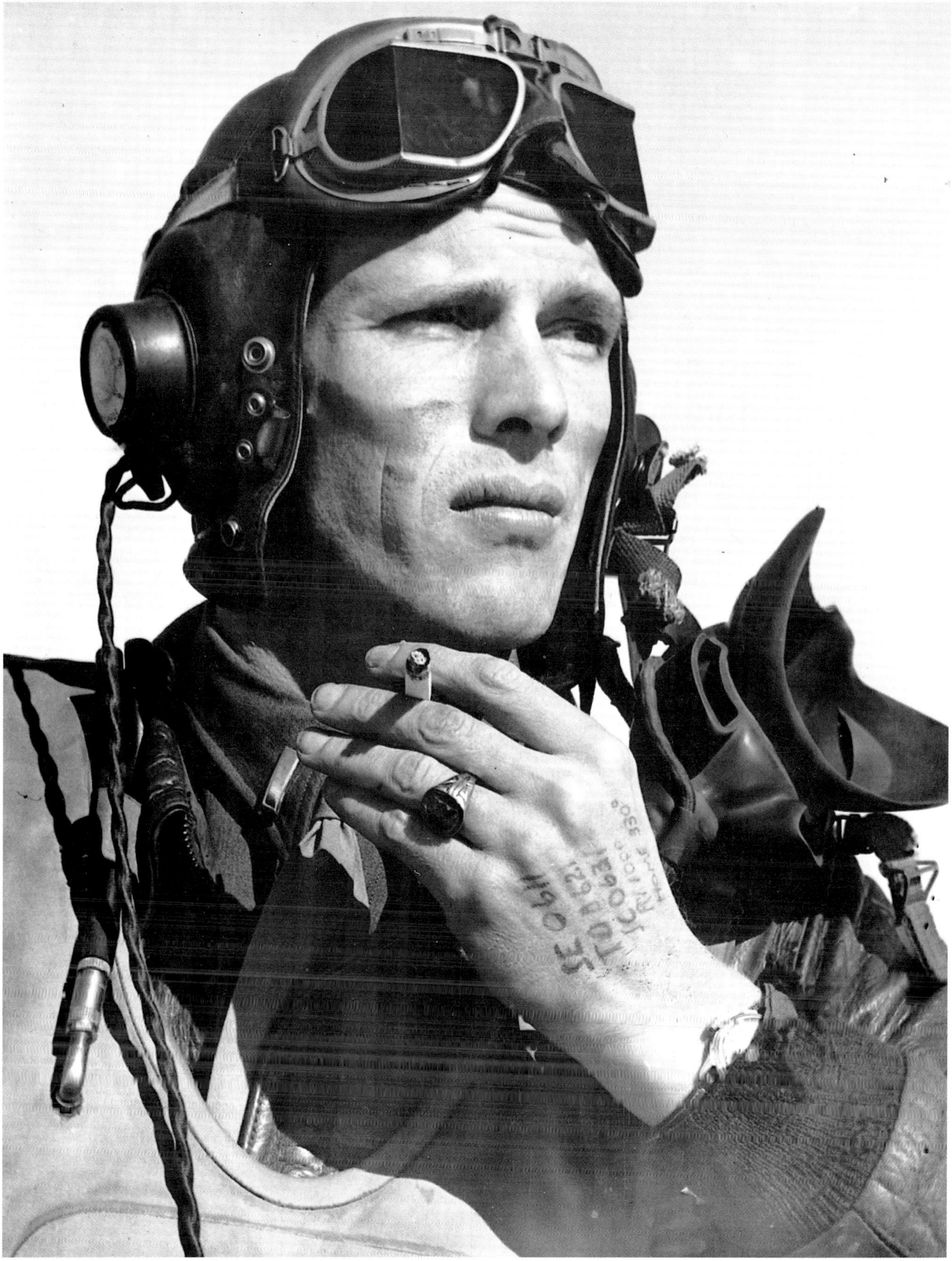

Crandell was in a dive attempting to catch up with his element leader when he noticed two Messerschmitts closing on him from behind. He immediately began evasive action and, in the process, became so excited he forgot to call for help. "The [enemy aircraft] continued to follow," he reported afterward, "and after flying [northeast] for several minutes without running across any friendly fighters, I decided to fight it out and allowed them to gain." Timing the approach of the two German fighters, Crandell broke into a series of tight turns during which he was able to pull enough deflection to open fire. Suddenly, the two Messerschmitts – still side-by-side – broke into a climbing turn into the sun. Lining up on the wingman first, Crandell fired one long burst from 100 yards causing the German to explode. When the leader broke away in a dive, Crandell rolled his P-51 over to follow and soon dispatched the fighter from dead astern.[35] Receiving credit for both victories following assessment of his gun-camera film, Jack Crandell would not have long to bask in his achievement. Almost two months later to the day, he would be killed while strafing ground targets.

Perhaps the most drawn-out of the group's combats on June 25 involved Lt. Col. Roy Webb who was leading the 374th Squadron on the escort that day. Once bandits were called out by Lt. Col. Kruzel, Webb immediately ordered his squadron to drop tanks, then led the way to the combat area from 22,000 feet. Searching for Germans as the Norman landscape loomed below, he spotted two FW-190s and immediately gave chase with his flight in trail. When the two fighters split up to flee in different directions, the chase was on and Webb ordered his second element after one while he pursued the other. Piloting "Sweet Thing IV", his recently acquired P-51D, Webb pushed his throttle "through the gate" applying maximum power to try to close the distance as the German pilot squeezed every ounce of power from his BMW radial in an attempt to out-run him. "I closed very slowly and pulled as much as 70 inches of mercury," Webb recounted in his combat report. "While closing I tried 3 or 4 long shots observing hits on the left wing root. After approximately 50 miles, I closed to approximately 300 yds. and after following him through a series of evasive measures, finally blasted him to hell … He hit a house and exploded leaving both in flames. The pilot did not get out."[36]

In all, ten German fighters were claimed without loss during the 15-minute air battle. Capt. Charles Cummings of the 375th Squadron was able to claim an ME-109 while piloting Col. Christian's P-51D – the now immortal "Lou IV." A single Messerschmitt was also claimed by Capt. Richard Durbin of

Opposite: Lt. Vernon D. Richards of the 374th Fighter Squadron. *National Archives*

the 376th Squadron who remarked that during a four-minute pursuit and subsequent dog-fight, the German pilot failed to jettison his belly tank.[37] Capt. Hugh D. Chapman, of the 376th Squadron, was able to claim an ME-109 destroyed, as well as one shared with a 9th Air Force Mustang of the 363rd Fighter Group.[38] Finally, 1st Lt. Vernon Richards of the 374th Squadron downed an FW-190 and an ME-109 in rapid succession after parting company with Col. Webb.[39]

As an interesting side note, Richards' crew chief, Robert Bland, recalled many years later that he and the pilot had a regular practice before take off on select missions. According to Bland, the ritual began in early 1944 before a particular mission that "was expected to see great opposition. As we were hooking [Richards] up [in the aircraft cockpit] he reached into his inside pocket and took out a combination cigarette case and lighter, removed a cameo ring, and asked if I would see to it that they were sent back to his parents in case he didn't come back. From that time on for the rest of his tour, when they expected great opposition, no words were spoken but those items were placed in my hands." This gesture eventually came to be used to gauge the difficulty of missions by other ground crews in the 374th Squadron. "Some of the crew chiefs discovered the ritual between Vernon and me," recalled Bland, "and as soon as the aircraft were airborne, they would question me as to whether I had the items in my possession. Fortunately, I never had to follow up on [Richards'] request."[40]

The last encounters with enemy aircraft for the 361st during June 1944 occurred on the 29th – a month to the day since the climactic "day of days" in May. A massive operation typical of so many which the "Mighty Eighth" regularly staged, the strategic bombing effort for June 29 involved some thirteen targets, most of them aircraft plants in the vicinity of Leipzig, and employed nearly fourteen hundred fighters and bombers. With so many aircraft headed toward east-central Germany that day, the bomber stream at one point occupied some 200 miles of German airspace from end to end.[41]

Though the formations offered tempting opportunities for German interception, the *Luftwaffe* made only scattered appearances throughout the day. While accompanying B-24s of the 2nd Bomb Division against Oschersleben airdrome, Lt. Col. Roy Webb again rose to the forefront of attention by leading one flight in a strafing attack just as the last of the Liberators' salvos detonated around the field. Diving from 21,000 feet toward the smoke and dust rising from Oschersleben, Webb was accompanied by White Flight of the 374th Squadron comprised of veteran Lieutenants Robert Eckfeldt and Vernon Richards, along with the Group Operations Officer, Lt. Col. Wallace Hopkins. As the four pilots initially traversed the field amid the smoke and fire from the bombing, no German aircraft could be seen below. As the smoke began to clear, however, large numbers of parked aircraft were revealed, and amazingly, not a single German flak battery opened fire – most likely due to the effect of the bombing.

As the four pilots streaked across the south perimeter of the airdrome, they spotted some twenty FW-190s parked in a neat row spanning the length of one taxiway. Spread out into string formation, they commenced an east-west gunnery pattern and each pilot lined up on a target and commenced firing from fifty feet above the tarmac. As the tracers walked down the row of German fighters, flames erupted as .50 caliber rounds penetrated their fuel tanks. With no flak, eight passes – an un-

precedented number – were made before ammunition was exhausted and Webb ordered the flight to break off and head for the bomber stream. "On pulling off the field, I looked back and in moderate terms estimated 15 airplanes burning on the ground," Webb reported after returning to Bottisham.[42]

In all, 16 enemy aircraft were claimed destroyed and another eight damaged making this the Group's most successful strafing attack during 1944. It would not be until the following spring, with Germany on the verge of collapse, that elements of the 361st would have such free reign over a German airdrome. June 29 being the exception, attacking such heavily defended targets would be a costly business, indeed.

Roy Webb's keenness for action was well-known not only among the pilots of the 361st, but also among the ground crews. On one occasion, as Webb taxied out to take off for a mission, the tail wheel of his P-51 burst, bringing him to an abrupt halt.

A flight of 374th Fighter Squadron Mustangs in line-abreast formation, summer 1944. At right, closest to the camera is Lt. Robert Eckfeldt's "Bald Eagle." *National Archives*

"Two guys took a weapons carrier to get a new tire and wheel; two other guys ran to a revetment and got a tail jack," wrote crew chief Russell Severson who had been among the ground crew coming to their Squadron Commander's assistance. "In about ten minutes the guys were mounting the tail wheel. Webb never cut his engine off, so the crew chiefs back at the tail were really taking a beating." The moment the new wheel was in place "Webb put the power to it. The plane was still up on the jack; he pulled it right off. He took off right on the grass so that he made the mission."[43] Eventually finishing his combat tour in August 1944 with 9 victories to his credit, Lt. Col. Webb would take a desk job at 8th Air Force headquarters.

In addition to the remarkable strafing success for the 374th Squadron, June 29, 1944 was also a notable day for the 375th Squadron which, while Maj. Webb was leading his pilots against the airdrome, caught a number of ME-109s which tried to at-tack the bombers just after they turned off the target. 1st Lt. Robert C. Wright, reported that just after the B-24s finished "bombing their target, a formation of fifteen ME-109s equipped with belly tanks passed under us heading for the bombers." Wright led his flight after the Messerschmitts and was able to cut inside of two P-51s, apparently from another group, to de-stroy one of them. Climbing back to altitude with his flight, Wright spotted a lone B-17 and headed toward it to give cover. Before his flight could arrive, however, an ME-109 made a pass on the bomber and shot it down. Chasing the Messerschmitt down to the deck, Wright was able to score some hits, but over-shot the enemy fighter allowing his wingman, 2nd Lt. Sherman Armsby, to shoot it down.[44] Two more ME-109s were destroyed by pilots of the 375th Squadron during the encounter – one by Lt. Eugene Cole, and another by Lt. Thomas Brubaker – cap-ping off a highly successful day for the 361st Fighter Group.

With 42 missions completed and 5,915 operational flying hours contributed to the Allied cause, June 1944 was the busiest month in the operational history of the 361st Fighter Group.[45] Though 25 missions would be carried out during July – a heavy schedule by any standard – the month in comparison with June would seem a relatively quiet phase in Group operations. Returned almost exclusively to bomber escort duties, the "Yellowjackets" would conduct twelve long-range escort missions during July 1944. Despite the seeming likelihood of contact with the *Luftwaffe* which these missions introduced, German interceptors would be encountered on just three occasions in the course of the month: once over France and twice over Germany.

During the aerial encounters which did materialize, several of the Group's "rising stars" played conspicuous roles. On July 5 while accompanying bombers to the Beauvais region in France, 1st Lt. Dale F. Spencer of the 376th Squadron, who had distinguished himself on May 29 by downing four ME-410s, shot down a pair of ME-109s near Amiens. Two days later on a mission to the Leipzig area, Spencer duplicated the feat by downing a second pair of Messerschmitts, though he was not alone in turning in results. On the same mission, Spencer's element leader, 1st Lt. Ray S. White, aged 21 of Austin, Texas, was also credited with downing a pair of German fighters. On the same mission, 1st Lt. Robert C. Wright of the 375th Squadron was also able to destroy two German fighters. In total, July 7 was the Group's biggest day of the month with a total of nine aerial victories chalked up (Also credited with destroying enemy aircraft were 1st Lt. Dean Morehouse of the 375th, who downed an ME-109, and 1st Lt. Russell Sobieski, also of the 375th, who shot down an ME-410 and shared a claim of an ME-109 with 2nd Lt. David Morgan).[46]

During eleven successive missions following July 7 only a single aerial victory would be recorded by the "Yellowjackets," despite a target list which included four trips to Munich, and one each to Peenemunde and Schweinfurt. It was not until July 20 that German fighters were again engaged in numbers on a mission to the Leipzig area. Exhibiting a truly ruthless desire to destroy enemy aircraft no matter what the risk, two relatively unknown pilots would emerge into the limelight that day. In a remarkable series of dogfights, the conclusion to one of which may be unique in the history of the 8th Air Force, the 375th Squadron's 1st Lt. Sherman Armsby would down three ME-109s in rapid succession, the third after all his

374th Squadron ground crewman catch a moments relaxation on Bottisham's flight line, summer 1944. *Russell A. Severson*

ammunition was expended. Displaying the same zeal, 2nd Lt. William T. Kemp, Armsby's wingman, would unhesitatingly engage and destroy two enemy fighters on the trip home despite his leader's inability to assist with guns.

A mission of some five hours endurance, it had begun for Armsby and Kemp in the usual fashion. Making rendezvous with their assigned B-17s at 1050 hours, some fourteen minutes beyond the German city of Bayreuth, the "Yellowjackets" accompanied the Fortresses on a northeasterly heading toward an eventual attack on targets near Kothen. While scanning the combat boxes arrayed below, 1st Lt. Armsby, flying the number 3 position in White Flight of the 375th at 28,000 feet, spot-

375th Fighter Squadron "ace" Lt. Sherman Armsby, one of the "rising stars" in the summer of 1944. Bold and aggressive, Armsby would have just weeks to live after this photograph was taken. *Courtesy Leonard A. Wood*

ted a formation of German fighters making an attack on the bombers some 4,000 feet below. Glimpsing a lone B-17 under attack by an ME-109, he dropped his wing tanks and called for Kemp to follow him down on the bandit. Though not in time to save the bomber, the two pilots latched on to the Messerschmitt which immediately broke in a hard turn to the right attempting to shake the pursuers. Unable to get adequate deflection in a violent series of hard-banking turns, Armsby was about to break away when the German suddenly popped his canopy and bailed out – an increasing tendency among German pilots in the last year of the war.

After switching on his gun camera to record the parachute of his first victim, Armsby led his wingman back to rejoin the B-17s. During a casual sweep of the air below while set for climb, Lt. Armsby caught sight of two more aircraft diving for the deck well below his altitude. "We took after them in a dive with throttles cut back to prevent overshooting … As we closed to approximately 600 yards, I saw they were ME-109s and at that moment they broke left in trail and we followed them around in a Lufberry at 1000 feet." As the four planes vied for position in the tight circle, Armsby dropped ten degrees of flaps to allow a tighter turning radius enabling him to place the number two bandit in his gun sight. He fired a long burst after which the Messerschmitt exploded in a flaming mass. With Kemp in trail, Armsby set his sights on the remaining German who immediately broke for the deck.

"I pulled up flaps and started after him," Armsby reported after landing at Bottisham. "I followed him for 10 minutes through trees, power lines and every other ground obstacle he could find." Running on the deck at full throttle, the German pilot evaded numerous bursts from Armsby's four .50 caliber machine guns until ammunition was finally expended. "I called White Four [Lt. Kemp] to close up and shoot him down. White Four was about 800 yds behind and was unable to close up…." With the German skimming the ground with just feet to spare, and Kemp too far behind to open fire, Armsby abandoned all caution when he caught sight of a 15-foot railroad embankment looming ahead. "I pulled up and slid over the ME-109 to prevent him from pulling up and waited for the crash. As I passed over the embankment I heard a crunch and pulling into a tight chandelle to the right I looked back and saw a cloud of smoke and flames with pieces falling all around."[47]

Witnessing the crash in amazement, Kemp caught up with his leader, who photographed the burning debris before beginning the climb-out for home. Suddenly, when they had reached 1500 feet, Kemp spotted an ME-109 on a parallel course just ahead. Calling out the bandit, he closed from behind with Armsby in trail and opened fire at 350 yards. He gave the

375th Fighter Squadron "ace" Lt. William T. Kemp in the cockpit of his P-51D flanked by his ground crew. On Kemp's right is his crew chief, Sgt. Bernard J. Redden. *Courtesy B.J. Redden*

Messerschmitt a long burst and watched as the pilot abandoned the aircraft in a shallow climb. As the smoking fighter slowly fell away, a Focke-Wulf 190 suddenly appeared from behind and without hesitation Kemp engaged it. After a head-on pass in which three of his guns jammed, Kemp was forced to momentarily break off the attack. "I called White Three to take over until I could get into position to fire again. Climbing back up, I found the enemy aircraft in a Lufberry with White Three on his tail. As I slipped in between…the [German] reversed his turn sharply and took a few shots at White Three as he was passing by. I was closing rapidly on him when he reversed his turn again. Following him I closed to 15 yards 0 degrees deflection and opened up with a short burst." Using his one serviceable gun, he was able to get some strikes after which the German fighter flipped over and dove straight into the ground.[48]

"Rising stars" each, Armsby and Kemp serve to illustrate both the potential accolades and abject realities faced by the truly impetuous fighter pilot during World War II. The twenty-year-old Armsby, born in Baltimore, Maryland, had joined the Army in 1942 and had graduated from advanced flight training late the following year before joining the 361st as a replacement pilot in the spring of 1944. Kemp, who hailed from Peoria, Illinois, had turned 21 by the time that he, too, joined the Group as a replacement in the months before D-Day. Each earning the Distinguished Service Cross (though only Armsby for the July 20 mission) they would quickly achieve the status of "hot pilots" at Bottisham. While Kemp would eventually finish his tour with six aerial victories, Armsby would be dead within five weeks of his dramatic July 20 mission.

For the remainder of the month, the "Yellowjackets" would continue operations varying from long-range escort to ground attack in France. In the course of a two-day lull during July 26-

27, however, a number of the Group's pilots were detailed to participate in a wholly peaceful mission which would have far ranging consequences for the Group's collective memory. Perhaps because of the distinctive yellow paint scheme which adorned the propeller hub and noseband on each of their Mustangs, several flights of the 361st were used as subjects for a series of color publicity photographs shot by an Army Air Force photographer. From this series would emerge some of the most striking images of the P-51 captured during the war – images destined to reappear countless times throughout succeeding decades.

Among the most familiar of the series is the 375th Squadron finger-four led by Col. Christian in "Lou IV." Set against a brilliant cloud-studded sky, "The Bottisham Four" as it has become known to Group veterans, was destined to become a classic from the moment it was snapped.

Also appearing in the shot was Lt. Urban L. Drew of the 375th who supplied background details on the photo mission. "The pilots in the flight are Col. Thomas J.J. Christian commanding the 361st, myself in 'Easy Two Sugar' flying his wing. The third airplane…the element leader, is Capt. Bruce W. Rowlett who was Operations Officer of the 375th, and the fourth airplane, the old B model…was Capt. Francis T. Glankler who commanded D Flight at the time … The reason we were flying is quite accidental as most of these things are," Drew continued. "Glankler, Rowlett and I were…stood down that day and getting dressed to go to London when Col. Christian came in and said 'Gentleman, I'm afraid your London trip is off. The Air Force wants us to do some air-to-air photographs of Mustangs and they've selected us because of our colorful yellow noses. They've taken the guns out of the starboard side of a B-17 and installed cameras and you three have just volunteered to do it with me.' So the three of us got into our flying suits and went up. We made many, many passes by the bomber. They had us in finger-four, then they had us in echelon right then line abreast and then on the last one they said 'Hey Easy Two S, you're the closest to the camera, slip in as close as you can'" – hence the oft-used close-up of E2-S.[49]

Of all the P-51s flown during the war, "Lou IV" is perhaps the most universally familiar by virtue of the photographs. While it has become something of an icon for Second World War aviation enthusiasts, the image would always have an intensely personal significance for those who served under Thomas J.J. Christian, Jr. As a tribute to the Group Commander, and to the Group, which he formed and led overseas, "The Bottisham Four" is superb. Perhaps, if Christian had survived the war, he would have looked upon it as a symbol of a highpoint in his career. Within three weeks of the photo mission, however, the 28-year old Colonel would be dead.

Part 3: The Guns of August

The Group which had first assembled at Richmond in 1943 was still recognizable at Bottisham at the end of July 1944. Since the 361st's activation, Col. Christian had been a unifying figure among all three squadrons as well as the ground echelon. Demonstrative rather than flamboyant, he had led the Group through its baptism of fire some seven months previously and had continued active command through the hectic invasion summer. Though subordinates had increasingly assumed leadership in combat as the pace of operations accelerated during the spring, it seemed likely at the beginning of August 1944 that the tall West Pointer would continue to lead the Group well into the fall, if not beyond.

At the beginning of August, two of the three squadrons were still led by their original CO's – the 374th under Roy Webb, and the 376th under Roy Caviness. While George Merritt had been killed the day after D-Day, Roswell Freedman, another original since Richmond, had taken over the 375th in his place. Among the flight leaders and pilots, more than 50% of those on strength had moved overseas with the Group the previous December and among the ground echelon, who typically served "for the duration," the overwhelming majority had been with the 361st all along. By September, however, much of the air echelon's familiar makeup would be in transition as an increasing number of the Group's original pilots would complete their 300-hour combat tours and depart for home and/or reassignment. Increasingly, replacement pilots, fresh from orientation at the Goxhill Operational Training Unit, would arrive at Bottisham to take the place of departing veterans.

Though transferred from the 65th to the 67th Fighter Wing, the mode of operations for the "Yellowjackets" in August remained much the same. Escorts were carried out during the first three days of the month, though no German fighters were seen. On August 4, however, the 361st was detailed to provide support for an attack on Anklam Airdrome near the Peenemunde research facility. During the escort, elements of the 376th Squadron decided to seek out and strafe enemy aircraft on the ground.

2nd Lt. Robert Volkman of the 376th Squadron, who had joined the Group in mid-July as a replacement pilot, found himself assigned to the Anklam mission as wingman to Capt. Sam Wilkerson. Describing the mission years later, Volkman vividly recalled his first experience strafing an enemy airfield. "[O]ne thing I'll never forget: at the briefing … we were advised not to strafe that airfield – there were about forty heavy guns and 120 light guns around [it]. I've never forgotten those numbers. … We escorted the '17's and they bombed, and the field was covered with black smoke, and [Capt. Wilkerson] said, 'I'm going down and make a pass at it.' So we hit it a

Aircraft of the 376th Fighter Squadron in flight. E9-R is piloted by Lt. Victor Bocquin, and E9-D, farthest from the camera, by Lt. Robert Volkman. Col. Christian's P-51 is at the far left in the number 4 position. *Courtesy Robert Volkman*

little bit east … we dove down from 29,000 feet and headed for the airfield and the guy who was leading the squadron said 'I'll cover you' – that's like Mush Stubbins in the comics used to say 'I'll hold the coats, let's you and him fight.' But anyway we dove down and there was this train and I remember I thought 'jeez, I'd better check my guns out,' so I took a couple squirts at this train. And, you know, there's an overlap of about three seconds on the camera film so it continues to run when you stop pulling the trigger. Since I had taken a shot at this train it also showed me coming up on this airfield and I think I was almost going to hit the fence!"

Approaching the field at extremely low level, each of the pilots in Volkman's flight picked out targets among the parked German aircraft. As Volkman triggered his guns once more, the flak batteries came alive, lacing the air with tracing ammunition. "[W]hen we got inside the smoke," Volkman recalled, "it looked like red-hot baseballs coming at you from all directions. If you've ever played dodge ball as a kid – there's one ball and they try to hit the people in the center – the only difference is everybody's got a ball and they're shooting!"[50]

After scoring a few hits on a JU-88, Volkman was able to claim damage to his target aircraft, though it failed to burn. 1st Lt. Victor Bocquin, also in the attack, was able to claim one enemy bomber damaged and a second positively destroyed. Columns of smoke confirmed two JU-88s destroyed by Capt. Wilkerson but the flight leader soon found himself in trouble. Having sustained several hits from the flak emplacements ringing the field, oil and coolant streamed from Wilkerson's P-51D as he pulled away from his run. "I called him and told him

to head North," reported Bocquin later that day. "He called back and said he got two JU-88's and that he would stick with his plane as long as possible. He flew about four minutes and [his] plane began burning so he bailed out."[51] Once again, a defended enemy airdrome proved to be the most dangerous of all targets of opportunity, and the 361st lost one of its veteran pilots.

Capt. Wilkerson, who became a POW, was not the only loss suffered by the Group that day. 2nd Lt. Joseph Kapr of the 375th Squadron was returning with his flight over the Baltic that afternoon when he suddenly experienced engine trouble. "We started for home," reported his wingman, 2nd Lt. Edward Marevka, "and a few minutes later his engine started smoking. He then called and said he was bailing out – that was at 18,000 feet." Marevka and the remainder of Red Flight followed Kapr down in his parachute and watched him as he landed in the sea. "I observed him get out of his chute," Marevka continued, "and then we circled some fishing boats about a mile from him and tried to attract their attention." When Lt. Marevka then flew back over the spot where Kapr had landed, however, the sea was empty and the downed pilot was not seen again.[52]

On three of four days following the mission to Anklam, the "Yellowjackets" continued to make contact with the *Luftwaffe*, though under varying circumstances. On a trip to Magdeburg on August 5, pilots of the 375th Squadron engaged and destroyed five enemy planes in the air and another on the ground. First to "drop tanks" was the impetuous 1st Lt. Sherman Armsby who spotted four ME-109s below the formation and peeled off to attack. With characteristic abandon, Armsby

Officers and men of the 374th Fighter Squadron photographed at Bottisham, July 31, 1944. Among the pilots of the 374th, this photo showed many of the "old hands" who would soon complete their 300-hour combat tours and return home. Their places would shortly be filled by new replacements as the summer of '44 drew to a close. *Courtesy George Lichter*

picked out a Messerschmitt and chased it down to 8,000 feet before the bandit straightened out – though not before another ME-109 made a head-on pass at Armsby's plane hitting the tail section with machinegun fire. Undeterred, Armsby continued to chase his target down to 3,000 feet where debris from the stricken '109 struck his own plane when he closed to 50 yards while firing.[53]

When Armsby headed his battle-damaged Mustang homeward, his flight leader, Capt. William J. Shackelford, found himself alone and joined up with the first friendly aircraft he saw – a flight of green-nosed P-51s of the 359th Fighter Group. While heading eastward, Shackelford spotted several aircraft parked on Alhorn Airdrome from 16,000 feet and peeled off to strafe – though the 359th pilots apparently declined to accompany him down. Heading across the field at low-level, he lined up on a Dornier-17 which burned following a long burst from his six .50 calibers. "I also fired on two objects along side of the east-west runway observing hits," he reported. "As I approached them, they appeared to be in a small [aircraft] under brown camouflage netting. I presumed these to be jet [aircraft], as they had very short fuselage and tail in proportion to the wing."[54] Very likely, these strange aircraft were examples of the rocket-powered ME-163 *Komet* first employed in mid-1944.

Originally identified by the generic term "jet," it was only two weeks earlier that elements of the Group first reported the telltale vapor trails made by the ME-163 in flight. Within two months, the appearance of the ME-262, a true jet, would clarify the difference.

Contact with the enemy again took place on August 7 when three pilots of the 375th Squadron suddenly found themselves intermixed with some 40 German fighters in an unforgettable chance encounter. Returning from escort to the Bordeaux region at approximately 1415 hours, three second lieutenants – Urban Drew, William T. Kemp, and Leonard A. Wood – were on the deck looking for targets of opportunity near Chartres, some 30 miles southwest of Paris. Having strafed several trucks and flak towers, most of their ammunition was gone as they approached the vicinity of an airdrome believed to have been vacated by the Germans. Flying in line-abreast formation just

A Messerschmitt ME-163, the rocket-powered interceptor used against American daylight bombers beginning in the second half of 1944. *National Archives*

under 1500 feet, the pilots continued to search the hazy landscape for German activity when suddenly they spotted a swarm of ME-109s and FW-190s taking off and forming up over the airfield just ahead. Before they could finish a hurried debate whether or not to engage, the three P-51s cut through the center of the gaggle which initiated a frenzied melee just above the treetops.

Apparently taken by surprise, many of the German pilots panicked, broke formation and attempted to land on nearby fields and roads as the Americans appeared in their midst. Firing at a pair of ME-109s in a head-on pass, Drew could only claim one damaged before his guns jammed.[55] Lt. Kemp, also low on ammunition, was able to damage an FW-190 with a short burst and then destroyed another as his guns began to fail. Finally, with one working .50 caliber, he went after an ME-109 attempting to land on a road and strafed it with his last few rounds.[56] Kemp's wingman, Lt. Wood, also scored several hits on the taxiing Messerschmitt though he could only claim damage as it failed to burn.[57]

With fuel reaching the critical stage, Kemp finally broke north along the deck with Wood and Drew in trail leaving the scattered Germans behind. After reaching Manston, the emergency landing field in Kent, virtually on fumes, the three pilots sent a hurried message back to Bottisham: numerous enemy aircraft on the ground at Chartres Airdrome. Despite the speed with which a strafing mission was dispatched against the field, the elusive French-based arm of the *Luftwaffe* stayed ahead of the game. By the time the "Yellowjackets" returned to Chartres that evening, the airdrome was deserted.[58]

Combat again took place on August 8 when three enemy fighters were claimed during an area support mission to the Stuttgart region. Group Operations Officer Lt. Col. Wallace E. Hopkins led the mission in which he claimed two FW-190s destroyed. Lt. Jacob L. Rawles of the 374th Squadron, however, was lost to enemy fighters during the action.[59] In the first eight days of August, a total of 13 German planes were claimed destroyed by the Group; the loss of Lt. Rawles on August 8 raised the MIA total to four during the same period. While the ratio of victories to losses was favorable, August had yet to exact its price from the 361st. Daily operations continued, and, indeed, intensified before any respite was felt.

August 12, 1944 would be a memorable day in 361st's operational history on three counts. Profoundly influenced by events on the ground in France, it would be the busiest day of August with four separate fighter-bomber missions departing Bottisham by day's end. It would be the costliest day of the month too as four pilots failed to return to base, including the universally admired and respected Col. Thomas J.J. Christian, Jr.

August 12 could truly be described as a "maximum effort" on the part of the 8th Fighter Command. As Allied armies in France rushed to close the Falaise pocket in the hope of trapping some 100,000 enemy troops west of the Seine River, the German transportation web in northern France was placed under attack by Allied airpower. With special priority given to rail targets that day, the Eighth Fighter Command would dispatch some 700 of its aircraft against marshalling yards and railroad junctions in the hope of disrupting enemy movement in the vital sector.[60]

Left: (LtoR) Lieutenants Urban Drew, Billy Kemp and Leonard Wood of the 375th Fighter Squadron photographed at Bottisham following their remarkable combat near Chartres on August 7, 1944. *Courtesy Leonard A. Wood* Right: Col. Thomas J.J. Christian, Jr. seen at his desk at Bottisham, summer 1944. *Courtesy Mrs. Jean Shackelford*

"Today was another 'never to be forgotten day'" declared Maj. John Stryker in his unit diary entry for August 12. "it started off like another 'D' day – briefing at 0400 and then another at 0600 and so on through the day   four missions were flown …"[61] Divided into "A" and "B" sections, each with half the Group's aircraft, the 361st's Mustangs, equipped with 500 lb. bombs, ranged across northern France attacking railroad equipment and targets of opportunity. No sooner had the aircraft landed from a mission when ground crews immediately began preparing them for the next sortie. During the morning and early afternoon, the "Yellowjackets" dive-bombed and strafed six railroad marshalling yards, along with several railroad bridges, and numerous trains and locomotives across northern France. Large concentrations of rolling stock and supplies, as well as evidence of camouflaged German airfields, were noted for later attacks. The first loss of the day was suffered over the marshaling yard at Bar-le-Duc in northeast France when 2nd Lt. John Engstrom of the 375th Squadron bailed out after a fuel line in his P-51 was cut by ground fire.[62]

The Group's fourth and final mission that afternoon would be a dive bombing attack on the marshalling yard at Arras led by Col. Christian. According to David C. Landin of the 376th Squadron, the Group Commander had been particularly concerned with dive-bombing accuracy during the pre-mission briefing. " Col. Christian had gotten us in the briefing room and our effectiveness in dive bombing was horrible and we all knew it," Landin recalled. "He said 'We need to do this mission and I'll lead it. We're releasing our bombs too high, we're not coming close enough to the target, we're not holding on the target long enough, we're not compensating for wind' and

that sort of thing …"[63] Landin's recollection of Christian's frame of mind at briefing may well provide an important clue to understanding what transpired over Arras that afternoon.

Take off for the mission commenced at 1403 hours and after joining up in flights over the field, Christian led his twenty-four P-51s on a southeasterly heading toward northern France. Steadily gaining altitude, the six flights of Mustangs had made landfall and were passing over Lille by 1454.[64] Although the landscape below was partially shrouded in haze, a large number of boxcars were sighted as they approached the marshalling yard near Arras. With the target area in sight, Col. Christian prepared to lead one flight down to bomb the stationary freight cars. His wingman, 2nd Lt. Robert Bain of the 376th Squadron, described what happened next: "We approached … from the north east direction at an altitude of 11,000 feet. We circled the target receiving instructions from Colonel Christian to make the bomb run from south to north, pulling up to the left after bombing. We were then in string formation, my position number two trailing our leader. Colonel Christian executed a half roll and split-s from an altitude of 11,000 feet. I watched his descent to at least 6,000 ft., and then made my dive. Pulling out at 3,000 feet., I banked left and climbed to 6,000 feet and looked for our leader. [The] Number three ship pulled near me, but neither he nor I could find Colonel Christian. I repeatedly called our leader over the radio but never received an answer."[65]

Lt. Landin's flight, along with several others, was circling in the vicinity of the target when Christian commenced his bomb run. "He went straight down and there was just a ball of fire. And the whole Group…I cannot tell you how we finished that mission, I know that we did, but the whole Group was just horrified."[66] Continuing with the mission, two more Mustangs of the 375th Squadron were lost against ground targets. 1st Lt. Clarence E. Zieske of the 374th Squadron bailed out of his flak-damaged aircraft near the Somme River, but was killed when his parachute failed to open.[67] 1st Lt. Merle Rainey of the 375th, also abandoned his P-51 after his engine quit, and was able to evade capture until several weeks later when he made contact with British troops.[68]

The cause of Col. Christian's death would never be fully determined. Perhaps mechanical failure prevented his pulling-out after releasing his bombs. Possibly enemy fire had disabled his plane – though flak over the target had been meager. Christian may even have dived too close to the target and the concussion of his bombs may have crippled his aircraft – once he disappeared into the smoke and haze over Arras, it was impossible to say. Though equally undetermined, the best evidence suggests that Col. Christian's final resting place is an unnamed grave in a British military cemetery near Arras.

"War must have its toll, even sometimes at a price that may seem unreasonably high," began Capt. J.F. O'Mara's monthly Group historical report for August 1944. "Our Group paid the price when the Group and Station Commander Colonel Thomas J.J. Christian, Jr. was reported MIA on 12 August 1944," O'Mara continued, "...Words are but silent testimony to the efficiency and admirable qualities of leadership displayed by this officer. His loss is noted in reverent tribute by all who had the pleasure to know, or serve under him."[69] While Capt. O'Mara summed up the contemporary feelings of loss, time has not diminished the esteem with which the surviving 361st veterans regard their original Group Commander.

Looking back on his own career, Joe Kruzel, who retired from the Air Force as a Major General, had nothing but praise for "Jack" Christian. "Actually, there were just a few officers in my 30 years of service who had a profound or a good and favorable influence in helping me complete a successful career in the military – Jack Christian was certainly one of those few. I have no doubt that had he survived [he] eventually would have attained 3 probably 4-star rank." Though home on leave and unaware of Christian's death at the time it occurred, Kruzel would be shocked at the loss of a close friend, but also would recall instances of grim fatalism which the Group Commander had confided to him. "He spoke in terms of having a premonition that he wasn't going to last the war, that he wasn't going

Col. Christian's P-51D "Lou IV" going into a half-roll. *Courtesy J.J. Kruzel*

to make it," Kruzel recalled years later. Referencing his wife and new-born daughter in the States, Christian at times told his Executive Officer that, "'I'm never going to get to see that baby of mine, Joe.'" Though Kruzel did his best to bolster the young Colonel's spirits saying " 'Oh, Jack don't talk like that,'" Christian spoke resolutely saying, "'No, I have a strong feeling.'"[70]

375th Squadron "ace" Urban Drew summarized his own impressions of Christian in terms which echoed most of those in the Group. "Colonel Christian was a leader a cut well-above anyone else," Drew remarked years later. "Certainly there was no one after him that I served with in the Army Air Forces who could hold a candle to him. He was a great leader and everybody loved this man. He had a charisma; he was a quiet and soft-spoken man, he wasn't loud. Whatever he had, he was an officer and a gentleman."[71]

Despite the sense of loss which permeated Bottisham in the days following Colonel Christian's disappearance, the pace of operations made no exceptions for sentiment. Since Lt. Col. Joe Kruzel was on leave in the United States when Christian was declared MIA, temporary command of Station F-374 was given to Col. Ronald F. Fallows, Executive Officer of the 65th Fighter Wing, who arrived at Bottisham on August 14.[72] As Station Commander, Fallows' role would be largely administrative and he would take no active part in the day-to-day flying operations of the Group. Until Kruzel returned on September 20, air leadership would fall on the shoulders of Group's squadron commanders and headquarters staff.

A variety of ground-attack and escort missions over France and Germany were carried out during the remainder of August. Two more pilots were lost during a dive-bombing mission on August 13 as pressure was maintained during the Falaise battle. Two days later, the Group accompanied B-24s as they bombed Wittmundhafen airdrome. Following the bomb run, elements of the 375th Squadron dropped down to strafe the field claiming three aircraft destroyed and several damaged, though 1st Lt. Sherman Armsby's Mustang was badly shot up.[73] 1st Lt. Billy Kemp of the 375th, was also hit and wounded in the arm by light flak around the airdrome. According to his crew chief, Sgt. Bernard J. Redden, Kemp was headed home when he spotted a large number of German fighters preparing to attack an unescorted formation of B-24s. Turning his P-51 toward the German fighters, Kemp made a head-on pass at their formation after which they dove away. Considering the incident years later, Redden commented that Kemp's action

Lt. Clarence Zieske of the 374th Fighter Squadron who was lost on August 12, 1944. *Courtesy Joseph Zieske Ormond*

"probably prevented the attack on the bombers [and] earned him the Distinguished Service Cross with the full endorsement of the B-24 Crewman. Kemp's wounds were not serious, but he was one weak puppy when he finally made it back home."[74]

Contact with the *Luftwaffe* by the "Yellowjackets" was again made on August 25 when the Group carried out a long-range escort mission to the Baltic city of Rostock. During the escort, the 361st's top scoring strafer, Capt. Martin Johnson of the 375th Squadron, nearing the end of his combat tour, underwent the most trying test of his dog-fighting skills he would

A memorial erected in the village of Boisleux Au Mont, near Arras, France, honoring Col. Thomas J.J. Christian, Jr. whose aircraft crashed nearby on August 12, 1944. *Courtesy Laurent Wiart*

experience with the Group. Johnson was leading Red Flight of the 375th that morning when he was ordered to investigate an unidentified combat wing of bombers reported some 15 miles north of the specified bomber track. Placed behind schedule after completing this periphery task, he planned to make up the time by taking Red Flight directly to the target where they could eventually rendezvous with the original force rather than attempting to find them at a particular point in the flight plan. When Johnson's flight arrived over Rostock shortly before 1200 hours, they were 15 to 20 minutes early and no bombers were yet in sight. Taking the initiative, Johnson decided to conduct a sweep south of Rostock in the vicinity of Muritz Lake, and it was there that they spotted a dogfight in progress between a gaggle of P-38s and ME-109s.[75]

Applying full power to close the distance, it was several moments before Red Flight joined the fight which was moving steadily southeast. When Johnson ordered his pilots to drop their tanks and engage, the jumble of P-38s and ME-109s were some 5,000 feet below them at 15,000 feet. Diving into the fray, Johnson and his wingman, 2nd Lt. Robert E. Geck, were forced to break several times when P-38 pilots mistook them for Germans. At one point, they were fired at from behind by Lightnings while several Messerschmitts made head-on passes – "Most discouraging, ME-109s in front of you and P-38s behind, all shooting," Johnson commented after the action.[76]

When he finally shook off the P-38s, Capt. Johnson picked out an ME-109 and attempted to close but was soon frustrated by the German whose skills were well above average. "He was definitely a 'hot rock'," Johnson declared. "When I first encountered him he was giving a lone P-38 one hell of a battle. I took him on just as he had gained the advantage on the '38, who quickly pulled out and left me with the '109. For several round abouts all I could get was a 90 degree deflection shot and this is where I made my mistake…We went through some of the most violent and beautiful, to say the least, maneuvers I've ever seen… I kept firing at him every chance I could and on 3 different occasions he led me down and across the city of Rostock and the airfield there at 2,000 feet. They really threw up the flak then. Finally I got on his tail to stay and with only one gun firing I managed to get my last burst into what appeared to be his cockpit. He then went into a spiral from about 4,000 ft and at about 2,000 feet he flipped over on his back and went straight in." Though eventually credited with 8 German planes destroyed on the ground during his tour, this would be Johnson's only aerial victory. With amazing doggedness, Lt. Geck managed to cover his leader throughout, to Johnson's enduring admiration: "My wingman, bless his heart, stayed right on my tail during the fight."[77]

A wounded Lt. William T. Kemp shows remnants of enemy fire which struck his P-51 on the mission to Wittmundhafen Airdrome on August 15, 1944. *Courtesy B.J. Redden*

Johnson was not the only pilot to encounter a better-than-average opponent that day. Flying as Red 3, 1st Lt. David R. Morgan was forced to break into an ME-109 as Red Flight of the 375th initially engaged. He suddenly found himself alone with the German, and the two rapidly became embroiled in a contest of skills: "… I managed to get on his tail but found it very difficult to close on him as he employed violent evasive actions – doing slow rolls and chopping his throttle as he came out of them and whipping his plane up on its wing in an attempt to get on my tail." As the contest progressed, the two ended up in a series of Lufberry circles during which Morgan applied as much as 20 degrees of flaps in order to pull enough deflection for a shot at the Messerschmitt. Despite the appearance of a second 109, which began making passes on Morgan, the young Lieutenant succeeded in scoring with a lucky deflection shot in a turn so tight that his opponent disappeared from sight beneath the nose of his P-51.[78] Witnessing the destruction of the ME-109 was Capt. Johnson who arrived in time to chase the second Messerschmitt away, though as soon as he did, disaster was narrowly averted when another gaggle of P-

38s, apparently from the 479th Fighter Group, mistook the Mustangs for Messerschmitts. Recognition problems, particularly in the heat of combat, would be a recurring problem since the silhouettes of the ME-109 and the P-51 were similar.

2nd Lt. Urban Drew was also a participant in the dogfight near Rostock and was able to claim an ME-109 destroyed after three of his four guns ceased to function. More remarkable was the fact that he nearly aborted the mission earlier due to mechanical failure just prior to takeoff. So eager was Drew to make every mission, however, that after the Group departed Bottisham, he took a spare 375th Squadron Mustang, and headed off on his own to join Capt. Johnson's flight over Denmark just prior to the fight.[79]

Two missions were fielded by the 361st on August 26, 1944. The first was an uneventful one in which 36 of the Group's Mustangs escorted B-24s of the 2nd Bomb Division from the target area over Ludwigshaven. On the second mission, in which elements of the Group were detailed to strafe railroad marshalling yards in northeastern France, the 375th Squadron would experience the Group's final losses in August. While strafing railroad cars at Thionville, 2nd Lt. Jack S. Crandell was killed when his P-51 was hit by ground fire and crashed.[80] 1st Lt. Sherman Armsby, who had been awarded the Distinguished Service Cross for his actions on July 20, disappeared in a fiery conflagration during the same sortie. 2nd Lt. Leonard Wood of the 375th was flying as Armsby's wingman when the two began to strafe a large concentration of railroad cars in the marshalling yard. "I was on the right wing of Lt. Armsby and behind," Wood reported following the mission. "Lt. Armsby had just finished firing and was just starting to pull up … I had fired at about 25 cars when [those] just to the right and just behind Lt. Armsby exploded, the flames reaching an altitude of nearly 1,000 feet. I never saw Lt. Armsby after that."[81]

Like so many in the summer of '44, Armsby's death was sudden and violent. The invasion summer had been the most intensive period in the operational history of the 361st and had

Lt. Martin Johnson of the 375th Fighter Squadron photographed next to his P-47 Thunderbolt in the spring of 1944. One of the Group's original pilots, Johnson built up the highest number of strafing claims in the history of the 361st Fighter Group. He was able to down an ME-109 on August 25, 1944 during a protracted dogfight over the German city of Rostock. *National Archives*

placed demands on the Group which it rose to meet. The unit which emerged at the end August was being transformed. Gone or soon to leave were many of the old hands who had left Richmond the previous November. And many others were dead, captured or missing. As the Allies advanced through France toward the borders of Germany, the "Yellowjackets," thus changed, would return to the escort role for which the Group had been created.

NOTES

1 Steve Gotts, *Little Friends: A Pictorial History of the 361st Fighter Group in World War II* (Dallas: Taylor Publishing Co., 1993), pp. 165-68.

2 361st Fighter Group, "Historical Report for May 1944," p. 7.

3 Ibid., p. 13.

4 Henry B. Lederer, Interview with The Author, November 13, 1995.

5 David C. Landin, Interview with the Author, October 15, 1995.

6 Roger A. Freeman, *The Mighty 8th War Diary* (New York: Janes, 1981), p. 258.

7 Walter J. Kozicki, Escape and Evasion Report # 1271, August 30, 1944.

8 Wesley Parks, "Historical Record: Operational Engineering Sections (Aircraft), AAF Station F-374, June 1944.

9 Robert O. Bland, Correspondence with The Author, December 8, 1996.

10 James Golden, Interview with the Author, November 27, 1995.

11 361st Fighter Group, Mission Summary Reports, June 6, 1944.

12 Golden.

13 Ibid.

14 George R. Rew, "Encounter Report," June 6, 1944.

15 George L. Merritt, Jr., "Encounter Report," June 6, 1944.

16 Dean R. Morehouse, "Sworn Statement" contained in Missing Aircrew Report #5521, June 6, 1944.

17 Ray S. White, "Sworn Statement" contained in Missing Aircrew Report # 5522, June 6, 1944.

18 Edward R. Murdy, "Sworn Statement" contained in Missing Aircrew Report #5520, June 6, 1944.

19 Golden.

20 Ibid.

21 Russell A. Severson, Correspondence with the Author, October 18, 1995.

22 Sherman Armsby, "Sworn Statement" contained in Missing Aircrew Report #5523, June 7, 1944.

23 James Hastin, "Sound Off," *361st Fighter Group Association Newsletter*, Vol. XI, February 1993, p. 6.

24 Gotts, p. 54.

25 Freeman, *War Diary*, p. 270.

26 Gotts, p. 55.

27 Glenn T. Fielding, Correspondence with James T. Collins, August 30, 1984.

28 Stryker, June 19, 1944.

29 Thomas J.J. Christian, Jr., "Combat Report," June 20, 1944.

30 William D. Rogers, "Sworn Statement" contained in Missing Aircrew Report # 5955, June 20, 1944.

31 Joseph J. Kruzel, "Encounter Report" June 25, 1944.

32 Ibid.

33 Martin Johnson, "Encounter Report," June 25, 1944.

34 Urban L. Drew, Interview with the Author, August 8, 1994.

35 Jack S. Crandall, "Encounter Report," June 25, 1944.

36 Roy A. Webb, "Encounter Report," June 25, 1944.

37 Richard M. Durbin, "Encounter Report," June 25, 1944.

38 Hugh D. Chapman, "Encounter Report," June 25, 1944.

39 Vernon D. Richards, "Encounter Report," June 25, 1944.

40 Robert O. Bland, Correspondence with the Author, December 8, 1995.

41 Freeman, *War Diary* , p. 282.

42 Roy A. Webb, "Encounter Report," June 29, 1944.

43 Severson.

44 Robert C. Wright, "Encounter Report," June 29, 1944.

45 Jack B. Pierce, "Statistical Report, 361st Fighter Group," May 1945, p.7.

46 Wentworth, p. 4.

47 Sherman Armsby, "Encounter Report," July 20, 1944.

48 William T. Kemp, "Encounter Report," July 20, 1944.

49 Drew.

50 Robert R. Volkman, Interview with the Author, August 3, 1994.

51 Victor E. Bocquin, "Encounter Report," August 4, 1944.

52 Edward J. Marevka, "Sworn Statement," contained in Missing Aircrew Report #7737, August 4, 1944.

53 Sherman Armsby, "Encounter Report," August 5, 1944.

54 William J. Shakleford, "Encounter Report," August 5, 1944.

55 Drew, "Encounter Report," August 7, 1944.

56 William T. Kemp, "Encounter Report," August 7, 1944.

57 Leonard A. Wood, "Encounter Report," August 7, 1944.

58 Drew, Interview, August 8, 1994.

59 J.F. O'Mara, "Station History, Station F-374 (361st Fighter Group) for August 1944," September 1, 1944, p. 15.

60 *The Mighty Eighth*, p. 323.

61 Stryker, August 12, 1944.

62 361st Fighter Group, "Mission Summary Report, Field Order 506," August 12, 1944.

63 David C. Landin, Interview with the Author, October 15, 1994.

64 361st Fighter Group, "Mission Summary Report, Field Order 506 B2," August 12, 1944.

65 Robert Bain, "Sworn Statement," contained in Missing Aircrew Report # 7784, August 13, 1944.

66 Landin.

67 Missing Aircrew Report # 7618, August 14, 1944.

68 Merle Rainey, "Sound Off" *361st Fighter Group Newsletter* Vol. XII, June 1993, p. 6.

69 O'Mara, p. 1.

70 Kruzel, December 7, 1975.

71 Drew, Interview, August 8, 1994.

72 O'Mara, p.2

73 Stryker, August 15, 1944.

74 Bernard J. Redden, Correspondence with the Author, February 4, 2001.

75 Martin Johnson, "Encounter Report" August 25, 1944.

76 Ibid.

77 Ibid.

78 David R. Morgan, "Encounter Report," August 25, 1944.

79 Urban L. Drew, "Encounter Report," August 25, 1944.

80 Stryker, August 26, 1944.

81 Leonard A. Wood, "Sworn Statement" contained in Missing Aircrew Report # 8538, August 27, 1944.

six

Autumn Escorts

September 1944 would continue the transition set in motion the previous month. From the beginning of September on, new faces began to appear as many of the original pilots completed their combat tours and were replaced by new personnel. "More of the old timers received their orders to return to the Z.O.I. [Zone of the Interior]" read Ground Exec Maj. John Stryker's unit diary entry for September 15, 1944.[1] By the end of the month, the makeup of the air echelon of the 361st would mainly consist of a few "old hands" in key positions who had opted for a second tour of duty, pilots who had arrived as replacements for combat losses during the spring and summer, and brand-new replacement pilots fresh from the States.

2nd Lt. Harry Chapman began his combat tour with the 361st in the fall of 1944. Fresh from advanced flight school in the States, he spent a week at Goxhill, the Operational Training Unit near Hull, before reporting to the 361st as one of several replacements in early October 1944. Of his initial introduction to the Group, Chapman recalled that after being assigned to the 376th Squadron "we got about four training flights with the flight commander to find out if we knew how to fly battle formation because they didn't want anybody dragging along behind. And they just flat told you that if you didn't stay up 'We'll send you home' – meaning back to [base] from the mission, not back to the States."

Considering the experience level at the time of his arrival, Chapman commented that "there wasn't really that big a gap between my position as a wingman and this guy who's the element leader – he's been there maybe a month longer than I have…we're flying with a flight commander who's probably been there for say three more months … and his boss went home and he inherited the flight and got promoted to captain

or something – but he hadn't been out of flying school much more than maybe eight or ten months ahead of me."[3]

Chapman's own experience flying the P-51 when he reported to the 361st was confined to those hours he received at Goxhill. "I aborted my first mission for a rough engine," he recalled years later. "Nobody told me anything about rough engines and just about the time we hit the [North Sea] climbing out I thought that airplane was going to disintegrate right there and leave me sitting over Norfolk! … I didn't want to bail out over the North Sea, it's cold, and I also didn't want to lose an airplane on my first mission so I turned around and went back, and landed. [I] taxied in [and] the crew chief jumps up (the crew chief's face just falls when their airplane aborts, I mean, that's not good) and he wanted to know what was the matter.…I said the engine's about to fall out of the airplane. And he said 'Did you clear it out?' and I said 'I don't know what you're talking about.' And so I got out of it, he got in it without ever shutting it down or anything and taxied it over to wherever you had to be to run an engine up, and put chocks under it and ran that throttle up to full power for about two minutes and when he throttled it back it was just ticking like a Swiss watch   I guess this guy was about thirty years old or so [and] I'm twenty. He said 'They should have told you about it. The way to do it now, if it ever happens again, Son, just push it to the firewall and that will burn off the carbon.'[4] Though perhaps embarrassing at the time, operational flying would make a quick learner of Lt. Chapman.

Among the "old hands" still to be found in the Group's air echelon in the fall of 1944 were Lt. Col. Roy Caviness, CO of the 376th Squadron who assumed much of the burden of operational leadership for the Group following the loss of Col.

Christian, Lt. Col. Wallace Hopkins, who had served as Group Operations Officer since Richmond days, and Majors George Rew, Roswell Freedman, and James Cheney who took over command of the 374th, 375th and 376th Squadrons respectively after long service with the Group.

In terms of overall command of the 361st, the void created by the loss of Col. Christian on August 12 would never be fully redressed. Lt. Col. Joe Kruzel, who was most able to provide a sense of continuity in Group leadership, would return from leave in the States in mid September to assume command of the Group. His tenure, however, would last only through the end of the following month when he was ordered home to assume a key role in the stateside training of combat pilots.

Another transitional feature which September 1944 would bring to the "Yellowjackets" would be the mode of operations. After a summer of mixed ground support and bomber escort, September brought a return to the longer-range strategic escort missions for which the 361st was primarily equipped and trained. As the pace of the Allied land drive across France and the Low Countries began to slow with the extension of supply lines, and as units of the 9th Tactical Air Force established their forward bases on the Continent, fighter groups of the 8th Air Force would find themselves tasked less frequently with specific ground-support missions, and more frequently with the long-range bomber escort trips to targets in Germany. Of all the periods in the operational history of the 361st, the autumn of 1944 would be characterized by the missions of greatest range and endurance, and also of the largest individual air battles with the *Luftwaffe*.

The German Air Force in the fall of 1944 was geared almost entirely toward the air defense of the *Reich*, though it was increasingly unable to protect German airspace from the American daylight raids. Now faced with an increasingly ca-

Maj. George Rew, West Point Class of 1942, who took command of the 374th Fighter Squadron in the fall of 1944. *Courtesy George Lichter*

Maj. James Cheney who took over command of the 376th Fighter Squadron in the fall of 1944 and became a POW a short time later. *Courtesy J.J. Kruzel*

Left: Maj. Roswell Freedman who commanded the 375th Fighter Squadron in the fall of 1944 after long service with the Group. *Courtesy J.J. Kruzel*

pable and numerous adversary in the form of long-range American escort fighters, the *Luftwaffe* was further handicapped by shortages of fuel and experienced pilots to make up growing losses. Amid these decreasing fortunes, the *Luftwaffe's* fighter arm would make progressively fewer mass appearances over their home airspace during the autumn months, and *Luftwaffe* strategy shifted toward conserving resources for selected "knockout blows" rather than piecemeal depletion.[5]

In terms of actual contact with German aircraft, September would be the "Yellowjackets'" busiest month of 1944's last quarter and they would be able to claim some 38 enemy planes destroyed in the air and another 11 on the ground. In 22 missions carried out during the month, the pilots of the 361st would meet German fighters in the air on 8 separate occasions.[6]

For three days in succession beginning September 11, the 8th Air Force carried out major attacks on synthetic oil plants throughout Germany – targets so critical to the Nazi war effort that the *Luftwaffe* would, indeed, rise *en masse* to protect them.[7]

September 12 would see the "Yellowjackets" engaged in a major air battle with German fighters deep in enemy territory. Accompanying B-17s of the 3rd Bomb Division to refineries in the Magdeburg area, in weather conditions described as unusually clear, the 375th and 376th Squadrons sighted a large number of ME-109s approaching the bombers just as they reached their target. 2nd Lt. Billy Kemp, who was leading Yellow Flight of the 375th Squadron, described how the first group of 10 ME-109s was sighted flying on a perpendicular course to

the bombers and then turned and headed away. "They then dropped their belly tanks and turned 180 degrees into us," Kemp related after returning to Bottisham. "We were waiting for them, and our ten ships broke into a Lufberry with their ten." Two of the Messerschmitts fell to Kemp's guns in rapid succession at the start of the engagement, and then a third after Kemp dove to "the deck" on an ME-109 in pursuit of a Mustang.[8]

2nd Lt. Charles Narvis of the 375th Squadron also shot down a Messerschmitt, though he broke away from his first opportunity in order to assist another pilot in trouble. "A P-51 went by racked up with an ME-109 on his tail, so I broke away from the one I was following … and got in two two-second squirts from 50 yards, 65 degrees deflection. As I mushed by and above him, I saw strikes from half way back on the cowl, through the cockpit and on the wing roots. The enemy aircraft appeared to stop in mid-air, then fell into a vertical spiral with great billows of black smoke trailing behind him."[9]

Among the pilots of the 376th Squadron, 2nd Lt. Donald Vulgamore, flying as Yellow Four, followed his flight leader after an ME-109 from 24,000 down to 8,000 feet when he sighted a lone Messerschmitt and gave chase. The rapid loss of altitude, however, caused the windscreen of Vulgamore's Mustang to frost over, making his gun sight useless as he followed the German into a tight turn. "I closed to approximately 50 feet on the inside of the turn and looking out of the clear side panel, fired a 5 second burst, observing hits on the left wing root," Vulgamore reported at the mission debriefing that day. "He

Lt. William T. Kemp holds up three fingers symbolizing three enemy planes personally destroyed on the mission of September 12, 1944. *Courtesy Bernard J. Redden*

Lt. William R. Beyer of the 376th Fighter Squadron seated in the cockpit of his P-51, 1944. *Courtesy William R. Beyer*

immediately caught fire and went into a steep diving turn to the left." Obtaining a picture of the crash site, Vulgamore's claim was additionally substantiated by squadron mates who witnessed the engagement.[10]

In all, the pilots of the 375th and 376th Squadrons would claim fourteen enemy aircraft destroyed, giving the 361st the day's highest total of German planes downed throughout the 8th Air Force. Among those who recorded aerial victories was 2nd Lt. Claire P. Chennault of the 376th Squadron, whose father, the legendary Maj. Gen. Claire Chennault, had led the famous American Volunteer Group (known as "The Flying Tigers") in China before the U.S. entered the war. 1st Lt. Dale Spencer claimed one and one-half ME-109s destroyed raising his total to 9.5 aerial victories, just three days before he departed for the States at the close of his tour. Spencer's record would stand as the top score on the 361st Group victory list. For all the success of September 12, one pilot, 2nd Lt. Robert E. Geck of the 376th Squadron, failed to return to Bottisham.[11]

September 17, 1944 would be the next occasion in which elements of the 361st encountered German aircraft. On that day, while carrying out a fighter sweep in support of Operation Market-Garden, the daring airborne and armored invasion of Holland, 1st Lt. William R. Beyer of the 376th Squadron found himself involved in a protracted dogfight with an extremely skilled German pilot. Beyer, age 21, was a native of Danville, Pennsylvania, where he had worked in a local factory until enlisting in the Army just over a month after Pearl Harbor. After an initial stint as a glider pilot, he completed regular flight training in late 1943 and arrived at Bottisham as a replacement in April 1944.[12] In the early afternoon of September 17, as the "Yellowjackets" patrolled eastern Holland in the vicinity of the German border, some 15 ME-109s emerged through hazy overcast to bounce the 376th Squadron, then flying as top cover for the Group. Lt. Beyer, leading Blue Fight of the 376th, called for his flight to break while singling out an ME-109 for pursuit. "The ME-109 I followed used every evasive action to lose me, flying through clouds and doing several split-esses between 15,000 feet and the deck," Beyer recounted after the mission. "He chopped his throttle and threw down flaps at 1,000 feet and did another split-ess. I did the same and got on his tail on the deck. I began firing at 200 yards using about 40 degrees deflection and got a few hits around the cockpit. He tried to continue his turn but went straight on into the ground, the pilot apparently dead."[13] Later investigation revealed that the crashed ME-109 was piloted by none other than Maj. Klaus Mietusch of JG 26, a *Luftwaffe* "Ace" of 72 victories.[14]

The following day, on September 18, while much of the 8th Air Force's strength was committed to supporting Market-Garden, the 361st would find itself flying to the other end of Europe as part of a shuttle mission to the Soviet Union codenamed "Frantic VII." The first of the "Frantic" missions involving the 8th Air Force had taken place in the weeks following D-Day when a force of B-17s from England, accompanied by P-51 escorts, bombed targets in Germany and continued to land at bases in Russia. Historic in their own right, "Frantic" missions demonstrated the prowess of Allied air power in crossing German airspace at will, and bolstered cooperation with the Soviet Union. On the mission of September 18, the B-17s of the 3rd Bomb Division were not attacking targets in Germany, but rather were loaded with 1,248 containers of arms and supplies for the Polish Resistance fighting desperately against the Germans in the famous Warsaw Uprising.[15]

While the 43 Mustangs fielded by the 361st would not accompany the bombers all the way to Russia, the flight took them well east across the Baltic Sea for a total of five and one-half hours in the air. In the course of the escort, a pair of ME-109s were downed by Lieutenants Will Butts and Claude Hanley of the 376th Squadron, and 1st Lt. Urban Drew of the 375th Squadron was able to down a Heinkel HE-111K which he spotted well below the American formation, skimming the waves over the Baltic. Recalling the mission years later, Drew recounted that, "when you see an airplane flying low over the water, you don't see the airplane, you see the shadow bouncing on the waves, and I saw this shadow and I picked up this twin-engined airplane…I did not want to call "bogies at 1 o'clock low" because the whole 8th Fighter Command would have gone out, so I called 'Cheerful' [the Group Leader] and I said 'Permission to investigate unidentified aircraft,' and everybody said "WHERE, WHERE, WHERE??" And I didn't answer that, I took [my flight] down and got in behind a Heinkel and it was a piece of cake … I got the right engine and I overshot him a bit and swung back and got the left engine and he went in."[16]

The downed HE-111 was the fourth of an eventual seven aerial victories for Drew with the 361st, but it was not the only contact with German aircraft he would experience on the September 18 mission. After rejoining the escort, Drew observed a number of German seaplanes at anchor while flying over the German base at Bug Auf Rugen on the Baltic coast. When he received permission to strafe the enemy aircraft, Drew took his flight toward the German anchorage. "I dropped down out of the sun from 13,000 feet and hit the base from southwest to northeast," he reported later that day. Lining up on a very large six-engined seaplane, Drew opened fire at 800 yards range, raking the plane from wing tip to wing tip. Lieutenants Lee C. Travis and William D. Rogers, flying in trail behind their flight leader, also got numerous hits on the aircraft which burned and sank following their attack runs. Returning to Bottisham, Drew reported that the aircraft in question was "believed to be a [Blohm & Voss] BV-222" which was how the claim would be officially logged.[17] Some thirty years later, however, additional details of the seaplane came to Drew's attention when living in London. Contacted by the BBC for an interview regarding the mission of September 18, 1944, he was told that the unusually large seaplane destroyed by his flight that day had, in fact, been a unique example of a Blohm & Voss 238, the largest seaplane built during World War II.[18]

Two days after the seaplane encounter by Drew's flight, the "Yellowjackets" returned to skies over the Netherlands in support, once again, of Operation Market-Garden. Though the top-cover patrols over Holland yielded no contact with the enemy, the mission of September 20, 1944 would be memorable primarily for the dramatic demonstration of England's notorious weather hazards which the return to base provided. "Another bad day for the boys that fly," was how Maj. Stryker described the effect of near-zero visibility at Bottisham after "heavy fog lying almost on the ground" rolled in while the Group was airborne.[19] Although the pilots were able to reach the vicinity of the base that evening with the assistance of ground control, landing their aircraft suddenly became a daunting prospect when they saw that the Cambridgeshire landscape was blanketed in fog.

Recalling the mission years later, former crew chief Russell Severson of the 374th Squadron had a vivid recollection of the difficulties faced by the pilots as they followed their leaders down through the swirling fog to land. Standing near his revetment awaiting the return of his pilot, Severson described how difficult the landings appeared from the ground as individual flights "were flying around the base, just missing each other. The tower took over and got [them] in some kind of order. Now Bottisham had no runway lights, so they started to shoot amber flares at the beginning of the runway, forming an arch. They must have fired thousands of flares, because that arch never faded until all the planes had landed." With wingmen clinging to their leaders in the dense fog, all the pilots, save one, were able to make it safely onto the runway. Severson's plane, flown by 2nd Lt. Edward Knickman, failed to appear, however, and the crew chief became anxious. A short time later he was surprised to see Knickman walking toward him carrying his parachute rig. "The first thing he said to me was 'I just wrecked our plane.'"[20]

A rare photo of the massive Blohm & Voss 238 flying boat destroyed by Lt. Urban Drew's flight on September 18, 1944. In the inset is Lt. Urban Drew. *Courtesy Urban L. Drew*

Recalling the mission years later, Knickman described how, as a wingman, he merely followed his leader in for the landing – though he got more than he bargained for. "I was flying the number two position … and we can't find the field and they're firing flares – and when you're flying formation, you don't look at anything except the guy you're flying on. So I was stuck to [my leader] and could hear all this talking on the radio … 'What's your position.' 'Where are you,'[etc.], and then I could see a red flare and the next thing you know [my leader is] making a tight turn because we went past it and he's letting down and I can see the ground going by and all of a sudden BAM! I hit something and I'm skidding through this field. There are haystacks over there built like a house … I hit the peak of one and it sheared my right wheel off and it just threw me down in this field. I skidded along and stopped maybe a hundred yards from a hedgerow." When emergency vehicles arrived on the scene, Knickman was not immediately found, though he appeared in the midst of the search to assure the rescue personnel that he was, in fact, the pilot in question.[21]

Sgt. Severson would always be amazed at the pilots' resolve despite the hazards they regularly faced. Shortly after Knickman's crash, he accompanied the young lieutenant to Flight Operations where "...he had to sign the Flight Book …

374th Squadron crew chief Russell Severson (l) and assistant crew chief John Couch (r) seated on the wing of Lt. Edward Knickman's P-51D "Joe Ghost." *Courtesy Russell A. Severson*

The thing I'll never forget was when he signed the book his hand wasn't shaking at all. I always thought he was the bravest man I ever met."[22]

Harry M. Chapman, who retired from the Air Force as a Brigadier General shortly after commanding a reconnaissance wing in Vietnam, reflected on his own experience and commented that the weather hazards over England did not seem as daunting to a twenty-year-old pilot in 1944 as they might in retrospect. "There were days when your base would shut down and you'd have to go land somewhere else, get a little fuel, and maybe come home the next morning, but some place was generally open. I don't ever recall being in a panic over it – I think, though, it was ignorance on my part – if I knew then what I know now I'd have been scared to death every time I got in that airplane, because we just did things that you're not supposed to do ... like letting down into the blind, and flying along on the treetops" home from another base. "But I didn't know it," Chapman continued, "I was flying wingman. I think it was just as tricky for my leader as it would have been for me because none of us had any decent ... instrument flying training at all ... As kids you consider yourself invulnerable – they still do," he added.[23]

While September 20 was notable for the difficult landing conditions faced by the Group's pilots, it also marked the return to Bottisham of one of the 361st's most familiar command personalities. Lt. Col. Joe Kruzel, having finished his leave in the United States, arrived on the Station to take over command of the Group. Having served as Air Exec since Richmond days, Kruzel was naturally familiar with the mode of operations at Bottisham, but returned to the Group with mixed emotions. "The thought of Jack Christian's death weighed heavily on my mind," Kruzel commented years later. Although he had been confident at the time of his departure for the States in July that his chance to command the Group would come in due course, Col. Christian was a close personal friend and the news of his death, which he received just as he left the States on his way back, came as a shock.[24]

Despite sadness over Christian's loss, "the preoccupation of getting on with the job at hand," recalled Kruzel, quickly dominated his mindset. "I thought I had what was a going concern. We had some tremendous pilots and I looked forward to at least six months, possibly a year, of excitement. The troops were beginning to move out on the Continent and I was all set to carry on."[25]

Though Kruzel would not personally start leading missions again until the beginning of October, it was not long after his assumption of command that his optimism about the Group's future would be further increased. September 27, 1944 would

Lt. Edward Knickman of the 374th Fighter Squadron, fall 1944. *Courtesy Russell A. Severson.*

stand out as one of the key dates in the operational history of the 361st featuring one of the major air battles of the autumn of 1944. On that morning the 376th Squadron found themselves heavily engaged with a large force of German fighters as they accompanied B-24s of the 2nd Bomb Division against tank and vehicle factories in Kassel, Germany.

With nearly 1200 B-17s and B-24s airborne over Europe, September 27 was a day of massive activity for the 8th Air Force. 462 B-17s of the 1st Bomb Division were dispatched against targets near Cologne, while another 415 Fortresses of the 3rd Bomb Division attacked targets in Ludwigshaven and Mainz. The 2nd Bomb Division, for its part, fielded 315 B-24s, divided into three separate combat wings, against Kassel that day. To ward off German fighters, the Kassel force was accompanied by some 200 escorting fighters including 45 P-51s of the 361st.[26]

Led by Maj. Roswell Freedman, the "Yellowjackets" departed Bottisham, climbed out over the North Sea and joined their assigned B-24s at 0855 hours, 22,000 feet over the Dutch city of Apeldoorn. From that point they would accompany the bombers to the target, and then back along the withdrawal route.[27] As the formations of Liberators made their way east toward Kassel, the landscape below was hidden by a near solid layer of undercast which would force their navigators and bombardiers to rely on H2X radar to find the target once its vicinity was reached. Following an approach to the target, the pilots of the 361st watched as their assigned B-24s released their bomb loads between 0943 and 0946 hours amid moderate but accurate flak.

While the B-24s were flying their withdrawal course following "bombs away," a group of approximately 40 German FW-190s suddenly appeared high above the formation, and commenced a diving attack through the bombers silhouetted against the undercast below. When the attack took place, the fifteen P-51s fielded by the 376th Squadron that day were patrolling just below the B-24s. Leading the 376th was 1st Lt. Victor Bocquin, a 22-year old native of Reading, Kansas, who had been commissioned in November 1943 and had reported to Bottisham as a replacement pilot the following spring. Recounting the mission later that day, Bocquin described how the battle began. "About five minutes after the bombers had bombed, they were attacked. I was sweeping back and forth from our box to another box that had fallen back and out to the side. When the enemy aircraft hit, I was between two boxes of bombers."[28]

Bocquin issued split-second orders for his squadron to follow the bandits down as they dove toward the cloud layer below while the remainder of the 361st continued the escort. During the fight that ensued, the pilots of the 376th Squadron would find themselves operating singly, or in groups of two or three, in a frenzied pursuit of the enemy. After giving his squadron the order to "drop tanks," which greatly increased maneuverability while reducing the explosive hazard presented by auxiliary fuel, Bocquin was able to bring his guns to bear on the first of three German fighters which he would personally destroy that day. "I caught an FW-190 just before we hit the clouds and began shooting at 300 yards getting good hits," he later reported after returning to base. "I followed him into the overcast and lost him but saw a 'chute when I came out and his plane spinning down." After re-joining Lt. Homer Powell, his wingman, Bocquin destroyed two more FW-190s in addition to covering Powell who also downed two Focke-Wulfs.[29] Referencing the second of the two fighters he shot down, Powell reported that "The [German] pilot flew closer to the trees than I have ever seen any plane fly; in fact, he hit them three times. As a last resort, he let down full flaps. I saw it in time and let

Lt. Col. Joe Kruzel who returned from the States to take command of the 361st Fighter Group on September 20, 1944. *Courtesy J.J. Kruzel*

Consolidated B-24 Liberators release their bomb loads on targets in Kassel, Germany. *National Archives*

mine down. I chased ... until he filled about 3/4 of my sight and gave him a long one. He dove straight into the trees."[30]

Elsewhere in the 376th Squadron, the fight had begun similarly as pilots latched on to individual enemy aircraft above and below the undercast. At the start of the engagement, 1st Lt. William R. Beyer, Red Flight Leader, closed in within 100 yards of an FW-190 which was diving toward the cloud layer below. "I got hits all over [the] fuselage and wings knocking pieces off and he started smoking... I throttled back to see what he was going to do and he came back up so I opened fire again getting more hits. He jettisoned his canopy and disappeared into cloud in a spiral to the right."[31]

Breaking through the clouds, Beyer found himself alone, but sighting another '190, he immediately gave chase. Soon to join with Beyer was 2nd Lt. Robert Volkman of White Flight. "We dove through the clouds and as the '190's would pop through…to head back to wherever they came from – they came from several different airfields – we were picking them off," Volkman described years later. "I got separated and I saw a '51 shooting at a '190; I found out later it was Bill Beyer."[32] Immediately joining up to cover the other Mustang, Volkman would watch Beyer destroy four FW-190s, while bagging one himself.

With Volkman now flying his wing, Beyer pressed home the attack. "I got on the '190's tail and he did his best to lose me, doing split-s's and tight turns … I followed through his maneuvers until he started to climb. I opened fire on him at about 100 yards getting hits. He jettisoned his canopy and bailed out." Now down to 1000 feet of altitude, Beyer made a turn to the right to record the crash of his second victim on his gun camera. Sighting another '190, however, he quickly engaged it and after a short burst, the German pilot abandoned his aircraft giving him his third victory.[33]

While Beyer was dispatching his third German, Lt. Volkman spotted an FW-190 which was attempting to slip behind him in a tight turn. Recounting the incident in his Combat Report, Volkman described how an "FW-190 came in on [Beyer's] tail and I made a pass at it. Before I could fire, he jettisoned his canopy and bailed out."[34] Later analysis revealed that Volkman had, in fact, fired 140 rounds, scoring hits on the German – though in the heat of the moment, he was unaware that he had triggered his guns. Considering the incident nearly fifty years later, Volkman recalled that in seeing the '190 mak-

Lt. Robert Volkman photographed in front of his P-51, autumn 1944. *Courtesy Robert Volkman*

Lt. Victor Bocquin who led the 376th Fighter Squadron on the September 27, 1944 mission to Kassel. *Courtesy Robert Volkman*

An FW-190 captured in the gun camera of a US fighter. Note the cloud layer below. Scenes like this would have been typical of those witnessed by the 376th Squadron in the opening moments of the Kassel battle. *USAF Museum*

ing a pass "I racked the airplane around so hard I almost did a high speed stall, but I cut him off, and … my combat film does show that I hit him. It was a full deflection shot and I was just lucky."[35]

Rejoining Beyer, Lt. Volkman watched the Red Flight Leader down two more FW-190s. Beyer's final victory, recalled Volkman, came at the end of an extended chase at low altitude. "One of the '190's, I thought, had a really good 'bag of tricks.' He was right on the deck, full throttle – we were full throttle: 3000 rpms, 65 inches of mercury – and [the FW 190] popped just over some high tension wires in hopes that Beyer and I would hit them. We stayed right on his ass and then he dumped flaps. You're not supposed to dump flaps above a certain airspeed because you might tear them off, but when somebody in front of you is dumping flaps and trying to end up on your tail, you dump the flaps too. He knew he couldn't get away and he tried to belly in." In the final event, the bullet-riddled Focke Wulf crashed into a nearby farmhouse and exploded. By that time low on fuel and nearly out of ammunition, Beyer and Volkman turned west to head for home.[36]

2nd Lt. Robert Myers of Red Flight was another pilot who found himself on his own shortly after breaking through the cloud layer at the start of the battle. When he spotted an FW-190, however, he immediately gave chase and was able to open fire at 250 yards range while following the German into a tight turn. "Because of the lag between firing and the appearance of the strikes," he reported afterward, "I at first thought somebody else was shooting at him, so I pulled up to look around. The enemy pilot took this opportunity to bail out."[37]

In watching the '190 plummet to earth, Lt. Myers spotted another German fighter above him and began climbing to engage. Before he was in range, however, Flight Officer Walter Chapin of Yellow Flight had spotted the Focke-Wulf and opened fire. "I fired until four of my guns ran out of ammunition," Chapin reported. The German pilot "took violent evasive action, including dropping flaps and a barrel roll. I overshot him but managed to pull up and get back on his tail. Then his engine stopped and I followed him down shooting as I went. He made a rough belly landing in a field, the canopy falling off on the first bounce. The pilot didn't get out and as I made a pass from the side to photograph him I could see him slumped in the seat."[38] The crashed '190 would be the second of two aerial victories claimed by Chapin on the Kassel Mission.

While the majority of the squadron's claims were in air-to-air combat, a few were made against German aircraft on the ground. 1st Lt. William J. Sykes, who was leading Blue Flight when the attack first started, pursued an FW-190 down to 1,500 feet before destroying it. "During the engagement," Sykes re-

lated in his combat report, "I had noticed a small airfield about 10 miles south of Kassel." Alone while downing the '190, Sykes was later joined by 2nd Lt. Donald F. Vulgamore who had become separated from White Flight. Together the two pilots decided to have a closer look at the German field. Spotting several enemy aircraft on the ground, they commenced strafing from low altitude. Met by only light and inaccurate flak, Sykes and Vulgamore were able to make repeated passes, expending all their ammunition. "There were seven parked ME-410s and 2 ME-109s that had bellied in on the field," Sykes reported. In three passes, he claimed two ME-410s destroyed, while Vulgamore, who also destroyed an FW-190 in the air before joining Sykes, claimed one ME-410 destroyed and one damaged.[39] Separated from the rest of their squadron, the two pilots set a westerly course for the trip home.

Though the encounter near Kassel was extremely successful, one member of Blue Flight, 2nd Lt. Leo H. Lamb, would not return to England. The sole 376th Squadron casualty of the day, Lamb had become separated from the rest of his flight at the start of the engagement and was not seen again. As another pilot in Blue Flight later reported, "Over the R/T [radio telephone] I heard someone calling for help. I believe it was Lamb. He said he had more than he could handle. While he was calling, I could hear his guns firing over the R/T." His Mustang apparently rammed by a German fighter, Lamb's body was recovered from the wreckage of his aircraft and interred by German authorities.[40]

By approximately 1030 hours, the combat involving the 376th Squadron had ceased and the scattered elements began to make their way toward friendly airspace. Credited with a total of 18 German aircraft destroyed in the air, and another three on the ground, the squadron had set a temporary record among the fighter groups of the Eighth Air Force for enemy aircraft destroyed by a single squadron on a single mission.[41]

Though no enemy aircraft would be destroyed on September 28, it was, nonetheless, an important day in the history of the 361st. When the Group's aircraft returned from an uneventful mission to Brussels, they did not land at Bottisham, but rather, touched down at Station F-165, Little Walden, Essex. The arrival of the Group's Mustangs at the base was the last major step in a process in which the ground echelon had been engaged for weeks — change of station. A note of sentimentality made it into Maj. John Stryker's unit diary entry that day when he wrote that "This was the last mission from good old Bottisham – when the planes returned they landed on the new Airdrome…all units are now mostly on the new Station – some equipment still to be hauled from old base, but should be completed in a couple days."[42] Located some eleven miles south-

Pilots of the 376th Fighter Squadron photographed at Little Walden, autumn 1944. *Courtesy Robert Volkman*

east of Cambridge between the villages of Saffron Walden and Linton, Little Walden would officially be home to the 361st for the remainder of the war.

The improved facilities of the new base were apparent as soon as the Group's personnel arrived at the new station. "We never realized how bad Bottisham was until we moved to Little Walden," recalled 374th Squadron crew chief Russell Severson years later. "At Little Walden [we had] three concrete runways, much better living quarters, mess hall, huge hangar, etc. At Bottisham, [we had] one metal runway [and] our living quarters were two miles from base – at Little Walden, maybe 3/4 of a mile."[43] 375th Squadron Crew Chief Bernard J. Redden concurred that "Little Walden was a much better base," but added that as "strange as it may seem…memories are more vivid of the time we spent at Bottisham than those of Little Walden."[44] Despite the improvements in living conditions, Little Walden was a comparatively isolated station for officers and airmen used to the close contact of Bottisham village, and the six-mile vehicle or bicycle ride into Cambridge. For many of those who came over from the States with the Group, which included the

vast majority of the ground echelon, Bottisham would always be "home" whatever its shortcomings.

Operationally, the "Yellowjackets" would carry out just 15 missions from their new base at Little Walden during the month of October. Poor weather over England hampered flying, and on just two missions which the Group carried out that month would its pilots see action. October 7, however, would be a red-letter day in the operational history of the 361st. On that day, 50 of the Group's P-51s accompanied B-17s of the 1st Bomb Division deep into Germany to attack the oil refineries at Brux and Ruhland near Berlin. During the return portion of the escort, an estimated 50 to 75 ME-109s and FW-190s attacked a combat wing of bombers just to the rear of that which the 361st was escorting. Hearing reports of large numbers of bandits to the rear, elements of each of the Group's three squadrons immediately detached themselves and went in search of the enemy aircraft. During combats ranging from 26,000 feet down to the deck six German fighters were shot down for no losses.[45]

The most dramatic encounter of the mission, however, was yet to come as the 375th Squadron, led that day by 1st Lt. Urban Drew, reached the scene of reported combat to find the enemy planes gone. "I had left my Red Section with the bombers and had just one flight with me due to a number of previous [early returns]," Drew reported later that day. "I couldn't locate our bombers so I joined up with some red-tailed B-17s that were short on escorting fighters." While searching the skies above and below the B-17s, Drew observed that the formation was passing over Achmer airdrome, and from 15,000 feet he could clearly see German aircraft preparing for takeoff.[46]

Achmer Airdrome, near Osnabruck in northwest Germany, was home at that time to a special unit of the *Luftwaffe* known as the *Erprobungskommando Nowotny* that had been established to demonstrate the potential of a new type of aircraft then beginning to appear in increasing numbers over Germany – the ME-262 jet fighter. The unit was commanded by the legendary 258-victory ace Maj. Walter Nowotny.[47] The menace posed by the ME-262 by the autumn of 1944 was one of the more daunting prospects faced by American fighter pilots and bomber crews alike in the course of the air war. The world's first operational jet fighter, Messerschmitt's remarkable twin-engined *Schwalbe* (Swallow) outclassed the best piston-engined fighters in every category save maneuverability. With the then-phenomenal capability of 540 mph in level flight at 19,000 feet, a climb rate superior to any Allied fighter, and the highly effective armament of four nose-mounted 30mm cannon, the ME-262 had the potential to fundamentally affect Germany's fortunes had it been properly exploited.[48]

Lt. Drew had been the first pilot in the 361st to encounter one of the German jets during a mission on September 26, 1944, and although he was able to attain a speed of 500 MPH as he dove on the unsuspecting enemy aircraft from well above, the

"Good Old Bottisham." Maj. John Stryker, the Ground Exec and dedicated unit diarist, photographed outside Bottisham Hall with his pet Russian Wolfhound. After September 1944, Bottisham would be just a memory for the Group's personnel. *Courtesy J.J. Kruzel*

Messerschmitt easily pulled away from his P-51. During a low-level chase which followed, in which 2nd Lt. Daniel F. Knupp was lost to flak, Drew was unable to gain any advantage over the German jet.[19] On October 7, when the opportunity to catch a number of ME-262s at a disadvantage presented itself, Drew acted immediately.

Describing the action which took place over Achmer following his return to Little Walden on October 7, Drew reported that when he saw aircraft on the field he "watched them for a while and saw one of them start to taxi. The lead ship was in

A Messerschmitt ME-262, the world's first operational jet fighter. Heavily armed and capable of 540 miles per hour in level flight, the ME-262 proved to be a dangerous adversary in the fall of 1944 and spring of 1945. *National Archives*

take-off position on the east-west runway and the taxiing ship got into position for a formation take-off. I waited until they were both airborne and then I rolled over from 15,000 feet and headed for the attack with my flight behind me. I caught up with the second ME-262 when he was about 1,000 feet off the ground, I was indicating 450 MPH and the jet aircraft could not have been going over 200 MPH."[50] Recalling the event years later, Drew described how he made his attack. "They didn't see me and I pulled in behind the number two man and the first burst hit his starboard fuel tank where the wing fares into the fuselage, and he exploded – I mean complete explosion, there was nothing left." Still indicating 400 miles per hour, Drew was able to close with the leader and opened fire at 400 yards range. "If he'd have 'cobbed' it, if he'd have thrown the throttle wide open, if it wasn't already there, I think he'd have gotten away. But he started a tight climbing turn to the left…" Drew recounted. "I pulled up and my bullets started hitting… then he was losing speed which enabled me to pull in tighter, and my bullets walked up to the cockpit and I saw the canopy blow off but I never saw him [the pilot] go over the side. As it turned out, he did go over the side."[51]

When Lt. Drew returned to Little Walden that day, he was without witnesses to his combat. One member of his flight had turned off to avoid the intense flak over Achmer, and Drew's wingman, 2nd Lt. Robert McCandliss, was shot down by flak as the two passed at low level near Rheine Airdrome on the way home.[52] To make matters worse, the gun camera in Drew's P-51 malfunctioned and no combat film was on hand to substantiate his claim. "Now the first thing your armament man does when you shut your engine down and they block the wheels is he reaches up for the gun-camera film," Drew recalled in an interview years later. "And that morning, he had told me before I left, that the squadron leaders that day in the Eighth Air Force were going to be given color film for the first time. We'd always used black and white, the Navy had used color film for years in the Pacific but we never had it … unfortunately the cartridge with that color film was slightly out of size and it jammed. So here my wingman is shot down, I've got no pictures and I say 'Hey, I shot down two jets.' and they say 'Really, what else is new, Drew?' At any rate, General Doolittle, when he saw the report of the 262's gave me credit for the two airplanes. That's what made me an ace. I had been put in for the DSC [Distinguished Service Cross] … because I had no gun camera film and my wingman was shot down, I was never awarded it until forty years later."[53]

An ME-262 captured in the gun camera of a US fighter. Close to the ground and with wheels down, this scene bears similarity to Lt. Drew's famous encounter over Achmer on October 7, 1944. *National Archives*

Some twenty-two years later, in early 1967, official confirmation of Drew's victories came from the West German government which, based on the eyewitness testimony of a former *Luftwaffe* pilot present at Achmer on October 7, 1944, informed Drew of the identities of the ME-262 pilots whom he had downed that day. *Leutnant* Kobert, was flying the second jet to take off and was killed in the combat. Kobert's leader, *Oberleutnant* Bley, survived a low-level bail-out that day, but was killed in a crash later the same month. Bley had been a successful pilot with some eight victories to his credit includ-

Urban L. Drew photographed after finishing his tour with the 361st. *Courtesy Urban L. Drew*

ing four P-38s shot down on a single mission in the Mediterranean theater.[54] In the end, it was not until sixteen years after the disclosure of the two pilots' identities that the final chapter in the affair was played out. In May 1983 Urban L. Drew was awarded The Air Force Cross in recognition of his actions on October 7, 1944.

Considering the incident years later, Joe Kruzel, who was in command of the 361st in October 1944, commented that "a good portion of the 8th Fighter Command didn't know much if anything about the ME-262 at the time and I'm sure the more that they learned about it, the more they respected Drew for what he did."[55] Indeed, effective countermeasures against the jet were a matter of some concern once the ME-262 made its appearance as an interceptor. With no hope of catching the new fighter in level flight, certain tactics were suggested to minimize the jet's advantage during attacks such as maintaining several thousand feet of altitude above the bombers which, it was hoped, would give American pilots the chance to catch up to the jet in a dive. Turning directly into an attack, another tactic for the escorts, provided a split-second chance to inflict damage before the jet reached the bombers. A lucky hit on a vital part even at maximum range might slow the Messerschmitt sufficiently for the escorts to catch and destroy it.[56] While these measures offered at least a chance of success, no entirely satisfactory solution to the problem of the ME-262 was ever reached during the war.

While at a distinct disadvantage in their piston-engined P-51s, the pilots of the 361st would do their best to keep the jets at bay as they encountered them in the last months of 1944, and into the spring of 1945. "I don't think they knew what they had, really, because we couldn't touch them," remarked 374th Squadron pilot Edward Knickman recalling encounters with ME-262s during the last six months of the war. "I mean we couldn't even get close to them. Now Drew, he got them the only way – catch them either taking off or landing when they had to slow up, because shooting them down was practically impossible unless you bounced them and they didn't see you … you had to come down at practically full power just to attain their speed because they cruised so much faster than we did."[57]

As was the case with many of the Third Reich's wonder-weapons, the ME-262 was a matter of too little, too late. Despite glowing reports on the aircraft's performance after initial test flights, and requests by Fighter Arm Commander Adolph Galland that the new aircraft be put into production at the expense of all other types, the jet was initially relegated to the role of bomber by order of Hitler and the production lag in the fighter version was enough to delay large scale use against the bombers until the war was effectively lost.[58]

Following Lt. Drew's combat over Achmer, the 361st saw little enemy opposition in the ten missions carried out during the remainder of the month. On a mission on October 15, however, Maj. James Cheney, CO of the 376th Squadron, was forced to bail out over Germany due to flak damage sustained while strafing ground targets. Captured shortly after hitting the ground, he remained a POW through the end of the war.[59]

The arrival of November brought the news of a major command change at Little Walden. On the second day of the month, Lt. Col. Joe Kruzel, who had hoped to stay with the Group into 1945, received orders rotating him home to take part in training pilots for combat in the Pacific Theater. Selected along with Kruzel were a number of other highly experienced 8th Air Force group commanders including Col. Don Blakeslee of the 4th Fighter Group, Col. Joe Mason of the 352nd, and Col. William Cummings of the 355th. Knowing that Kruzel had hopes of remaining with the 361st, Gen. William Kepner contacted him personally with the news. "He said that he knew that I wasn't particularly pleased about going back, and neither was Don Blakeslee, and he asked if there wasn't anything he might do as a token of appreciation of our service with the 8th Fighter Command," Kruzel explained. "I told him that I would like an opportunity to visit Europe before I left. At that time the troops had got beyond Brussels so he said 'Sure, why not? The four of you are anxious to go, why not go ahead and take your P-51s and take about a week or ten days' – which we did. Don Blakeslee, Joe Mason, Bill Cummings and I, took off and…spent a couple days in Paris then flew on to Brussels and spent the remainder of our time there…and came on back to our respective bases. A few days later we departed for the States."[60]

The departure of Lt. Col. Kruzel for his tour of the Continent in early November, 1944, ended another chapter in the Group's history. Having joined the 361st less than a month into its existence, and eventually leading the Group on no fewer than 49 combat missions with credit for 3.5 German aircraft destroyed in aerial combat, Joe Kruzel was truly one of the "Yellowjackets'" most remarkable leaders. Kruzel's replacement, chosen from outside the Group, would not arrive at Little Walden until the beginning of December, and Lt. Col. Roy Caviness, another of the Group's long-time leaders since Richmond days, would serve as the interim Group Commander – just as he had done following Col. Christian's death. Remarkable in his longevity, Caviness would remain with the 361st during its entire wartime operational history in the ETO first commanding the 376th Squadron, then later serving as Group Air Exec, and ultimately as its Commander during the waning weeks of hostilities.

Though possessing a vast amount of combat time with the 361st, Lt. Col. Caviness, like the Group's original CO, Col. Christian, would never be credited with destroying an enemy plane in the air, though he had several ground victories from strafing. Caviness, "believed in much discipline, adherence to orders, and [flying] the mission as ordered," recalled Billy D. Welch, a former pilot with the 376th Squadron. "Our mission, most of the time, was to protect the bombers. This he did! ... On several occasions, Col. Caviness could have left the bombers and gone after enemy fighters. He didn't because he knew that they were probably 'decoys' trying to lure us away from our primary job... He probably saved many a 'Big Friend' by accomplishing the mission as briefed," Welch added.[61]

November 1944 brought a continuation of the strategic raids on German resources by the 8th Air Force. Under repeated attack during the month was the German oil industry – a resource so vital that large-scale attacks on oil refineries frequently brought about a major reaction by the *Luftwaffe*. As later analysis would show, the effect of bombing on the German petroleum industry did more to undermine the Nazi war effort than any other priority target. Aircraft and armaments for the *Reich* would continue to be turned out in surprising numbers despite the onslaught; petroleum, however, would be hit hard and production would decline precipitously in the last quarter of 1944.[62]

On November 2, the 361st provided target area escort to the B-17s of the 1st Bomb Division which were attacking synthetic oil plants at Merseburg/Leuna, a day on which German fighters rose to attack the American bombers in greater numbers than at any time during the previous six weeks.[63] In all the 1st Bomb Division lost 26 Flying Fortresses during the raid[64] – though the increasingly heavy concentrations of flak proved at least as damaging as German fighters. During the escort, the 361st was able to engage and destroy 8 FW-190s and ME-109s, though two pilots from the 375th Squadron, Lt. Charles Narvis and Lt. Charles Moore, were killed. Lt. Narvis was observed attempting to pull out of a dive after shooting down an ME-109, but was not seen again after disappearing into a cloud layer.[65] Later in the mission, Lt. Moore's P-51 was seen to crash and burn while flying at low-level, possibly due to flak damage.[66]

The November 2 interception cost the *Luftwaffe* dearly, as 8th Air Force fighters and bombers claimed over 100 German planes destroyed that day.[67] Though overall claims tended to exceed by varying degrees the number of German casualties listed in *Luftwaffe* records, the punishment inflicted on Goering's fighter arm in these missions meant that fighter activity for much of the remainder of November would be weak

Capt. Richard M. Durbin who was killed returning from a combat mission on November 9, 1944. *Courtesy J.J. Kruzel*

to non-existent. The "Yellowjackets'" sole aerial combat for several weeks took place on November 6, when 2nd Lt. William J. Quinn of the 374th Squadron was lucky enough to inflict fatal damage to an ME-262 while escorting B-17s to bomb a canal bridge over the Weser River at Minden. Spotting a pair of the jets being pursued by P-51s of another group, Quinn watched as the Messerschmitts "made a long diving turn...and we were able to gain on them." When another P-51 opened fire, one of the jets turned toward Quinn who also opened fire. "I was turning inside of him and my next two bursts I observed strikes along the fuselage and canopy ... He went into a spiral to the right at approximately 2,000 feet" which ended in a fiery crash.[68]

Pilots in the 361st would continue to encounter the German jets for the remainder of the war, and although they were usually not seen in great numbers on any one mission, they were a persistent menace to the bombers and were treated as such. In all, the "Yellowjackets" would be credited with downing six ME-262s in the air by the time the Group's final mission was completed in April 1945.[69]

Following Quinn's successful encounter on November 6, a quiet phase of operations was experienced by the Group – though the dangers of a flying operation were always present even when enemy opposition was not a factor. As a case in point, at the conclusion of a mission on November 9, 1944, Capt. Richard Durbin, a highly experienced pilot originally assigned to the 376th Squadron but who later transferred to Group Headquarters, was killed while landing at Little Walden. Attempting to touch down in a cross-wind, Durbin's P-51 went out of control and crashed.[70]

November 26, 1944 would be an exceptional day in the history of the 361st Fighter Group, as well as that of the 8th

Air Force in general when some 300 "heavies" of the 1st and 2nd Bomb Divisions were tasked with destroying the synthetic oil refinery at Misburg, near Hannover, in northern Germany. Assigned to penetration, target, and withdrawal support for a combat wing of B-24s, the "Yellowjackets" were destined to encounter the largest German fighter reaction in the Group's history as an estimated 350 bandits attacked in waves as the bombers reached their Initial Point (IP - point at which a formation turned onto its final bomb run heading). Heavily engaged throughout the 45-minute air battle, the Group's three squadrons would be split into flights and elements as they attempted to cope with a series of attacks against their assigned combat wing. Ultimately, as full details surfaced and scattered elements returned to Little Walden in the days following the mission, November 26 would emerge as the 361st's most successful day of the war resulting in 23 enemy aircraft destroyed in the air, two probables, and another nine damaged for no losses.[71]

The task assigned to the 361st on November 26 would be to pick up the assigned combat wing of B-24s bound for Misburg over western Holland, accompany the bombers through to the target, and then cover their withdrawal across the Netherlands before breaking escort. Commencing with take-off from Little Walden shortly after 1000 hours, the mission progressed as planned and the 361st joined its assigned combat wing, consisting of the 389th and 445th Bomb Groups, some seventy-five minutes later over the Dutch city of Zwolle. On the way to pick up the bombers, and again during escort over Holland, evidence of the latest German terror-weapons could be seen as several V-2 rockets left their launching pads bound for the vicinity of London. Though they posed no threat to air operations, the pilots noted the appearance of what they called the "Big Bens" and attempted to pinpoint their launching points for use by Intelligence.[72]

As an indication of the intensity of the German flak defenses then being experienced by bomber crews, a squadron of B-24s of the 491st Bomb Group, which dropped its bombs 15 miles short of the target when its lead bombardier accidentally toggled his bomb load, separated itself from the remainder of the Group during the approach to Misburg rather than fly through the heavy flak anticipated over the target. This maneuver, which gave only secondary consideration to the threat of attack by fighters, was later cited as a primary cause for the loss of fifteen of that group's Liberators on the mission.[73]

At approximately 1210 hours, the lead combat wing of the Misburg force, escorted by the P-51s of the 361st, was approaching the Initial Point – the city of Wittingen, some forty miles northeast of the Hannover-Misburg area. Just as the B-

2nd Bomb Division B-24 Liberators in formation, bound for targets in Germany, November 1944. *National Archives*

24s were preparing to turn onto the bomb-run heading, the first signs of what would be a massive *Luftwaffe* reaction appeared. Approaching from the east, slightly above the American formation, a wave of 100-plus FW-190s and ME-109s was sighted preparing for what appeared to be a head-on attack against the bombers.[74] At that moment, the Mustangs of the 376th Squadron, under Capt. John Duncan, who was also leading the Group, were posted ahead and slightly above the lead combat wing. Spotting the huge gaggle of bandits nearing the formation, Duncan attempted to get the squadron in a favorable position to intercept. "The Group Leader started a turn to get up sun of them but by the time I got half way through, the [enemy aircraft] were on us and I had to turn into them," reported Capt. William Beyer of the 376th Squadron. "They fired at us in the head-on pass but didn't hit anybody."[75] Remarkably, the Germans inflicted no damage on the B-24s but continued westward after a single pass. The 376th immediately broke escort and gave chase, leaving the 374th and 375th squadrons to continue the escort.

Though most of the German aircraft in the first attack continued west at high speed, a few turned to engage the pursuing fighters. Capt. Beyer, with his flight in trail, quickly latched onto an FW-190 as it streaked away from the bombers. The German pilot pulled into a loop but Beyer was able to keep the Focke-Wulf in his gun sight throughout, scoring numerous hits after which the German dove into the ground. Climbing back toward the bombers, Beyer spotted an ME-109 which he destroyed after a chase in which the pilot jettisoned his canopy following an attempt to throw-off his pursuers.[76] Simultaneous with this attack, three more FW-190s were engaged by members of Beyer's flight, and one each was destroyed by Lieutenants Hanley, Scott and Ford.[77]

While the skirmish involving the 376th was taking place, a second crisis for the escorts emerged as another group of German interceptors appeared from the north. Capt. Elroy Neely was leading the 375th Squadron, posted at 26,000 feet, just above the assigned combat wing, when bandits were reported at nine o'clock to the bombers. "I took [the] Squadron over to investigate and found about two hundred [enemy aircraft] about twenty miles northeast of Brunswick, mostly FW-190s, but about 20 ME-109s, at about 25,000 ft.," Neely related in his combat report. Gaining a favorable position high and six o'clock to the Germans, he ordered the squadron to engage. "I fired at a '190 from about 400 yards dead astern, and saw a few hits, but broke off when two other Mustangs closed on him from my left and behind." Neely later reported. "I discovered that my wingman had become lost from me then so I went into a one-man Lufberry , trying to join up with someone. The enemy aircraft weren't aggressive, and most of them split-s'd for the deck." Hearing from number 3 in his flight that the bombers were under attack, Neely climbed back toward the last combat box of B-24s which was under attack over the target, by then temporarily joined by another P-51. "I saw two bombers

burst into flame and disintegrate, no chutes." Picking out an FW-190 positioning itself for an attack on the bombers, Neely shot it down from astern, the pilot bailing out. "I looked back and found that my wing man was gone again and I had a 190 in his place. I broke into this one, got on his tail in about two turns, and he started diving for the deck. I got in two long bursts from about 2-300 yards dead astern ... the enemy aircraft burst into flames all along the fuselage."[78]

As Capt. Neely reported, when the 375th attacked from behind, most of the German fighters broke and split-s'd for the deck. A few, however, were caught from behind while still in formation. 1st Lt. Robert Adams, Blue Flight Leader, spotted an FW-190 dropping down from top cover onto his wingman's tail and immediately went into a Lufberry circle. When the German attempted to break out of the circle by pulling up into the sun, Adams raked the Focke-Wulf from 300 yards, sending the plane spiraling earthward.[79] 2nd Lt. Paul Klees, flying as Blue 3, picked out an ME-109 from the rear of the German formation and brought it down when the pilot attempted to dive away following a series of desperate maneuvers. Finding that he and his wingman, 2nd Lt. Lee Travis, were then alone, the

Capt. Elroy Neely who led the 375th Fighter Squadron on the mission of November 26, 1944 which saw the greatest air battle in the history of the 361st Fighter Group. *Courtesy Leonard A. Wood*

Lt. Paul Klees of the 375th Fighter Squadron who downed an ME-109 and an FW-190 on the mission of November 26, 1944. *Courtesy Leonard A. Wood*

two began climbing back toward the bomber track when they spotted two unidentified aircraft heading eastward, side-by-side at 15,000 feet. Diving down to investigate, they quickly recognized them as FW-190s. Indicating that Travis take the aircraft on the left, the two brought down the German fighters nearly simultaneously after closing undetected from astern.[80]

Shortly after the 375th Squadron detached itself from the bombers to engage the enemy fighters, a third German attack wave approached the Misburg force from the east. Their well-timed arrival, with just one squadron of escorts left to cover the first combat wing, led to later speculation that the first waves were specifically intended to draw the escort away.[81] When this third attack wave of approximately 60 FW-190s and ME-109s appeared around 1220 hours, Capt. Lucius LaCroix, leading the 374th Squadron, gave the order to drop tanks and break into the German formation.[82] From that point on, the squadron would be reduced into flights, elements, and single aircraft in a protracted dogfight lasting more than thirty minutes and ranging down to the deck.

Following the initial head-on pass, 2nd Lt. Barry Hicks of the 374th turned after an FW-190 with his wingman, 2nd Lt. Richard Chandler, in trail. "I opened up at about 100 yards, my gun sight and radio went out then. This 190 did a split-s and I went after him. I closed in to 50 yds, and less several times hoping to get hits on him. A couple of times I saw strikes on the underside of his ship below the cockpit. We went all the way down to the deck."[83] At that point Hicks discovered that his guns were jamming and he was limited to one working .50 caliber machine gun. Having no luck with the single gun, he pulled away to the right and allowed his wingman, Lt. Chandler, to open fire. After watching the Focke-Wulf crash into a wooded area below, Chandler spotted another FW-190 and attacked from the rear. When the enemy pilot prepared to bail out, the discarded canopy struck his propeller hub causing an oil leak which obscured his windscreen.[84] In the meantime, Hicks encountered yet another Focke-Wulf whose pilot also chose to bail out after several hits were scored from his single working gun. Between them, Hicks and Chandler would be credited with two destroyed and two damaged.

2nd Lt. Judd G. Vear of the 374th Squadron found himself alone shortly after the fight started, and after joining onto another P-51 which turned out to be from another fighter group, spotted a Mustang being chased in a turn by an FW-190 some 5,000 ft. below and broke away to assist. "Evidently the P-51 must have seen me because he reversed his turn to the right bringing him back towards me. The '190 was so close to the '51 that I had to hold my fire until I was almost upon the enemy aircraft. At about 200 feet I fired a fairly short burst and

An FW-190 in flight, seen from below. Fighters such as this were hurled in great numbers at the bombers attacking the synthetic oil plants on November 26, 1944. *USAF Museum*

observed hits all over the canopy and right wing. I had too much speed to continue firing so I pulled…50 feet above him. The pilot released his canopy and was trying frantically to unstrap himself. The plane went into a sharp spiral to the left and crashed in the edge of [some] woods. I did not think the pilot could have escaped as we were only at 1500 feet. However, just after the plane crashed I saw a chute open and the pilot landed in a field about 100 yards from his plane." Later, after climbing back toward the bomber track, Vear was able to damage another FW-190 before heading for home.[85]

Among the many notable events of the mission, 2nd Lt. Robert J. Farney of the 375th Squadron would achieve a rare distinction when he downed an FW-190 on only his first combat mission. Farney, age 23, was born in Croghan, New York, and had arrived at Little Walden as a replacement pilot at the end of October. On November 26, he found himself assigned as a wingman to 1st Lt. Leonard Wood.[86] After watching Wood overshoot an FW-190, Farney was able to fire on the German fighter scoring hits until "…the FW-190 slowly rolled over on its back and went down."[87]

1st Lt. George Vanden Heuvel of the 376th was also able to claim two victories in the engagement – his 18th combat mission. Older than many in his squadron, the 27-year-old Vanden Heuvel, who originally hailed from Mt. Vernon, New York, had joined the 361st only two months prior after serving stateside as a flight instructor." After initially running into the German formation that day, Vanden Heuvel became separated from his flight during a high-speed dive, and finally managed to pull out at 10,000 feet. "I climbed up southwest along the bomber track looking for some one to join up with. I was at about 20,000 feet when I saw 10 plus FW-190s ahead and they broke into me," he later reported. Maneuvering onto the tail of one, Vanden Heuvel fired several bursts when all but one of his guns ceased firing. "While I was on this FW-190's tail, several other FWs were making side passes at me but scored no hits ... Two FW-190s, coming from opposite sides, were closing in and shot from about an 80 degree deflection angle. I dumped the stick and made a steep diving turn. The two FW-190s collided almost head-on and exploded..."[89] Low on fuel, Vanden Heuvel headed west and was eventually forced to land at a Belgian airfield before returning to England the following day.

The mission to Misburg on November 26 was the high point of the Group's long-range escort battles during the fall of 1944. Never again in the operational history of the 361st would enemy aircraft be seen in such vast numbers, nor would such unprecedented success be attained. Throughout the last autumn of the war, the "Yellowjackets" had carried out their primary mission to the deepest targets in Germany. By the beginning of December 1944, two trends at Little Walden would be evident to all: the continued transformation of the air echelon through turnover of the remaining "old hands," and the apparent nearness of Germany's collapse. While the first of these was undeniable, the second would prove to be more elusive.

NOTES

[1] John Stryker, Unit Diary Entry, September 15, 1944.

[2] Harry M. Chapman, Interview with the Author, October 29, 1994.

[3] Ibid.

[4] Ibid.

[5] Roger A. Freeman, *The Mighty Eighth* (New York: Janes 1981), p.180.

[6] Steve Gotts, *Little Friends: A Pictorial History of the 361ˢᵗ Fighter Group in World War II* (Dallas: Taylor Publishing Co., 1993), pp. 167-168.

[7] *The Mighty Eighth* , p. 178,

[8] William T. Kemp, "Encounter Report," September 12, 1944.

[9] Charles Narvis, "Encounter Report," September 12, 1944.

[10] Donald Vulgamore, "Encounter Report," September 12, 1944.

[11] Stryker, September 12, 1944.

[12] *The Escorter* (Newspaper of the 361ˢᵗ FG) Vol. 1 #17, October 7, 1944.

[13] William R. Beyer, "Encounter Report," September 17, 1944.

[14] Gotts, 81.

[15] Roger A. Freeman, *The Mighty Eighth War Diary* (New York: Janes, 1981) p. 349.

[16] Urban L. Drew, Interview with the Author, August 8, 1994.

[17] Urban L. Drew, "Encounter Report," September 18, 1944.

[18] Drew, August 8, 1994.

[19] Stryker, September 20, 1944.

[20] Russell A. Severson, Correspondence with the Author, October 13, 1994.

[21] Edward Knickman, Interview with the Author, September 23, 1992.

[22] Severson, Ibid.

[23] Harry M. Chapman, Interview with the Author, October 29, 1994.

[24] Joseph J. Kruzel, Recollections Recorded December 7, 1975 and transcribed by Paul B. Cora, October 2000.

[25] Ibid.

[26] 8ᵗʰ Air Force, "Intelligence Summary No. 150," September 27, 1944.

[27] 8ᵗʰ Fighter Command, "Narrative of Operations, Field Order 1201'590," September 27, 1944.

[28] Victor E. Bocquin, "Encounter Report," September 27, 1944.

[29] Ibid.

[30] Homer G. Powell, "Encounter Report," September 27, 1944.

[31] William R. Beyer, "Encounter Report," September 27, 1944.

[32] Robert R. Volkman, Interview with the Author, August 3, 1994.

[33] Beyer, Ibid.

[34] Robert R. Volkman, "Encounter Report," September 27, 1944.

[35] Volkman, August 3, 1994.

[36] Ibid.

[37] Robert Myers, "Encounter Report," September 27, 1944.

[38] Walter F. Chapin, "Encounter Report," September 27, 1994.

[39] William J. Sykes, "Encounter Report," September 27, 1944.

[40] "One Lost Fighter Pilot" *8ᵗʰ AF News*, Vol. 15, No. 1, January 1989, p. 15.

[41] *The Mighty Eighth*, p. 355.

[42] Stryker, September 28, 1944.

[43] Severson, October 18, 1995.

[44] Bernard J. Redden, Correspondence with the Author, February 10, 1996.

[45] 361ˢᵗ Fighter Group, "Mission Summary Report, Field Order 600," October 7, 1944.

[46] Urban L. Drew, "Encounter Report," October 7, 1944.

[47] Hans Ring, Correspondence with Urban L. Drew, February 18, 1967.

[48] William N. Hess, *Fighting Mustang: Chronicle of the P-51* (Garden City NY: Doubleday, 1970)p. 67.

[49] Drew, "Encounter Report," September 26, 1944.

[50] Drew, "Encounter Report," October 7, 1944.

[51] Drew, Interview, August 8, 1994.

[52] 361ˢᵗ Fighter Group, "Mission Summary Report, Field Order 600," October 7, 1944.

[53] Drew, Interview.

[54] Ring, Ibid.

[55] Kruzel, Recollections, December 7, 1975.

[56] *The Mighty Eighth*, p. 193.

[57] Knickman, Ibid.

[58] *Fighting Mustang*, p. 67.

[59] Gotts, p. 99.

[60] Kruzel, Ibid.

[61] Billy D. Welch, Correspondence with the Author, February 13, 2001.

[62] *The United States Strategic Bombing Survey Vol. 1* (New York: Garden City Publishing, 1976), p. 43.

[63] *The Mighty Eighth*, p. 180.

[64] *The Mighty Eighth War Diary*, p. 375.

[65] Edwin E. Tinkham, Jr., "Sworn Statement" contained in Missing Aircrew Report # 10246, November 3, 1944.

[66] Caleb J. Layton, "Sworn Statement" contained in Missing Aircrew Report # 10244, November 3, 1944..

[67] *The Mighty Eighth War Diary*, p. 375.

[68] William J. Quinn, "Encounter Report," November 6, 1944.

[69] *Fighting Mustang*, p. 173.

[70] Stryker, November 9, 1944.

[71] 361ˢᵗ Fighter Group, "Mission Summary Report" November 26, 1944.

[72] Ibid.

[73] 2ⁿᵈ Bomb Division, "Tactical Report of Mission, Misburg and Bielefeld," November 26, 1944, p.1.

[74] 8ᵗʰ Air Force, "Intops Summary No. 210, " November 26, 1944, p. 3.

[75] William R. Beyer, "Combat Report," November 26, 1944.

[76] Ibid.

[77] 361ˢᵗ Fighter Group, "Mission Summary Report," November 26, 1944.

[78] Elroy Neely, "Combat Report," November 26, 1944.

[79] Robert Adams, "Combat Report," November 26, 1944.

[80] Paul Klees, "Combat Report," November 26, 1944.

[81] "Intops Summary No. 210" p.3.

[82] Milton F. Glessner, "Encounter Report," November 26, 1944.

[83] Barry Hicks, "Encounter Report," November 26, 1944.

[84] Richard Chandler, "Encounter Report," November 26, 1944.

[85] Judd Vear, "Encounter Report," November 26, 1944.

[86] Danny Morris, *Aces and Wingmen II, Volume 1* (Washington State: Aviation Usk, 1989), pp. 170-172.

[87] Robert J. Farney, "Encounter Report, " November 26, 1944.

[88] Morris, p. 188.

[89] George R. Vanden Heuvel, "Combat Report," November 26, 1944.

seven

"Watch on the Rhine"

The first day of December 1944 brought with it a new Group Commander for the 361st. Arriving at Little Walden that day was Lt. Col. Junius W. Dennison, Jr., who would officially take the place of Joe Kruzel. Col. Dennison took over the Group with a fairly sparse operational background as far as the ETO was concerned. As Maj. Stryker recorded in his unit diary after meeting the new CO, "he hasn't had a great deal of fighter time, nor has he had much combat, but he seems eager to get into it."[1] Having sufficient flying time to earn a Command Pilot rating, Dennison had seen several years of service as an Air Attaché to several foreign governments in South America before serving with a training wing in Florida immediately prior to his arrival at Little Walden.[2] While he would remain in command of the Group through the spring of 1945, the day-to-day operational leadership of the 361st would primarily fall to those who had lengthy combat records with the "Yellowjackets."

December 2, 1944 brought the only contact with the *Luftwaffe* which the "Yellowjackets" would experience until the end of the month. While escorting B-24s of the 2nd Bomb Division to attack the railroad marshalling yard at Bingen, the 374th Squadron was able make good use of ground radar warnings to break up an attack by some 30 FW-190s. Advised by ground control that radar contacts were detected heading toward the bomber formation they were escorting, Capt. Jerome R. Mau, leading the 374th, was ready to intercept as soon as the bandits were sighted visually. When ground control reported that enemy aircraft "were in the immediate vicinity and that they would be coming in on the last box," Capt. Mau put his squadron into position to catch the German fighters from behind before they reached the B-24s. "I had just crossed behind the last box when White 3 (Capt. La Croix) called me and told me there was a gaggle of bogies at the bombers' 4 o'clock

coming in at them. They were in ragged formation flying about 7 abreast and about 5 deep… I called the Squadron and told them that we were going down. We dropped tanks and came in at their six o'clock. I picked out an FW-190 that had just come in on a B-24's tail. As he had just started to fire at the B-24, I opened up at maximum range (800 yards)." Observing no hits, Mau applied throttle to close the distance and fired again, this time seeing strikes all over the Focke-Wulf which spiraled downward and away trailing smoke. With enemy aircraft still in the vicinity, Capt. Mau continued to search for German fighters as he circled his P-51D back to the rear of the bombers. He then sighted three more FW-190s diving away into a layer of undercast and detailed part of the squadron to remain with the B-24s while taking the remainder in pursuit. After attaining an indicated airspeed of over 500 MPH while diving after the Germans, Mau caught another FW-190 which he chased down to 500 feet, firing, before the German pilot bailed out.[3]

The encounter on December 2, in many ways, showed where the balance lay in the air war over Europe at the end of 1944. Directed by radar, the 374th Squadron was able to gain an advantageous position over the approaching bandits and break up their attack, destroying three enemy planes, and damaging another without loss to themselves or the bombers. Often inexperienced and hastily trained, German fighter pilots, when making their comparatively rare appearances in the fall of 1944, frequently chose to dive away when intercepted by American fighters. Clearly, the *Luftwaffe* was being bested in the eyes of the pilots at Little Walden, and like views were shared throughout the 8th Air Force at that point in the war.

The beginning of December 1944 was a time for optimism not just in the 8th Air Force, but for the Allies in general. All along the western borders of Hitler's Reich, the armies were

Ground crewman of the 361st seen at their makeshift mess hall at St. Dizier, France, the forward base to which the Group was transferred during the Battle of Bulge. *Courtesy Russell A. Severson*

Capt. Jerome R. Mau who led the 374th Fighter Squadron on the mission of December 2, 1944. *Courtesy J.J. Kruzel*

preparing to push onto German soil, and in the east, the Red Army was placing equal if not more pressure on the retreating German forces. However, while Germany's fortunes ebbed as 1944 drew toward a close, and as the western Allies looked forward to crossing the Rhine, a tremendous shock was being prepared by Hitler's dwindling armies. Code-named "Watch On the Rhine," Germany's last major offensive in the west would be known to history as the Battle of Bulge. Employing some ten carefully hoarded armored and twenty infantry divisions, the German offensive was planned by Hitler himself and would ultimately be the largest battle involving American troops ever fought. Hitler's plan was to capture the Belgian port of Antwerp which he believed would split the Americans and British causing such a shock that they would consider a negotiated peace.

Throughout the Normandy Campaign and the Allied drive across France, a decisive factor in the German defeat had been the overwhelming Allied air superiority across the entire front. As German armies retreated through France, American and British fighter-bombers made daylight movement over roads all but impossible while completely negating the possibility of German air support for their own units. "Watch on the Rhine" was carefully planned to nullify Allied air power by taking advantage of weather conditions that would ground American and British aircraft. By planting meteorological teams in the Arctic in the final months of 1944, the Germans were able to predict when such a weather pattern, lasting a week or more, would begin. After receiving a forecast for an extended period of rain, snow and heavy fog arriving in western Europe during the middle of December, the German armies prepared to attack along a lightly held portion of the American front in the Ardennes region of eastern Belgium and Luxembourg.

Just before daybreak on December 16, the German offensive was launched, initiating the most desperate period of the European war for the Americans. In succeeding days, the offensive pushed into the Ardennes with overwhelming local superiority, forcing the surrender or withdrawal of thousands of American troops. In the opening days of the offensive, with heavy fog blanketing the treetops throughout much of western Europe, American units fought desperately to stem the seemingly overwhelming German drive without the benefit of air support. At Bastogne, in eastern Belgium, the U.S. 101st Airborne Division doggedly refused to yield, enduring a dramatic siege which bought time for reinforcements to be brought up. As the Germans pushed deeper into Belgium in their drive toward Antwerp, the strategic maps began to reveal their progress in the form of a broad salient or "bulge" jutting westward through the Allied line.

2nd Bomb Division B-24 Liberator bombers in formation. *National Archives*

For the 8th Air Force, the period of December 16 through 22, 1944 was one of extremely limited activity as the German weather forecast proved to be all too accurate. Though attempts would be made to bomb German communication centers and railroad hubs which supported the Ardennes offensive, these were largely unsuccessful due to weather complications. For three days beginning December 20, the fog was so bad that the 8th Air Force was grounded, with the exception of a few weather reconnaissance flights.[4] For the units of the 9th Air Force, whose primary job was the tactical support of American ground forces, the situation was no better during the first days of the German offensive, and their forward bases in France and Belgium were largely inactive until the weather improved.

At Little Walden, the middle of December was a time of poor weather even before the start of the German offensive. Beginning December 13, heavy fog made operations impossible and the Group would be almost continually grounded for the remainder of the week that followed. On December 16, Maj. Stryker noted the opening of the German offensive, commenting that the "situation on the front [is] not looking too good in the Ardennes area – no air support for a couple of days now."[5] The following day, as the Group's aircraft remained on the ground, Stryker noted the departure of several pilots who had completed their combat tours and were homeward bound. "Nothing unusual today except the signing out of three good pilots, namely: W.T. Butts, Choppin and Neely – signed out with remarks as follows: 'I'm through,' 'Me too,' and 'Watch my smoke'…"[6] The brevity of their remarks on finishing with the Group underscores the strain of combat flying for the average pilot. Faced with a significant chance of death, capture and/or maiming every time they left the ground, the completion of a combat tour produced anything but feelings of sentimentality. As Henry Lederer of the 374th Squadron put it many years later, the stresses of combat flying were enormous – "like walking that last mile at Sing Sing three or four times a week and you didn't know whether you were coming back or not."[7]

The first large-scale effort by the 8th Air Force to strike at German lines of supply and communication supporting the Ardennes offensive took place on December 18. While the P-51s of the 361st were called on to take part, the weather deteriorated so much over the Continent that the mission was recalled, and during the next four days, the story would be much the same. On December 22, 1944, with a forecast calling for partly clearing skies over both England and the Continent on the following day, large scale operations were once again planned.

For the 361st, December 22 not only brought news of the Group's likely participation in major operations the following

Lt. Caleb W. Layton of the 375th Fighter Squadron who was shot down and killed on December 23, 1944. *Courtesy Leonard A. Wood*

day, but also confirmed a dramatic operational change for the Group. Effective December 23, the "Yellowjackets" were to be transferred to the Continent where they would provide top cover to 9th Air Force units that would bear the brunt of the tactical support needed to turn back the German thrust. According to orders received for December 23, 60 of the Group's P-51s and pilots, along with 9 ground officers and 137 enlisted men would depart for Airdrome A-64, St. Dizier, France, located some 70 miles southwest of the fighting front. The Group's Mustangs would first carry out an escort mission, after which they would land at the French field; the maintenance personnel and ground officers would depart in transport aircraft, arriving directly at the new base.[8]

Among the pilots selected to go to France on December 23 were most of the more experienced "hands." A total of 55 of the Group's yellow-nosed P-51s took off from Little Walden shortly after 1230 hours that day bound for the Trier area of western Germany, where they would provide area support for Allied operations along the front. Though the weather was marginal, the 8th Air Force dispatched over 400 "heavies" and nearly 600 fighters against railroad marshalling yards and communication centers east of the Ardennes battle area in an attempt to cut German lines of supply.[9]

While the Group was patrolling that afternoon some 25 miles southeast of Bonn along the Rhine, two pilots of the 375th Squadron ended up in a low-level dogfight with German fighters in a scrap that showed just how quickly the individual fortunes of war could be turned. 1st Lt. Caleb Layton, flying as Number 3 in White Flight of the 375th Squadron, reported sighting a pair of unidentified aircraft on "the deck." Layton and his wingman, 1st Lt. William H. Street, were detailed to investigate and when they dove to overtake the pair of eastward-flying aircraft, they quickly recognized them as FW-190s. Street provided cover as Layton rapidly downed both German fighters who were taken completely by surprise. As the two American pilots watched the second German fighter fall away and crash from an altitude of just 100 feet, an ME-109 suddenly appeared and attacked Layton's P-51 from five o'clock high. "Lt. Layton broke to the right … and started flying around hills and down in the gulleys," Street reported afterward. "The '109 followed him at about 500 yards and I was on the '109's tail. After turning around one of the hills, the '109 pulled up and I lost sight of Lt. Layton." While Street had not seen the enemy fighter firing on his leader, Layton's plane was critically damaged by the Messerschmitt, and a tell-tale pall of black smoke marked the place where his Mustang had gone in.[10] As the ME-109 pulled up to gain altitude, Street was able to score hits on the German fighter, which in turn crashed and burned.[11]

With the exception of the combat involving Lieutenants Layton and Street, the sweep of the Rhine area carried out by the 361st on December 23 turned up no more enemy aircraft. Using the French city of Metz as a checkpoint on the return trip, the Group's Mustangs set course southwest to land at St. Dizier as they had been briefed. Arriving shortly before 1600 hours that afternoon, the pilots were greeted by members of the Group's ground crew who, having been instructed to pack their personal belongings and tools, had been flown from Little Walden to St. Dizier in C-47s earlier that day. Commenting on the disruption caused by the move, Maj. Stryker described December 23, 1944 as a "mighty busy day in the history of this Group – men and baggage waited patiently on the line for transport to take them to the Continent … about half of the personnel got off today – rest will leave tomorrow weather permitting … everybody on the Station wants to go to the Continent with the other crew."[12]

While the excitement of transferring closer to the fighting front may have seemed an interesting change of pace for those of the ground echelon who were left behind at Little Walden, the realities of St. Dizier were soon evident to the new arrivals. A former *Luftwaffe* base which the 361st had actually dive-bombed during the previous spring, and on which other Allied

Ground crewman of the 361st digging fox holes in frozen ground, St. Dizier, December 1944. Their proximity to the fighting front during the Battle of the Bulge heightened the awareness of the potential need for defensive preparations. *Courtesy Russell A. Severson*

Mess kits in hand, 361st personnel line up for chow at St. Dizier. *Courtesy Russell A. Severson*

361st ground crewman servicing one of the Group's P-51s during a snow storm at St. Dizier. Note the absence of gloves, made necessary by the task at hand, despite the cold. *Courtesy Russell A. Severson*

outfits, as well as the Germans themselves, had left their respective marks, St. Dizier would be far more primitive than anything Group personnel had experienced thus far. Most of the buildings left standing were badly damaged, and living conditions were challenging. "At St. Dizier, we had no hangars, blisters, or any buildings on the line. Being an old German base, they more or less destroyed most of the buildings," recalled Russell Severson of the 374th Squadron who had been among the first ground personnel to arrive there,[13] Norman Baer, a crew chief in the 375th Squadron, described the field as "a wreck and covered with snow…we stayed in a building without a roof, door or windows," he added. "Three days after we arrived, the crew put a tarp over the roof – it helped keep out the snow, but not the cold."[14]

Ground crews and pilots alike would share the privations, living as best they could within the damaged buildings and eating meals cooked and served in the open air. Aircraft maintenance was frequently uncomfortable due to weather conditions at the best of times, and would be especially so for the Group's personnel at the forward French base. "In the cold and snow, maintenance was difficult," Norman Baer commented with regard to the routines necessary to keep the Group's P-51s flying. "Most times we had to work without gloves as it was close quarters. We had [sheepskin] boots, pants, and jackets … We never took them off for weeks as we lived in the open."[15]

A shortage of fresh water at St. Dizier was another difficulty added to the list. Among Russell Severson's worst memories of the nearly six weeks spent at St. Dizier that winter was the difficulty of bathing which, at times, necessitated desperate measures. "Imagine going to bed with grease and oil from the planes on your hands!" Having gone for an extended period in the same clothes, and then undergoing the disappointment of arriving at a recently installed field shower only to discover that it had run out of hot water, Severson and two other ground crewman decided one snowy evening that enough was enough. Acquiring a 75-gallon drop tank from the flight line, they proceeded to construct a bath tub in their makeshift sleeping quarters. "…[W]ith over a hundred guys watching, we split the wing tank in half at the weld. Then we added two more guys to our team and we started melting snow on our little pot-belly stove. Have you any idea how much snow has to be melted to get enough hot water to take a bath?" After flipping a coin to see in what order they would bathe, each man took his turn while the others added more water from the snow. "What a feeling to be clean again," Severson recalled, but cautioned, "You don't want to know the condition of that water after the fifth man finished!"[16]

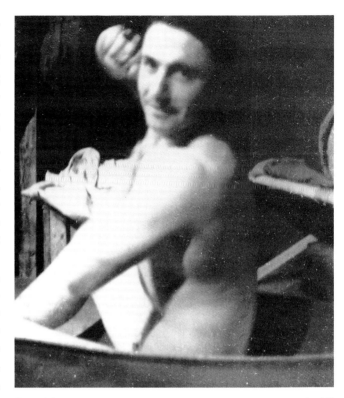

One of Sgt. Severson's team who turned a drop tank into a makeshift bathtub at St. Dizier. *Courtesy Russell A. Severson*

Christmas Eve 1944 brought the 361st's initial sortie from its new base in northeastern France. From St. Dizier's snow-covered dispersal points, ground crews prepared 36 of the Group's P-51s for a fighter sweep behind the "Bulge," which by that time had extended well into eastern Belgium. When the "Yellowjackets" took off from St. Dizier shortly after 1200 hours that afternoon, bound for a patrol of the Rhineland between Bonn and Trier, they were well aware that they would not be alone in the sky that day. December 24, 1944, the first day of relatively good weather since the start of the German offensive eight days earlier, would go down in history as the heaviest single day of operations by the 8th Air Force in the Second World War. Nearly 1,900 B-17s and B-24s, escorted by more than 800 fighters, pounded German airfields and communication centers behind the front dropping more than 5,000 tons of bombs. Virtually every aircraft capable of flying was put was into the air that Christmas Eve, redefining the concept of "maximum effort."[17]

Just prior to 1400 hours, as the "Yellowjackets" patrolled near the Rhine, hoping to catch German fighters responding to the massive raids in progress, a sharp dogfight in which both sides sustained losses took place. When 1st Lt. William J. Sykes, leading White Flight of the 375th Squadron, spotted unidentified aircraft silhouetted against the snow covered landscape

The 361st Fighter Group's snow-covered flight line at St. Dizier. Note the ground crewman carrying carbines. *Courtesy Russell A. Severson*

several thousand feet below the Group, he called out the bogies and took his flight down to investigate. The aircraft in question turned out to be ME-109s and Sykes called them out while tacking on to the nearest pair. Yellow Flight of the 376th Squadron, led by 1st Lt. Clarence E. Sullivan, also headed down to join in the fight and by the time they arrived, Lt. Sykes and his flight were fully engaged. Sullivan later reported that when he arrived on the scene, he saw "a yellow nose P-51 that must have been Lt. Sykes chasing two ME-109s. He was firing at the second one getting hits all around the canopy, coolant was streaming out and parts flying off. The ME-109 pulled straight up with Lt. Sykes following, still getting hits from about 50 yards range, while the first ME-109 made a sharp turn to the left." Sullivan followed the turning German and was able to score numerous hits on the Messerschmitt, which crashed.[18] Likewise, 1st Lt. George R. Vanden Heuvel of the 376th Squadron, was able to down an ME-109 at the start of the fight, but reported that after turning to rejoin his flight, he heard Sykes "call for 'some one to get this guy off my tail.' Down at my ten o'clock I saw an ME-109 firing at Lt. Sykes' plane from which pieces started flying off. Lt. Sykes called out that they got him, then jettisoned his canopy and bailed out the left side … I flew past [him] in his chute and he seemed to be alive and kicking," Vanden Heuvel added after returning to base.[19] Sykes was, in fact, suffering from wounds caused by German fire as he descended in his parachute, and was taken prisoner shortly after landing.[20]

Christmas 1944 passed all but unnoticed at St. Dizier as the 361st carried out four separate escort missions in squadron-sized units covering Martin B-26 Marauders of the 9th Air Force over the battle front. Back at Little Walden, a party for local children was held at the base, though preparations for the movement of additional personnel to the Continent went forward. Commenting in his unit diary the day before, Maj. Stryker wrote that the Group's personnel were "in an uproar, over half leaving and half staying here."[21]

December 26 saw the arrival of more of the Group's pilots and personnel at St. Dizier, and also four more missions – two fighter sweeps and two B-26 escorts over the "Bulge." On the morning fighter sweep, the 376th Squadron returned to the Rhineland in the hope of intercepting German aircraft bound for the battle front. Shortly before 1200 hours in the vicinity of Trier, 14 Mustangs of the 376th were patrolling at 17,000 feet when a group of 11 FW-190s passed in front of them on a perpendicular course, momentarily unaware of the Americans. The reaction was instantaneous as the 376th Squadron executed a diving turn to catch the German formation from behind. "We turned on them and they broke into us," reported 1st Lt. George Vanden Heuvel, who was credited with one FW-190 destroyed, and another shared with Capt. Jay Ruch.[22] The fight quickly devolved into a series of pursuits as the German pilots, in most cases, headed for the deck. Six were shot down without loss, and the 376th Squadron's pilots used to good effect the lead-calculating K-14 gun sight.

Introduced in the spring of 1944, the K-14 gun sight was fairly advanced for its time. It consisted principally of a piece of slanted, clear glass centered above the instrument panel directly in the pilot's line of sight. Onto the glass was projected a center dot of yellow light, known as a "pipper," which was surrounded by a circle formed of eight diamond shaped dots. Once the pilot set the known wingspan of an enemy plane using a knob on the sight itself, he then centered the pipper on his target and, using the control knob mounted on the throttle handle, expanded or contracted the diamonds so that they continually bracketed the target. The K-14 automatically calculated the amount of lead needed for the range of the target, and so long as the pilot kept the pipper centered on the enemy aircraft, and enclosed it tightly within the diamonds, he had an excellent chance of scoring hits.[23]

1st Lt. David Overholt, leading Yellow Flight, was able to bring down one of the Focke-Wulfs at extreme range after latching onto the enemy fighter at 800 yards distance. "He made a sharp turn to the left and I closed my pippers on the gun sight down as small as they would go and fired … I finished firing at about 600 yards and 65 degrees deflection." Seeing his bullets strike the German fighter repeatedly, he followed it visually as it went into a dive and struck the ground.[24] 1st Lt. Homer Powell also used the K-14 to its full potential as he followed an FW-190 into a steep climbing turn. "I put the pipper on him at about 45 degrees deflection and fired one long burst at 200 yards. He started smoking, burst into flame and spiraled aimlessly toward the ground."[25]

In the days following Christmas, American divisions fought their way into besieged Bastogne in addition to driving the Germans back and gradually retaking the ground lost since December 16. On December 27, elements of the 361st provided close escort to B-26 Marauders of the 9th Air Force as they attacked targets in Luxembourg, and accompanied C-47 transport planes over Bastogne where they dropped much-needed supplies and reinforcements to the 101st Airborne Division there. In the days which followed, a series of uneventful fighter sweeps were fielded by the 361st, including three on New Years Day 1945. While January 1 was an extremely memorable day for many American air units at forward bases which experienced the massive *Luftwaffe* raid known as Operation *Bodenplatte* ("base plate"), the "Yellowjackets" would see no enemy action that day. The *Bodenplatte* attacks, which involved an extraordinary 900 German aircraft of which approximately 30% failed to return, were intended to deal a surprise knockout blow to Allied airfields in Belgium and the Netherlands, but St. Dizier was not involved.[26] When the 361st ventured into Germany on three fighter sweeps later that day, the skies were clear and no traces of the *Bodenplatte* attackers were seen.

Four separate missions involving the "Yellowjackets" lifted off from St. Dizier on January 2, 1945. On the last of these, a late afternoon fighter sweep of the areas between Bonn, Frankfurt and Saarbrucken, the Group experienced one of its last multi-victory dogfights of the war when eight ME-109s were spotted and engaged by the 375th Squadron. When unidentified aircraft were sighted at 9 o'clock to the 375th, an extended pursuit began as the Germans dove away. "We turned to investigate and they poured on the coal with us all out behind them,"

Martin B-26 Marauders in formation. This type of medium bomber equipped numerous 9th Air Force bomb groups and was often escorted by the 361st during the last five months of the war in Europe. *National Archives*

reported 1st Lt. Anthony Maurice. "We closed on them west of Stuttgart."[27]

1st Lt. Donald L. Farrar, flying as Yellow Two of the 375th, was able to down an ME-109 as his flight leader overshot one of the German fighters then desperately fleeing the Americans. "I got in a 4 second burst from 400 yards," he reported after returning to St. Dizier, "and observed hits on both wings and fuselage. A second short burst from 300 yards … blew off his left wing and the enemy aircraft crashed into the deck in a mass of flames."[28] In all, five confirmed "kills" were awarded

Lt. Robert O. Adams of the 375th Squadron who destroyed an FW-190 during the Misburg mission of November 26, 1944, and who was lost in combat on January 25, 1945.

to 375th's Squadron pilots in the action, including one to 2nd Lt. James J. Sullivan of Red Flight who, unable to engage any of the Messerschmitts initially spotted, returned with his wingman to the vicinity of a German airfield which he had sighted a short time earlier. "As I approached the field, I saw an ME-109 at about 100 feet on a course of 90 degrees to me. I pulled up to 400 yards and opened up with a long burst closing to 150 yards 90 degrees deflection just as he started to turn to the left. I observed hits on the fuselage and cockpit area as he continued his turn. Almost immediately, however, he dove into the deck, exploded and burned."[29]

A lull in operations brought on by rain, snow and fog kept the "Yellowjackets" grounded until January 10 when combat operations resumed. In a total of 36 missions flown during the month, 14 were fighter sweeps and patrols, 8 were medium bomber escort missions and 9 were fighter-bomber sorties in which the Group's Mustangs, fitted with bombs instead of drop tanks, specifically went after ground targets in and behind the fighting front. On a notable fighter-bomber mission on January 15, 1945, a number of German railroad tunnels were blocked by pilots of the 361st using "skip-bombing" techniques. Only five of the Group's assigned missions were to escort heavy bombers, though one carried out on January 13 was notable as the first occasion when the Group's Mustangs accompanied RAF heavy bombers flying a daylight raid on Saarbrucken.[30] On January 25, 2nd Lt. Paul Dougherty and Flight Officer Wesley Hart of the 375th Squadron were able to catch a twin-engined ME-110 flying just above a layer of ground-haze while patrolling near Mannheim, sending it down in flames. On a later mission that day, 2nd Lt. Robert J. Farney, also of the 375th, was able to down a lone ME-109 hedgehopping some ten miles northeast of Speyer. These two were the sole encounters with the *Luftwaffe* for the entire month after January 2. During the same period, two pilots, both in the 375th Squadron, were lost. During a mission on January 22, Capt. Alton B. Snyder dropped down to strafe a German truck in the vicinity of Trier, but was hit by ground fire. Though shot at again while

375th Squadron armorers check the guns on a P-51D prior to a mission. Note the sheepskin flight jackets prized by the ground crews but by relatively few pilots who found the P-51's cockpit heating system more than adequate. *Courtesy Russell A. Severson*

making a forced landing, Snyder made a belly landing in a field and was later taken prisoner.[31] Not as fortunate two days later was 1st Lt. Robert G. Adams whose P-51 was hit by German fire near Mannheim and crashed before he could bail out.[32]

While the 361st remained at St. Dizier through the end of January, the crisis for he Allies on the western front had ended and the spirit of optimism that characterized the Allied camp at the beginning of December 1944 returned to an extent, following the German defeat in the "Bulge." Though the Allies would not allow themselves to again be lulled into a false sense of security, Germany was clearly on its last legs, and the end was in sight as the spring of 1945 approached.

NOTES

[1] Stryker, Unit Diary Entry for December 1, 1944.

[2] John F. O'Mara, "Station History for December 1944, Station F-165 (361st Fighter Group)." January 1, 1945.

[3] Jerome R. Mau, "Encounter Report," December 2, 1944.

[4] Roger A. Freeman, *The Mighty Eighth War Diary* (New York: Janes, 1981), p. 398.

[5] Stryker, December 16, 1944.

[6] Ibid., December 17, 1944.

[7] Henry B. Lederer, Interview with the Author, November 13, 1995.

[8] O'Mara, p. 6.

[9] *The Mighty Eighth War Dairy*, P. 398.

[10] William H. Street, "Sworn Statement" contained in Missing Aircrew Report # 11461, December 29, 1944.

[11] William H. Street, "Encounter Report," December 23, 1944.

[12] Stryker, December 23, 1944.

[13] Russell A. Severson, Correspondence with The Author, October 18, 1995.

[14] Norman Baer, Correspondence with the Author, 1996.

[15] Ibid.

[16] Severson, Ibid.

[17] *The Mighty Eighth War Diary* , pp. 399-400.

[18] Clarence E. Sullivan, "Combat Report," December 24, 1944.

[19] George R. Vanden Heuvel, "Combat Report," December 24, 1944.

[20] Steve Gotts, *Little Friends: A Pictorial History of the 361st Fighter Group in World War II* (Dallas: Taylor Publishing Company, 1993), p. 116.

[21] Stryker, December 24, 1944.

[22] Vanden Heuvel, "Combat Report," December 26, 1944.

[23] Clarence E. Anderson, *To Fly and Fight* (New York: St. Martins Press, 1990), pp. 96-97.

[24] David Overholt, "Combat Report," December 26, 1944.

[25] Homer G. Powell, "Combat Report, December 26, 1944.

[26] Danny S. Parker, *To Win the Winter Sky* (Conshocken, Pennsylvania: Combined Books, 1994), pp. 447-448.

[27] Anthony Maurice, "Encounter Report," January 2, 1945.

[28] Donald J. Farrar, "Encounter Report," January 2, 1945.

[29] James J. Sullivan, "Encounter Report," January 2, 1945.

[30] John M. Ellis, "Headquarters 361st Fighter Group, Office of Intelligence Officer, Historical Report," March 27, 1945.

[31] Missing Aircrew Report # 11918, January 23, 1945.

[32] Missing Aircrew Report # 11917, January 25, 1945.

eight

Spring of Victory

February 1945 brought transition once more to the 361st Fighter Group. While the majority of the air echelon had moved to St. Dizier the previous month, much of the headquarters and support staff, along with a few pilots, still remained at Little Walden where activities were largely confined to airlifting supplies and spare parts to the Group's French base. In late January, orders were received specifying that the 361st would change bases once again, this time moving north to a Belgian field at Chievres known as Airdrome A-84. Unlike the move to St. Dizier, the Belgian transfer would involve the entire Group, including the support elements at Little Walden, who were alerted to make preparations for transfer to the Continent.

The air echelon at St. Dizier departed for Chievres on February 1 and their ground crews followed closely behind in C-47s. Amid much hurried preparation, the movement of the remainder of the Group at Little Walden began on the afternoon of February 4 when an advanced party was airlifted to the Belgian base. Over the next two days, the remainder of the Group began what would be a much slower transfer. Organized into road convoys of heavy equipment, trucks and other vehicles, they departed Little Walden for Southampton, where they crossed to France by ship, and through a series of road journeys, route marches and train rides through France and into Belgium, finally arrived at Chievres on February 15.[1] "Someone once said that when taking a trip, half the fun can be in getting there," remarked Bernard J. Redden, a former crew chief in the 375th Squadron. "Such was not the case for those of us who went to Belgium in February 1945," he added. "Going by motor convoy … thence by Channel boat to LeHavre, we eventually wound up at a train station to complete the journey by rail. We were dismayed when we learned we would be traveling in the infamous '40x8's' [French boxcars with a carrying capacity of 40 men or 8 horses]. We were packed into each car so that finding a position of comfort for any length of time was impossible…it was quite an experience – not one we'd wish to repeat!"[2]

The base at Chievres, like St. Dizier, was a former *Luftwaffe* field, though, overall, the accommodations were far better. While some personnel were assigned to "tent cities" nearby, the pilots and headquarters personnel were accommodated at a number of chateaus in nearby Brugelette and Cambron-Casteau, or in the town of Lens.[3] Chievres compared very favorably to St. Dizier in the eyes of former 374th Squadron Crew Chief Russell Severson. "The crews really liked this base," he recalled, adding that there was "plenty of water, more food … [and] we had little hangars to work on the planes in bad weather. We even made a few engine changes," a task that was impossible in the spartan conditions at St. Dizier.[4]

As soon as the "Yellowjackets" established themselves at A-84, the nearby civilian population wasted no time satisfying their curiosity about the newly arrived Americans. They were worse off than the civilian population in England, and more numerous than those near St. Dizier. "This was our first experience with little neighborhood kids digging in our garbage cans for food," Russell Severson recalled years later. "Then our cooks started making more food than our guys could eat to feed these kids. They were all small for their age, and most wore wooden shoes like the Dutch." Severson went on to add that "Some of our men got very close to local families and learned to speak pretty good French in a short time. For a bar of G.I. soap, the women would do our laundry. Naturally, we gave them all the food we could sneak out of the mess hall."[5] The Group's Historical Officer, writing in March 1945, reported that "The civilians in both Lens and Brugelette opened their

Pilots of the 376th Squadron return from a mission in the spring of 1945. Second from the right is Lt. Harry Chapman; just to his left, Lt. George Vanden Heuvel. *Courtesy Harry M. Chapman*

houses to the Yanks and from the day of arrival the children were asking for 'chewing gum.' Some of them came out with the line 'Chewing gum pour moi, chocolate pour Mama, et cigarettes pour Papa' – in any event the kids used all the items. Soap spoke better than money...." Comparing the wartime experience of the population near Little Walden with that of Chievres, he went on to write that "After observing the rather strict adherence to rationing in England, it was a shock to a lot of the men to find the magnitude of black market operations in Belgium. The Belgians say that they have the best black market in the world and after a few days in the country one would not dare question that statement. Brussels has absolutely everything for sale – if you have the price, and the smaller communities are almost as good."[6]

Chievres, which became known as Station 181, was shared with the 352nd Fighter Group, another 8th Air Force outfit which had made a name for itself in the long-range escort battles of the previous 18 months. Even while the move of the support units from Little Walden was underway, the air echelon of the 361st continued operations without missing a beat.

Unlike January, February would see the "Yellowjackets" engaged almost exclusively in heavy bomber escort over Germany. Targets deemed appropriate for strategic attacks at that stage of the war were largely confined to synthetic oil plants

and related industries, and German transportation hubs – especially railroad marshalling yards. The special targeting of transportation centers was aimed at crippling the ability of German ground forces to continue their stubborn resistance to Allied advances in both east and west. Though the borders of the Reich were rapidly shrinking, and the resources of the *Luftwaffe* continued to dwindle each day, German defiance in the face ap-

361st ground personnel photographed with the wreckage of a German V-1 rocket at Chievres, Belgium. Note the intact building in the background which was a welcome change from St. Dizier. *Courtesy Russell A. Severson*

proaching defeat continued. German fighter interceptions became more rare, though intense flak barrages would continue to be thrown up at the raiders right through until the last days of the war.

A total of 23 missions were carried out by the 361st during February, and enemy aircraft were practically non-existent. With the exception of an HE-111 shot down while hedge-hopping on February 11, no claims against enemy aircraft would be made throughout the month. Two pilots, both from the 374th Squadron, would be lost during operations in February. On February 14, as elements of the Group made a second sweep of the Munster area after escorting bombers out, 2nd Lt. Thomas A. Kneifel of the 374th Squadron was forced to bail out of his P-51 when he ran out of fuel.[7] Twelve days later, 2nd Lt. Richard E. Chandler's Mustang caught fire after strafing a German train, forcing him to parachute out east of Gottingen.[8] Fortunately, both pilots survived their bailouts and relatively brief stints as prisoners.

Operations in March 1945 would bring practically the last aerial combats of the war for the pilots of the 361st. On March 9, the Group would experience its final encounters with piston-engined German fighters while carrying out a target area support sweep near Wiesbaden in western Germany. Shortly before noon, as the Group approached a homeward-bound formation of B-26 medium bombers, small numbers of enemy aircraft were spotted making attacks on a nearby formation. Capt. Anthony Maurice, leading the 375th Squadron, reported afterward that he at first noticed a formation of B-26s out to the side of the briefed course, and also saw "4 ships diving vertically in the rear of this formation. We were about five miles away so I dropped tanks and went over to investigate in a hurry." Arriving on the scene, Maurice immediately began chasing an FW-190 which was in the process of shooting down a P-51. Though he quickly found himself in an ideal position to bring down the German fighter, Capt. Maurice would have to make allowances for the unrestrained zeal of a Mustang pilot from another group. "A P-51 with a yellow or orange spinner then stuck his nose in ... As we both fired, the enemy aircraft's canopy was jettisoned and I was forced to cease firing immediately to prevent hitting the '51 which slid past and in front of me about 25 yards away."[9]

Indicative of the skill level and morale among the *Luftwaffe* pilots at the time, none of the B-26s were lost, and most of the German fighters dove away when the Mustangs of the 361st arrived on the scene. Two FW-190s, however, fell to the guns of the 374th Squadron during the fight. 1st Lt. Barry Hicks claimed one of these victories after spotting German fighters behind the rear box of B-26s. "We dropped our tanks and closed

361st personnel dine in the open air at Chievres. *Courtesy Russell A. Severson*

Capt. Anthony Maurice of the 375th Fighter Squadron photographed at Chievres in the spring of 1945. *Courtesy Leonard A. Wood*

in on one flight," Hicks reported later that day. Chasing the German fighters, which immediately dove away, Hicks latched onto an FW-190 which he pursued down through a layer of undercast, firing as he went. "I came out at 2,000 feet. I overshot him and cut my throttle to get behind. His engine was smoking and he ditched his canopy and bailed out." Climbing back through the clouds on instruments, Hicks rejoined his flight for the trip back.[10]

1st Lt. Thomas J. Moore, flying in the number 3 position of Lt. Hicks' flight, also claimed an FW-190 destroyed during the engagement. Chasing one of the German fighters, Moore was able to score numerous hits after holding the gun trigger down in several long bursts. After firing some 1,650 rounds at the German fighter, it "burst into flames and started a slow split-s into the overcast at about 350 mph."[11]

While the "Yellowjackets'" main effort under Lt. Col. Caviness was still airborne on March 9, other portions of the Group provided additional escort to bombers over Germany. While no enemy aircraft could be claimed destroyed by these sections, an ME-262 jet fighter was shot at from extreme range near Cologne, and another was spotted in the vicinity of Koblenz.[12] These were the first sightings of the German jets by pilots of the 361st since the fall, but they would not be the last. In the weeks that followed, combat with these advanced German fighters in the dying days of the *Luftwaffe* would be repeated numerous times.

On March 21 the "Yellowjackets" faced several attacks by German jets while escorting B-17s against the aircraft plant at Plauen in eastern Germany. At 0945, 1st Lt. Richard D. Anderson was flying as Red 3 in the 375th Squadron when "2 flights of ME-262s attacked the bombers from 6 o'clock high." Anderson spotted one of the jets which seemed to be lagging behind the others, possibly with engine trouble, and he began a steep climb at full power in an attempt to intercept it, but stalled out before he could close the range. "As I started down from my stall, one of the enemy aircraft which had made a pass on the bombers had started a turn to the left. I cut the ME-262 off in his turn and started firing at about 500 yards, 90 degrees deflection. The enemy aircraft started to make a head-on pass, but then reversed his turn putting me on his tail." Though still at extreme range, Anderson was able to fire from directly behind his target, apparently getting some strikes on the jet, whose pilot bailed out.[13]

Ten minutes after Lt. Anderson's combat, 2nd Lt. Harry Chapman, flying the number 3 position in Blue Flight of the 376th Squadron, was also able to claim a victory against a jet. When a flight of four ME-262s made a pass on a box of B-17s, one of them turned head-on at Chapman's flight giving him a split-second opportunity to fire at close range. "The number 4 man of the enemy aircraft flight kept turning into us until he was making a head-on pass at me. With a K-14 sight set at 2400 feet, I put the pip on his canopy and fired a 1 to 1 1/2 second burst …" Some of Chapman's .50 caliber rounds apparently found a fuel tank as the Messerschmitt was transformed into a fireball as it passed.[14]

Describing the event many years later, Chapman remarked that the encounter happened so fast that, at first, he had not been sure if the jets were, in fact, enemy planes. "We were escorting bombers and we had just crossed over them and gotten on the other side" when a flight of four unidentified aircraft appeared high above the formation. "I thought they were

The underside of a German ME-262 in flight, as it makes a hard, banking turn. This example was captured and returned to the United States for evaluation after the war. *National Archives*

Lt. Harry M. Chapman of the 376th Squadron in flight gear. *Courtesy Harry M. Chapman*

friendlies … and all of a sudden they started to dive down and started shooting at this box of bombers. Three of those four kept shooting and when they finished shooting they just went straight on down and left. The fourth one started turning into us, and I was the one who turned into him. I still got the impression it was a P-51 – [the jet engines] looked like two drop tanks hanging, and before I recognized him as a '262, he started firing at me and I already had the gun sight on him but I hadn't starting firing….When he started shooting I thought 'it doesn't make much difference – friendly or enemy if he's going to shoot at me I'm going to shoot back.' So I opened fire at about the same time and…he burst into flames and went past me and I didn't get a scratch so maybe my gun sight was better than his. We had a very good gun sight for that time, [the] K-14, it did a good job…[the ME-262]was probably doing around 400 and I was doing my regular 280, 300 – whatever we cruised at – so the combined speed was rather fast for those times."[15]

Three days after the combats of Lieutenants Anderson and Chapman, the 361st would have its most intense day of operations during the spring of 1945 as the Allies launched Operation Varsity, the crossing of the Rhine River. With elements of the Group airborne from 0600 that morning until 1900 hours that evening, the "Yellowjackets" put up no fewer than six separate missions patrolling German airspace east of the Rhine in the hope of intercepting *Luftwaffe* reaction to the crossings. While no German aircraft came into contact with elements of the 361st, Capt. Russell D. Wade of the 375th Squadron became one of the last few of the Group's pilots to lose his life during the war. While flying in the vicinity of Dortmund, Capt. Wade, leading Blue Flight of the 375th, dropped down to low-level in search of targets of opportunity. "As we were flying west, we approached the town of Soest when we were fired upon by heavy flak," reported 1st Lt. Richard Anderson who had downed the jet on March 21st, and who was flying in Wade's flight. "We immediately turned south for evasive action and in doing so went over a large lake 6 miles south of Soest. From a dam at the east end of the lake," continued Lt. Anderson, "we were fired on by light flak. We turned east again to avoid the fire and Capt. Wade started to climb. I could see he had been hit for dark gray smoke started to pour from the engine. At approximately 2500 feet, he jettisoned his canopy and rolled the ship over. I saw him fall from the plane, but his chute was a streamer; and it appeared as though some part of his airplane had caught in his chute. I never did see the chute open, and Captain Wade was spinning furiously."[16]

The days following Capt. Wade's death near the Moehne Lake would be an intensely hectic period for the 361st. During the final week of March 1945, eleven missions were carried

Lt. Robert G. Young, Jr., of the 374th Squadron photographed after returning from an escort mission to Berlin during the last week of March, 1945. Note the special identification tag worn around his neck at that stage of the war. On one side of the I.D. tag was an American flag, and on the reverse side was an inscription in Russian identifying the wearer as an American flier. The proximity of the Red Army in the East necessitated this measure in the spring of 1945. *National Archives*

out by the Group ranging from fighter sweeps to escort of heavy and medium bombers in squadron and group strength. On both March 30 and 31, the "Yellowjackets" bore the brunt of repeated attacks on their bombers by ME-262s. One jet would be destroyed and several more would be damaged as the Group's pilots did their best to stave off the attacks with their outclassed but more numerous Mustangs. Making passes on the bombers at high speed, the ME-262s were extremely difficult for the escorting Mustangs to counter. The tactics which promised the best chances of success – protecting the bombers – were to turn into the attacking jets forcing them to turn away, or gaining the best possible speed in a diving pursuit. If a P-51 pilot was lucky, he could close momentarily to get in a quick shot from moderate to long range. If he were very lucky, a jet would execute a turning movement allowing him to close the range by turning inside of his target. In all cases, success required split-second timing and anticipation on the part of the escorting fighters.

On March 30, the 361st provided free-lance support as over 1300 B-17s and B-24s carried out raids against U-Boat yards and other industrial targets in northern Germany.[17] During an afternoon patrol over the Schleswig Peninsula, 1st Lt. Kenneth J. Scott, leading Blue Flight of the 376th Squadron, had a rare opportunity to gain a good firing position behind a lone ME-262 which attacked the 376th from 11 o'clock high. "He was diving at about a 45 degree angle on a course which would have taken him across the front of my flight," Scott recounted after returning to base, "so I started a diving turn to the right to build up enough speed to catch him. I succeeded in cutting him off, and when I was about 60 degrees to him and 200 yards behind, the jet pulled up in a climbing turn to the right which gave me another chance to shorten the distance between us. I began firing from about a 10 degree deflection and 200 yards range. Just as strikes registered … the pilot stood up and bailed out."[18]

The following day more German jets appeared as the 361st escorted B-24s of the Second Bomb Division against the railroad marshalling yard at Bremen. Several claims of damage were made by Group's Mustangs as formations of the jets were repeatedly forced to break away in head-on passes, though none of them fell to the "Yellowjackets" that day. One pilot, Flight Officer Dean E. Jackson of the 374th Squadron did not return from the mission and was last seen following his leader, 1st Lt. John Cearley, in an extended pursuit of an ME-262. After landing at Chievres, Lt. Cearley reported that during the fight over Bremen, he and Flight Officer Jackson had spotted one of the jets executing a wide turn well below them and immediately dove to attack it. "We had dropped tanks so we had an excellent opportunity to cut him off with about 10,000 feet altitude on him. So I put the nose down in a 45 degree dive at which time I checked Flight Officer Jackson who was OK and following me down. We quickly built up air speed of 500 MPH

and succeeded in drawing up to just out of range of the jet which was now headed for a broken layer of cumulus cloud." Chasing the jet through the cloud layer, Lt. Cearley emerged below it to fire on the German fighter which then accelerated and sped away. When Cearley broke off the chase, he discovered that Flight Officer Jackson was nowhere to be seen and was ultimately presumed killed.[19]

Early April 1945 would bring the hectic activity to the 361st at Chievres which only another change of base could generate. Receiving secret orders on April 3, the Group undertook preparations for transfer from Belgium back to Little Walden. Like the previous moves, the operation began with a departure by air of an advance party whose primary job would be to prepare the base for the bulk of the Group's arrival several days later. On April 6, B-24s of the 2nd Bomb Division began arriving at Chievres in the role of troop transports, ferrying personnel back to England.[20] Russell Severson of the 374th Squadron was among the first of the ground crews to be flown back to Little Walden in a B-24, a flight which he recalled vividly due to confusion over wind direction on landing. "I was in the very first B-24 to come over our Little Walden runways," Severson described years later. "There was no one in the tower and … no wind sock or smoke. So naturally, the pilot picked the wrong wind direction and landed downwind and shot off the end of the runway. I was standing at the waist gun position and could see huge pieces of rubber flying off the tire – I imagine the pilot and co-pilot were standing on the brakes. However, no harm done – they towed him on to the runway the next day and he went home."[21] The B-24 flights continued daily for several days, and on April 10, they were augmented by C-46 and C-47 transports which took much of the heavy equipment to England. A road convoy of Group ve-

A 374th Squadron P-51 taxis along the perimeter track at Station F-165 Little Walden, Essex, to which the Group returned in early April 1945. *Courtesy Harry M. Chapman*

hicles left Chievres on April 12, and was transported across the Channel in Navy tank landing ships (LST's), ultimately arriving at Little Walden on April 15. "It might be of interest for the record," wrote the Group Historical Officer, "that there were very few in favor of returning to England. Even though we were only stationed in Belgium for approximately two months, all of the personnel seemed to prefer life there to that of England."[22]

While preparations for the return to Little Walden were underway on April 4, the "Yellowjackets" accompanied the B-24s of the 2nd Bomb Division on a mission which directly targeted Parchim airfield, known to be an active base for the *Luftwaffe's* jets. During the escort, the B-24s were hit repeatedly by ME-262s, and the pilots of the 361st were called on once again to put up a hectic defense against the much faster German fighters. Positioning themselves several thousand feet above the bomber formations, the Group's pilots awaited the appearance of the Messerschmitts. Ten miles south of Hamburg, as the B-24s were enroute to the target, 8 ME-262s appeared at 7 o'clock level to the bombers and commenced attack runs. 1st Lt. William H. Street, leading one of the Group's two escort formations, engaged two of the jets in rapid succession, though he could only claim damage to the enemy aircraft. Diving on the Messerschmitts as they made their first attack run, Street used his height advantage to gain firing position. "I made a steep pass at the jets and closed very fast, almost overshooting," he reported later that day. After firing a 5-second burst at his target, the jet sped away, its left engine belching a puff of black smoke indicating possible damage from one or more hits. Lt. Street's second opportunity occurred when another ME-262 pulled up from below him, passing directly in front of his P-51 at only 75 yards range. So quickly did the jet pull away, however, the he was only able to hold it in his gun sight long enough to score a few strikes on the fuselage.[23]

The story was much the same among all the pilots of the Group who engaged the jets on April 4, including 1st Lt. Leo Gendron of the 375th Squadron who claimed damage to four separate ME-262s in different combats during the course of the escort.[24] Overall, some 11 damaged jets would be claimed by the Group on the mission to Parchim airfield.

The final aerial encounter of the war for the 361st Group took place 5 days after the Parchim mission as the 2nd Bomb Division again targeted active jet airfields. During the escort, 2nd Lt. James T. Sloan of the 374th Squadron was first able to damage an ME-262 which passed beneath him at high speed before downing a B-24 in the bomber stream. Tracking the same jet through the bombers, Sloan elected to wait for a second chance to engage the German. "My rate of closure was too

Living quarters and mess hall at Little Walden. *Courtesy Harry M. Chapman*

slow to warrant chasing him," he reported after landing at Little Walden that day, "so I climbed … to an altitude of 25,000 feet and waited for him to make another pass. When he came in again, I cut him off and split-s'd down on him and fired. I did not observe hits, but he did not make his pass on the bombers." After climbing back to 25,000 feet, Sloan spotted another ME-262 below him making a pass on the bombers and dove his P-51 after the German fighter. Attaining an airspeed in excess of 500 MPH, Sloan opened fire at close range observing that the jet "went into a slight dive which developed into a spin. He crashed approximately 18 miles from the target."[25]

Sloan's flight leader, 1st Lt. Merne L. Waldusky, had his hands full as the jets made passes on the bombers, but he was later able to confirm that Lt. Sloan was seen in pursuit of the jet "going almost straight down. I saw some very good hits on the jet but didn't have time to observe the results."[26] Ultimately credited with destroying the Messerschmitt, James T. Sloan would have the distinction of obtaining the 361st's very last aerial victory of the war.

Operations from Little Walden continued virtually every day for the 361st into the third week of April 1945. As heavy and medium bombers attacked a diminishing number of targets in a rapidly shrinking area of Nazi-controlled Germany, the "Yellowjackets" continued close escort duties, or carried out free-lance patrols in search of targets of opportunity. On April 15, Lt. Col. Roy B. Caviness officially succeeded Col. Junius W. Dennison to become the Group's last wartime Commander – a fitting choice considering that Caviness had been with the Group since its earliest days at Richmond and had served continually in key posts. Now, he would lead the 361st in its last days of combat operations in the ETO.

While no further German planes rose against the 361st during the remainder of April, the "Yellowjackets" would continue to carry out hazardous missions and would lose pilots in their waning days of operations. On April 16, the Group escorted B-24s attacking the railroad marshalling yard at Landshut, and on a separate mission, carried out strafing attacks against a number of German airfields. Led by Lt. Col. Caviness, the 30 P-51s assigned to attack Reichersburg, Kircham, Pocking and finally Muhldorf airfields were able to claim 17 German planes destroyed on the ground between 1550 and 1620 hours. The score might have been higher, but many of the German aircraft had no fuel aboard and failed to burn despite repeated damage. Killed on the low-level mission were two pilots. At Reichersburg, 2nd Lt. Delmer Ford of the 376th Squadron disappeared into the smoke from burning planes which blanketed the field, and became separated from his flight. His element leader, 1st Lt. Allen Chalmers, reported later that he believed Ford was hit over the neighboring Kircham Airfield. "As I came off to the northeast of Reichersburg, I heard Lt. Ford calling in numerous aircraft on the field … He was firing as he talked." After his flight reformed, Chalmers attempted to contact Ford by radio, but no answer was received.[27] 2nd Lt. Russell E. Kenoyer, also of the 376th Squadron, did not pull up from a strafing run by his flight on Pocking Airfield. 1st Lt. Harry Chapman of Kenoyer's flight later reported seeing a crashed and burning P-51 on the airdrome and assumed that it was his plane when Lt. Kenoyer failed to reform.[28]

The following day, the 375th and 376th Squadrons carried out a strafing attack on Pilzen and Eger airdromes in Czechoslovakia, while the 374th Squadron escorted B-24s against nearby railroad targets. During the strafing attacks, a total of five enemy planes were claimed destroyed and another seven damaged, though the targets were sparse. Shortly after 1500 hours, 1st Lt. Walter Stevens of the 375th Squadron would have the distinction of destroying the Group's last enemy plane when he spotted a JU-188 at Eger airdrome and set it on fire on a low-level strafing run. While Stevens was commencing his attack on the German bomber, 1st Lt. Robert B. Wolfe was seen to crash into a line of trees on the edge of the field, his P-51 immediately bursting into flames. Though the cause – pilot error or flak – was uncertain, Wolfe was the last man to lose his life in combat with the 361st Fighter Group.[29]

The final combat mission of the war for the "Yellowjackets" took place on April 20, 1945 when the Group put up 55 Mustangs in support of B-24s attacking railroad bridges and marshalling yards in central Germany.[30] Following this sortie, operations at Little Walden went into a distinctive wind-down as all personnel awaited what everyone knew could not be prolonged – the surrender of Germany.

Like the 361st after April 20, the 8th Air Force began to suspend combat operations against a dwindling number of

An ME-262 photographed at extreme close range by the gun camera of a US fighter. During the last weeks of March and the first weeks of April 1945, the pilots of the 361st would repeatedly engage German jets while escorting bombers over the rapidly shrinking Nazi-controlled parts of Germany. *National Archives*

worthwhile targets in the Nazi-controlled areas of Germany. On April 21, some 400 heavy bombers attacked marshalling yards and airfields in Bavaria, and then following a lull, a final mission by the "heavies" to targets in southern Germany and Czechoslovakia took place on April 25. Six days later, in a kind of "swords to ploughshares" transformation, B-17s of the 3rd Bomb Division began dropping food parcels over Holland as the Dutch sought to recover from their final hard winter of occupation. These operations continued until May 7 – the eve of final victory for the Allies.[31]

"The month of May was very quiet and uneventful on this station," wrote the 361st Group's Historical Officer. "V-E Day was by far the biggest event of the month and, as in most places, it didn't come as any surprise."[32] At 1000 hours on the morning of May 8, Lt. Col. Caviness announced over Little Walden's loudspeaker system the end of hostilities in Europe after which "for the balance of the day, all personnel enjoyed the free beer and games arranged by Special Service."[33]

The news of the German surrender was welcome, but for many in the ground echelon it was not a source of unrestrained rejoicing. As Robert O. Bland, a former crew chief in the 374th Squadron put it, "We were slated to go to the Pacific Theater and were not really 'gung ho' about the end of the war in Europe. We were happy it was done, but we had another tour staring us in the face. Keep in mind that the enlisted men had been there from the word 'go' and were committed…to 'the duration plus six.'"[34]

For pilots who had been with the Group for the majority of a combat tour, returning home was a matter of waiting out the military machine which, by process of a point system based on combat hours, time overseas, etc., dictated whom would be sent home first. Those with over 85 points when all variables were factored in would be sent home beginning in June. Among the relatively new members of the Group's air echelon, the news of the German surrender had hardly worn off when training routines made their appearance. The United States was still at war in the Pacific and as the weeks of May gave way to June, the Group prepared for an anticipated deployment to the Far East. At the end of the month, however, it was learned that the 361st was scheduled for shipment home in September 1945.[35]

Ultimately, the last elements of the 361st Fighter Group departed Little Walden in late October bound for Southampton and a sea voyage home. Arriving at Camp Kilmer, New Jersey, the Group was officially deactivated on November 10, 1945.

Like most Americans, the pilots, ground crews, and support staff who had served with the 361st Fighter Group were eager to pick up where they had left off when their lives were interrupted by the war. While some stayed on in the Air Force, most returned home to begin careers, or continue their education through the opportunities available through the G.I. Bill. As time went on, however, they would begin to look back and to consider what their war experience had meant, and what, overall, the 361st had achieved.

"The 361st was not a 'glory' outfit," wrote former pilot Billy D. Welch looking back many years later.[36] True, the "Yellowjackets" did not lead the 8th Fighter Command in the

The 376th Squadron pilot's ready room at Little Walden. Note the prominent section titled "Pacific Headlines" on the bulletin board at left. *Courtesy Harry M. Chapman*

numbers of enemy aircraft destroyed, or the number of high-scoring aces within its ranks. The 361st, however, had its share of aces, and left behind its share of pilots who did their duty and never returned home as a result. Most importantly, the "Yellowjackets" never lost sight of their primary mission: to protect the heavy bombers which were the main weapons that the 8th Air Force employed in its war against Nazi Germany. Without the effort and sacrifice of the pilots and personnel of fighter groups like the 361st, the major contribution to the defeat of Germany made by the 8th Air Force would not have been possible.

376th Squadron P-51s in flight over England, summer 1945. Note the letters "WW" on the tail surface of the P-51B in the center. "WW" designated this aircraft as "war weary" meaning it was not to be flown in combat. The stresses caused by hard use in operations over time – heavy payloads, high speeds, etc., took a toll on the airframe. *Courtesy Harry M. Chapman.*

NOTES

[1] 361st Fighter Group, "Station History for February 1945, Station 181-B," March 1, 1945.

[2] Bernard J. Redden, Correspondence with the Author, February 10, 1996.

[3] "Station History for February 1945."

[4] Russell A. Severson, Correspondence with the Author, October 18, 1995.

[5] Ibid.

[6] 361st Fighter Group, "Historical Officer's Report," March 1, 1945.

[7] Missing Aircrew Report # 12331, February 15, 1945.

[8] Missing Aircrew Report # 12674, February 15, 1945.

[9] Anthony Maurice, "Encounter Report," March 9, 1945.

[10] Barry Hicks, "Encounter Report," March 9, 1945.

[11] Thomas Moore, "Encounter Report," March 9, 1945.

[12] 361st Fighter Group, "Mission Summary Report," March 9, 1945.

[13] Richard Anderson, "Encounter Report," March 21, 1945.

[14] Harry Chapman, "Encounter Report," March 21, 1945.

[15] Harry M. Chapman, Interview with the Author, October 29, 1994.

[16] Richard Anderson, "Sworn Statement" Contained in Missing Aircrew Report #13439, March 25, 1945.

[17] Roger A. Freeman, *The Mighty Eighth War Diary* (New York: Janes, 1981), p. 476.

[18] Kenneth J. Scott, "Encounter Report," March 30, 1945.

[19] John Cearley, "Sworn Statement" Contained in Missing Aircrew Report # 13966.

[20] Headquarters, AAF Station F-165 "Unit History, 361st Fighter Group, April 1945," 1 May 1945.

[21] Severson.

[22] "Unit History, 361st Fighter Group, April 1945."

[23] William R. Street, "Encounter Report," April 4, 1945.

[24] Leo F. Gendron, "Encounter Report," April 4, 1945.

[25] James T. Sloan, "Encounter Report," April 9, 1945.

[26] Merne L. Waldusky, "Supporting Statement" Contained in Encounter Report of James T. Sloan, April 9, 1945.

[27] Allen J. Chalmers, "Sworn Statement" Contained in Missing Aircrew Report # 13973, April 16, 1945.

[28] Harry M. Chapman, "Sworn Statement" Contained in Missing Aircrew Report # 13973, April 16, 1945.

[29] 361st Fighter Group, "Mission Summary Report," April 17, 1945.

[30] Gotts, p. 171.

[31] *The Mighty Eighth War Diary*, pp. 495-502..

[32] "Unit History – 361st Fighter Group – Station F-165 – May 1945."

[33] Ibid.

[34] Robert O. Bland, Correspondence with The Author, December 8, 1995.

[35] John B. Crandall, "Monthly Historical Report, Headquarters 361st Fighter Group" June 1945.

[36] Billy D. Welch, Correspondence with the Author, February 13, 2001.

Appendices

All textual information in the following Appendices was obtained from a statistical summary report compiled by Maj. Jack B. Pearce in 1945.

Appendix 1: 361st Fighter Group Aircraft in Profile

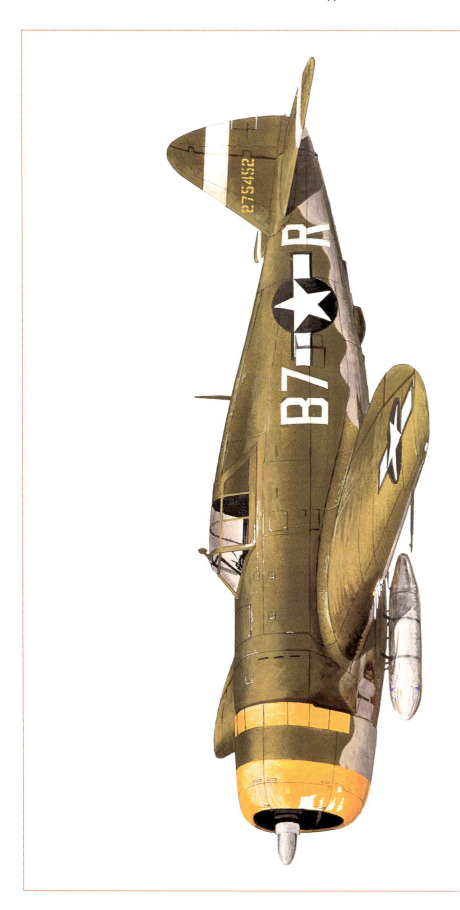

The 374th Fighter Squadron P-47D Thunderbolt "Tika" assigned to Lt. Vernon D. Richards. Note the yellow nose band that replaced the initial white band at the end of March 1944.

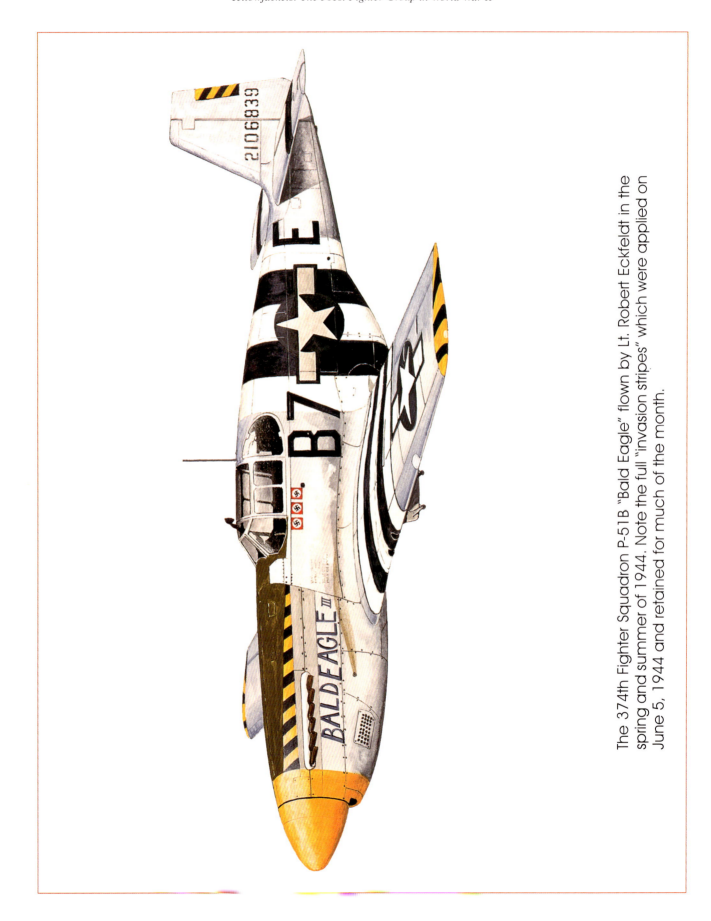

The 374th Fighter Squadron P-51B "Bald Eagle" flown by Lt. Robert Eckfeldt in the spring and summer of 1944. Note the full "invasion stripes" which were applied on June 5, 1944 and retained for much of the month.

The 374th Fighter Squadron P-51D Mustang "Sweet Thing IV" flown by squadron CO Lt.Col. Roy A. Webb, Jr. An aggressive commander, Webb led the 374th Squadron from the Group's early days in Richmond through the summer of 1944.

The 374th Fighter Squadron P-51D Mustang "Lil Bunyep" flown by Capt. Lucius LaCroix during the fall of 1944 and spring of 1945. The origin of this aircraft's name goes back to LaCroix's earlier service with the 7th Fighter Squadron in New Guinea where a "Bunyep," according to local legend, was a jungle demon of great power. Note the red rudder panel and canopy frame typical of the late-war markings adopted by each of the Group's three squadrons.

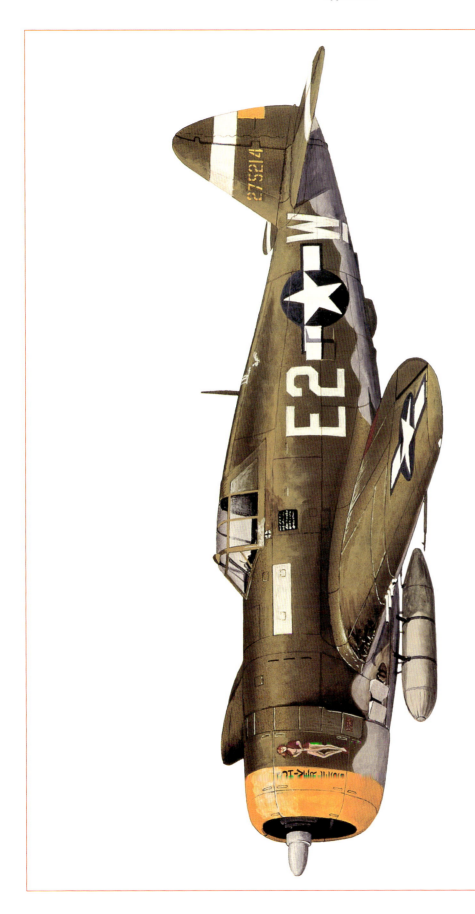

The 375th Fighter Squadron P-47D "Shiverless" flown by Lt. Stanley D. Rames in the spring of 1944. Rames was credited with downing an ME-109 on the mission of April 29 but was forced to bail out of his aircraft, becoming a prisoner the following month.

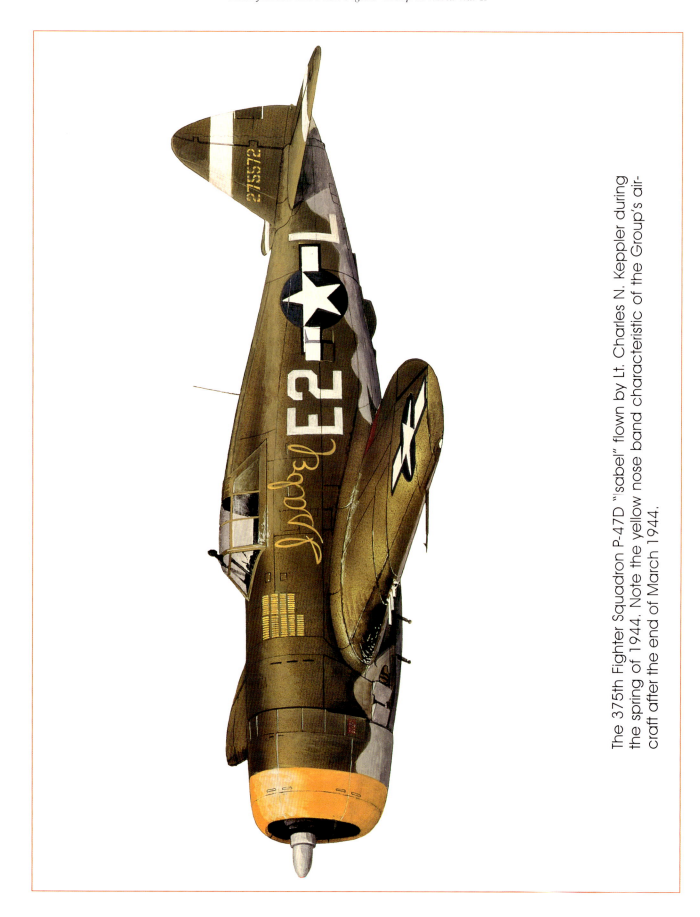

The 375th Fighter Squadron P-47D "sabel" flown by Lt. Charles N. Keppler during the spring of 1944. Note the yellow nose band characteristic of the Group's aircraft after the end of March 1944.

The P-51B Mustang "Lou III" flown by Group Commander Col. Thomas J.J. Christian, Jr. This aircraft was equipped with the British Malcolm Hood canopy allowing much greater visibility for the pilot. Note the full "invasion stripes" characteristic of the first weeks of June 1944.

The 375th Fighter Squadron P-51D Mustang "Betty Lee II / Marie" flown by Lt. William T. Kemp in the fall of 1944. Note the blue rudder panel characteristic of squadron markings in the fall of 1944 and spring of 1945.

The 376th Fighter Squadron P-47D Thunderbolt "Goona!" flown by squadron CO Maj. Roy B. Caviness. Caviness was one of the Group's longest serving officers and was ultimately its final wartime commander. Note the white nose band characteristic of 361st's aircraft during the first two months of combat operations.

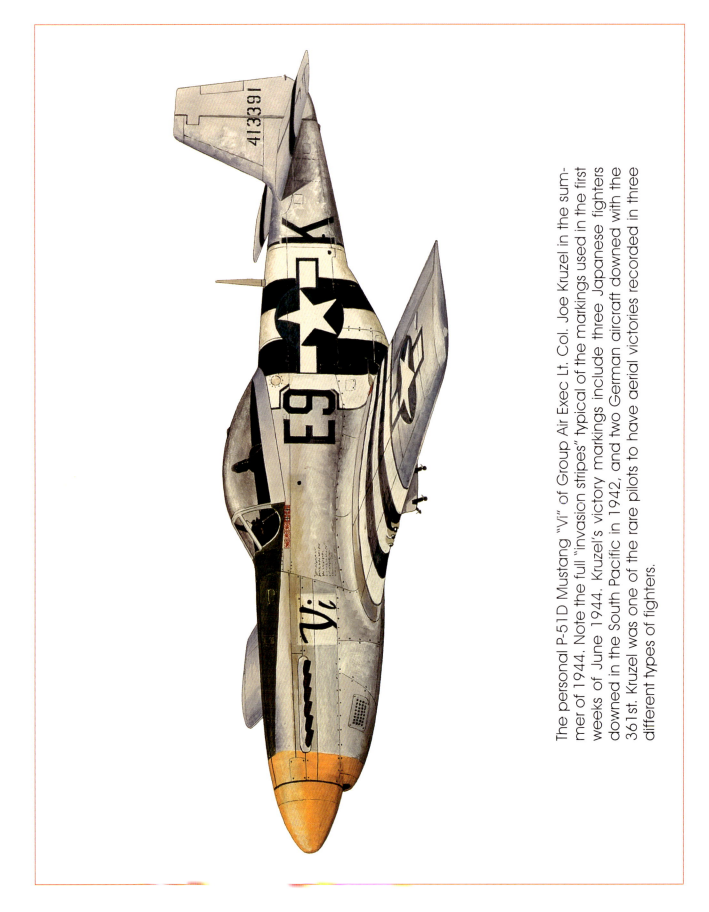

The personal P-51D Mustang "Vi" of Group Air Exec Lt. Col. Joe Kruzel in the summer of 1944. Note the full "invasion stripes" typical of the markings used in the first weeks of June 1944. Kruzel's victory markings include three Japanese fighters downed in the South Pacific in 1942, and two German aircraft downed with the 361st. Kruzel was one of the rare pilots to have aerial victories recorded in three different types of fighters.

The 376th Fighter Squadron P-51D flown by "ace" William R. Beyer during the late summer of 1944.

The 376th Fighter Squadron P-51D "Hilma Lee" flown by Capt. William J. Sykes in the fall of 1944. Note the yellow rudder markings used by the 376th Squadron in the fall of 1944 and spring of 1945.

Lt. Vernon Richards of the 374th Fighter Squadron at the controls of his personal P-51D "TIKA IV" in the summer of 1944. *USAF*

Group Commander Col. Thomas J.J. Christian, Jr. piloting his now well-known P-51D "Lou IV" during the summer of 1944. Note the yellow nose band extended almost to the firewall of the aircraft – a feature unique to this plane at the time of the photo. In the fall of 1944, the extended yellow nose band became a standard Group marking. US*AF*

"The Bottisham Four" – in one of the most well-known photographs of P-51 Mustangs ever taken, Col. Christian leads a flight of the 375th Fighter Squadron for the benefit of an Air Force photographer, July 1944. *USAF*

A P-51D of the 376th Fighter Squadron in flight, 1944. Note the 75-gallon drop tanks which were standard equipment for long-range bomber escort. *USAF*

Equipped with a pair of 500 lb bombs, Lt. Col. Wallace E. Hopkins pilots his personal P-51D "Ferocious Frankie" during the summer of 1944. Hopkins, who served as Group Operations Officer for much of his time with the 361st, was credited with destroying four German planes in aerial combat, and another four in ground strafing. *USAF*

Another of the famous "Bottisham Four" photograph series of late July 1944. *USAF*

A line-abreast shot from the famous "Bottisham Four" series. Note the contrast of the dark green upper surfaces with the shiny "natural metal finish" on the remainder of each aircraft's fuselage. *USAF*

Lt. Col. Hopkins releases his bombs for the benefit of the photographer. *USAF*

Appendix 2: Aces Of the 361st Fighter Group

	Air	**Ground**	**Total**
1st Lt. Dale F. Spencer	10		10
Capt. William R. Beyer	9		9
1st Lt. Urban L. Drew	6	1	7
1st Lt. William T. Kemp	6		6
1st Lt. George R. Vanden Heuvel	5.5	3	8.5
Capt. William J. Sykes	5	5	10
Maj. George L. Merritt, Jr.	5	6	11
1st Lt. Sherman Armsby	4.5	1	5.5
Lt. Col. Roy A. Webb, Jr.	4	5	9
Lt. Col. Wallace E. Hopkins	4	4	8
Capt. Victor E. Bocquin	4	1	5
Capt. Robert C. Wright	3.5	4	7.5
Capt. Robert T. Eckfeldt	3	4	7
Lt. Col. Joseph J. Kruzel	3.5		6.5*
1st Lt. Vernon D. Richards	2	3.5	5.5
Capt. Martin H. Johnson	1	8	9

Aces are customarily ranked by the highest number of aerial victories first, followed by the number of ground strafing victories.

* Includes 3 enemy planes destroyed in the Pacific Theater.

Appendix 3: Pilots Killed Overseas With the 361st Fighter Group in World War II

Group Headquarters:
Col. Thomas J.J. Christian, Jr.
Capt. Richard M. Durbin

374th Fighter Squadron:
1st Lt. Ethelbert Amason
2nd Lt. Clyde A. Arrants
1st Lt. Glenn T. Berge
1st Lt. John R. Bernert
2nd Lt. Harry G. Bosyk
1st Lt. David L. Callaway
1st Lt. Francis Christensen
2nd Lt. Alfred B. Cook
1st Lt. Lawrence E. Downey
Flight Officer Dean E. Jackson
Capt. Joe L. Latimer
2nd Lt. Charles C. McKivett
1st Lt. James M. Norman
1st Lt. Walter H. Sargent
2nd Lt. William V. Staples
1st Lt. Robert J. Stolzy
2nd Lt. John R. Wilson
2nd Lt. Robert M. Zelinsky
1st Lt. Clarence E. Zieske

375th Fighter Squadron
1st Lt. Robert G. Adams
1st Lt. Sherman Armsby
2nd Lt. Jack S. Crandell
2nd Lt. Donald D. Dellinger
1st Lt. Albert C. Duncan
1st Lt. James A. Eason
2nd Lt. Miles E. Elliott
Capt. Charles H. Feller
2nd Lt. Robert E. Geck
Capt. John W. Guckeyson
Flight Officer Cornelius G. Hogelin
2nd Lt. Joseph V. Kapr
1st Lt. Eugene W. Kinnaird
2nd Lt. Daniel Knupp
1st Lt. Caleb W. Layton
2nd Lt. John H. Lougheed
Maj. George L. Merritt, Jr.
2nd Lt. Charles E. Moore
2nd Lt. Charles W. Narvis
2nd Lt. Lawrence E. Perry
1st Lt. William A. Rautenbush
2nd Lt. James A. Rogers
2nd Lt. Collier W. Todd, Jr.
Capt. Russell D. Wade
2nd Lt. Warren D. Wherry
1st Lt. Joseph B. Wolf

376th Fighter Squadron
Flight Officer Walter F. Chapin
2nd Lt. Robert C. Clement
2nd Lt. Milton A. Dahl
1st Lt. Delmer R. Ford
1st Lt. Woodrow Glover
2nd Lt. Russell E. Kenoyer
2nd Lt. Leo Lamb
2nd Lt. Daniel B. Nazzarett
1st Lt. John J. Sadinski
2nd Lt. Dennis B. Weaver

Appendix 4: Commanding Officers of the 361st Fighter Group

Col. Thomas J.J. Christian, Jr.
Col. Ronald F. Fallows
Lt. Col. Joseph J. Kruzel
Col. Junius W. Dennison, Jr.
Lt. Col. Roy B. Caviness

Appendix 5: Squadron Commanders of the 361st Fighter Group

374th Fighter Squadron:
Lt. Col. Roy A. Webb
Maj. Robert E. Sedman
Maj. George R. Rew
Maj. Charles H. Bergmann

375th Fighter Squadron:
Maj. Barry E. Melloan
Maj. George L. Merritt, Jr.
Maj. Dayton C. Casto
Maj. Roswell Freedman
Maj. Charles N. Keppler

376th Fighter Squadron:
Lt. Col. Roy B. Caviness
Maj. James B. Cheney
Lt. Col. Roswell Freedman
Maj. William W. Patton

Glossary

Air Echelon: That portion of a group's complement made up of flying personnel.

Air Exec: The officer serving as second-in-command for the air echelon under the Group Commander.

B-17: Boeing B-17 "Flying Fortress." The most common type of four-engine American heavy bomber used in the ETO. The B-17 equipped the 8th Bomber Command's 1st and 3rd Bomb Divisions.

B-24: Consolidated B-24 "Liberator." Four-engine heavy bomber which equipped the 8th Bomber Command's 2nd Bomb Division. Slightly faster and capable of carrying a larger bomb load than the B-17, the B-24 was generally less able to absorb punishment or hold formation at altitudes above 20,000 feet.

B-26: Martin B-26 "Marauder." Twin-engine medium bomber typically flown by 9th Air Force units by the time of the 361st's arrival in the ETO.

Bandit: An airborne aircraft definitely determined to be hostile.

Belly Tank: Jettisonable auxiliary fuel tank fixed to the bottom of an aircraft's fuselage along the centerline. The P-47, and German fighters such as the ME-109 and FW-190, typically made use of centerline belly tanks for increased range.

Bogey: An airborne aircraft of undetermined identity – friend or foe.

Combat Box: Primary defensive formation used by the 8th Bomber Command's heavy bombers. In the combat box, aircraft of a bomb groups were flown in close formation with squadrons stacked low, middle and high positions. The formation allowed for maximum defensive firepower.

Combat Wing: A formation of two or more bomb groups arranged in combat boxes and tasked with the same target objectives.

Deck: Extreme low flying altitude; "treetop" height (and possibly lower).

Deflection: Aerial gunnery technique of "aiming off" in order to give proper lead to the target. This technique compensated for the relative position of one's own aircraft above, below, or adjacent to the target aircraft, as well as the lag in time required for bullets to reach the target.

Drop Tanks: Jettisonable auxiliary fuel tanks fixed under each wing of an aircraft such as the P-51.

Element: The basic two-plane fighter formation consisting of an element leader and wingman. Two elements made up a flight.

ETO: European Theater of Operations

Fighter Wing: An administrative, but not a tactical division, controlling several fighter groups. The 65th, 66th and 67th Fighter Wings made up the 8th Fighter Command.

Flaps: Airframe panels located beneath the trailing edge of an aircraft's wings which, when lowered, change the curvature of the wing in order to produce greater lift and increase the stalling speed of the plane. Flaps were intended to be used for take-offs and landings, however, fighter pilots sometimes used them in combat to rapidly slow the aircraft in order to make a pursuing enemy plane overshoot, or to allow a tighter turn in certain combat situations.

Flight: A formation of four aircraft made up of two elements and led by a flight leader. On operations, the four or more flights making up a squadron were designated by colors (i.e. white flight, red flight, etc.). Each aircraft was assigned a number with the flight leader as 1, his wingman 2, second element leader 3, and his wingman 4.

FW-190: Single seat German fighter aircraft built by Focke-Wulf and introduced into combat in 1942.

Group: An administrative and tactical unit made up of three squadrons and led by a Group Commander.

Ground Echelon: The non-flying portion of a group's complement consisting of administrative, maintenance and support personnel.

Ground Exec: The officer serving as second in command under the Group Commander for the ground echelon.

Hardstand: A concrete pad used for individual aircraft parking and maintenance. Hardstands were typically dispersed around the perimeter of the airfield.

Lufberry Circle: A defensive tactic in which a group of aircraft fly in a tight circle, making it difficult for enemy aircraft to break into and attack without themselves being attacked. Named for the World War I American fighter ace Raoul Lufberry.

ME-109: Single seat German fighter aircraft built by Messerschmitt which formed the backbone of the *Luftwaffe* fighter arm for much of the war.

PSP (Pierced-Steel-Planking)**:** Interlocking steel runway matting used primarily at forward airbases where rapid completion takes precedence over permanence. Also called "Sommerfield Track" by the British.

R/T: "Radio Telephone" or aircraft two-way radio.

Split-S: a flight maneuver enabling a fighter pilot to rapidly change direction by 180 degrees. Essentially, the split-s consists of a half-roll followed by a half-loop. The pilot half-rolls the aircraft so that it is inverted, then applies back pressure on the stick bringing the nose of the aircraft through the horizon and leveling off with the aircraft heading in a direction approximately 180 degrees from the start of the maneuver.

Squadron: A unit of approximately 16 aircraft divided into flights.

Bibliography

Anderson, Clarence E. *To Fly and Fight*. New York: St. Martins Press, 1990.

Bowman, Martin W. *Castles In The Air*. Great Britain: Patrick Stephens, 1984.

Craven, Wesley Frank and Cate, James Lea, ed. *The Army Air Forces in World War II*. Chicago: University of Chicago Press, 1950.

Ethell, Jeffrey L., et. al. *The Great Book of World War II Airplanes*. New York: Crescent Books, 1996.

Freeman, Roger A. *The Mighty Eighth*. London: Janes, 1970.

Freeman, Roger A. *The Mighty Eighth War Diary*. London: Janes, 1981.

Gotts, Steve. *Little Friends: A Pictorial History of the 361st Fighter Group in World War II*. Dallas, Texas: Taylor Publishing Co., 1993.

Hall, Grover C., Jr. *1000 Destroyed: The Life and Times of the 4th Fighter Group*. Dallas, Texas: Morgan Aviation Books, 1946.

Hamlin, John F. *The Royal Air Force in Cambridgeshire Part 2: The Histories of RAF Waterbeach and RAF Bottisham*. Great Britain: Privately Published, 1987.

Hess, William N. *P-51: Bomber Escort*. New York: Ballantine Books, 1971.

Hess, William N. *Fighting Mustang: Chronicle of the P-51*. Garden City New York: Doubleday, 1971.

Jablonski, Edward. *Double Strike*. Garden City, New York: Doubleday and Company, 1974.

Miller, Thomas G. *The Cactus Air Force*. New York: Harper and Row, 1969.

Morris, Danny. *Aces and Wingmen*. London: Neville Spearman, 1972.

Morris, Danny. *Aces and Wingmen II, Vol. 1*. Washington: Aviation Usk, 1989.

Parker, Danny S. *To Win the Winter Sky*. Conshohocken, Pennsylvania: Combined Books, 1994.

Stokesbury, James L. *A Short History of World War II*. New York: William Morrow and Company, 1980.

The United States Strategic Bombing Survey. New York: Garden City Publishing, 1976.

Index

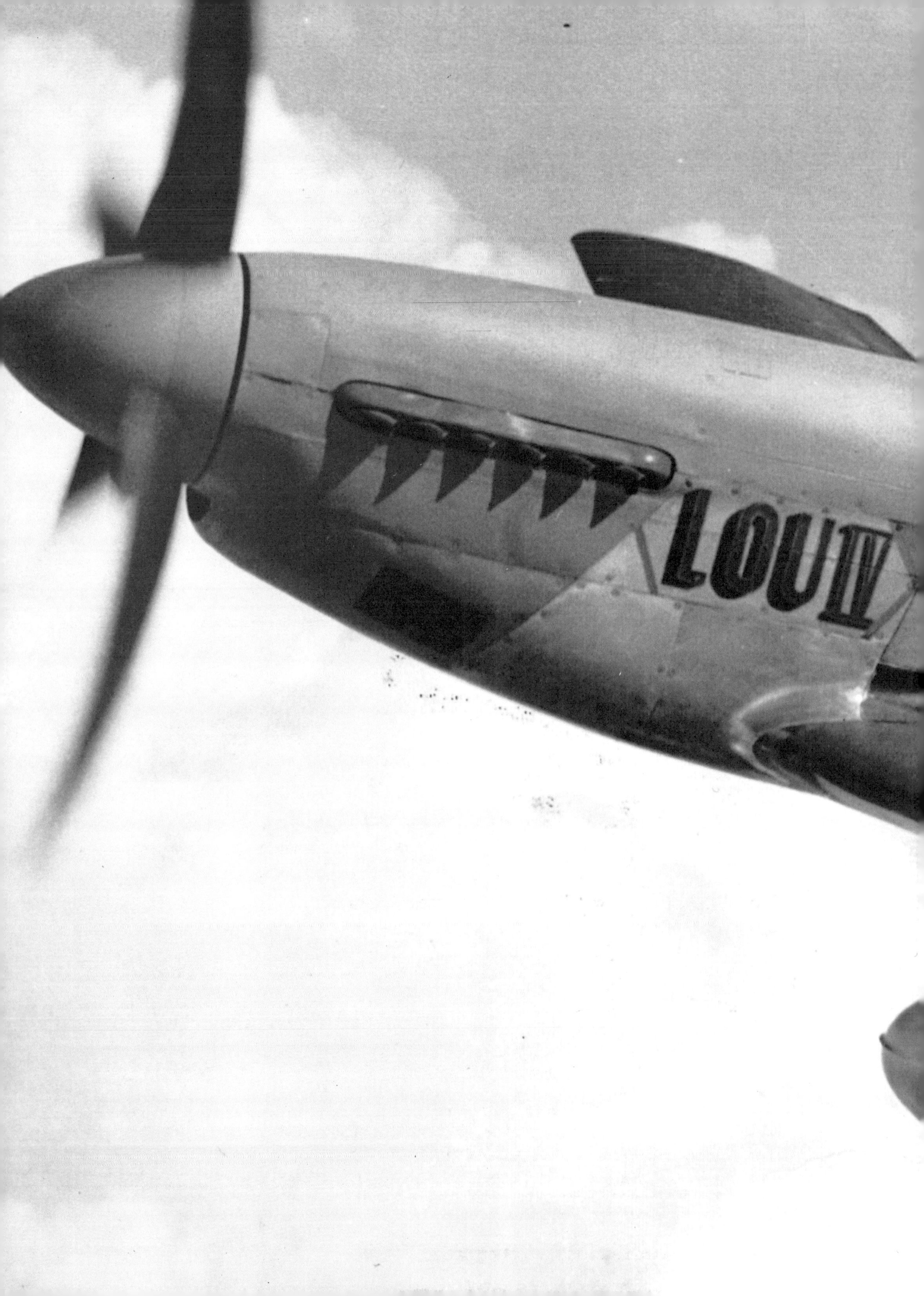
LOU IV